Contestations Over Gender in Asia

This book brings together the work of scholars from around the world in a consideration of how gender is contested in various parts of Asia – in China, India, Indonesia, Japan and the Philippines. Part I of this collection explores notions of agency in relation to women's domestic and everyday lives. While "agency" is one of the key terms in contemporary social science, scholarship on women in Asia recently has focussed on women's political activism. Women's private lives have been neglected in this new scholarship. This volume has a special focus on women's relational and emotional lives, domestic practices, marriage, singlehood and maternity. Papers consider how women negotiate enhanced space and reputations and challenge negative representations and entrenched models of intra-family and intimate relations. There is also a warning about too free feminist expectations of agency and the repercussions of the exercise of agency. The three essays in Part II examine the historical construction of masculinities in colonial and postcolonial South and Southeast Asia, and the ways that manhood is interpreted, experienced and performed in daily life in the past and in the present. They highlight the centrality and continued relevance of masculinity to analyses of empire and nation and underscore the highly gendered and (hetero)sexualized nature of political, military and economic institutions. Collectively, the essays explore a wide range of competing articulations and experiences of gender within Asia, emphasizing the historical and contemporary plurality and variability of femininity and masculinity, and the dynamic and intersectional nature of gender identities and relations. This book was published as a special issue of *Asian Studies Review*.

Lyn Parker is a Professor in Asian Studies, School of Social Sciences, The University of Western Australia, Perth, Australia. She is a social and cultural anthropologist who specializes in Indonesia.

Laura Dales is Assistant Professor in Asian Studies, School of Social Sciences at The University of Western Australia, Perth, Australia. She researches contemporary Japanese society, with a particular focus on gender.

Chie Ikeya is Associate Professor in the Department of History at Rutgers University, New Jersey, USA. Her research concerns the social and cultural histories of modern Southeast Asia, with a focus on women and gender, race, colonialism and nationalism in late nineteenth and early twentieth century Burma (Myanmar).

Contestations Over Gender in Asia

Edited by
Lyn Parker, Laura Dales and
Chie Ikeya

LONDON AND NEW YORK

First published 2015
by Routledge
2 Park Square, Milton Park, Abingdon, Oxon, OX14 4RN, UK

and by Routledge
711 Third Avenue, New York, NY 10017, USA

Routledge is an imprint of the Taylor & Francis Group, an informa business

© 2015 Asian Studies Association of Australia

All rights reserved. No part of this book may be reprinted or reproduced or utilised in any form or by any electronic, mechanical, or other means, now known or hereafter invented, including photocopying and recording, or in any information storage or retrieval system, without permission in writing from the publishers.

Trademark notice: Product or corporate names may be trademarks or registered trademarks, and are used only for identification and explanation without intent to infringe.

British Library Cataloguing in Publication Data
A catalogue record for this book is available from the British Library

ISBN 13: 978-1-138-90682-2

Typeset in Times New Roman
by RefineCatch Limited, Bungay, Suffolk

Publisher's Note
The publisher accepts responsibility for any inconsistencies that may have arisen during the conversion of this book from journal articles to book chapters, namely the possible inclusion of journal terminology.

Disclaimer
Every effort has been made to contact copyright holders for their permission to reprint material in this book. The publishers would be grateful to hear from any copyright holder who is not here acknowledged and will undertake to rectify any errors or omissions in future editions of this book.

Contents

Citation Information   vii
Notes on Contributors   ix

Part I: Everyday Agency of Women in Asia

1. Introduction: The Everyday Agency of Women in Asia   1
   Lyn Parker and Laura Dales

2. "Northern Girls": Cultural Politics of Agency and South China's Migrant Literature   5
   Wanning Sun

3. Left-behind and Vulnerable? Conceptualising Development and Older Women's Agency in Rural China   23
   Tamara Jacka

4. Problematic Conjugations: Women's Agency, Marriage and Domestic Violence in Indonesia   42
   Siti Aisyah and Lyn Parker

5. *Ohitorisama*, Singlehood and Agency in Japan   61
   Laura Dales

Part II: Masculinities in Asia

6. Masculinities in Asia: A Review Essay   80
   Chie Ikeya

7. A Collision of Masculinities: Men, Modernity and Urban Transportation in American-Colonial Manila   90
   Michael D. Pante

8. Obscenity, Moral Contagion and Masculinity: *Hijras* in Public Space in Colonial North India   111
   Jessica Hinchy

Index   133

Citation Information

The chapters in this book were originally published in the *Asian Studies Review*, volume 38, issue 2 (June 2014). When citing this material, please use the original page numbering for each article, as follows:

Chapter 1
Introduction: The Everyday Agency of Women in Asia
Lyn Parker and Laura Dales
Asian Studies Review, volume 38, issue 2 (June 2014) pp. 164–167

Chapter 2
"Northern Girls": Cultural Politics of Agency and South China's Migrant Literature
Wanning Sun
Asian Studies Review, volume 38, issue 2 (June 2014) pp. 168–185

Chapter 3
Left-behind and Vulnerable? Conceptualising Development and Older Women's Agency in Rural China
Tamara Jacka
Asian Studies Review, volume 38, issue 2 (June 2014) pp. 186–204

Chapter 4
Problematic Conjugations: Women's Agency, Marriage and Domestic Violence in Indonesia
Siti Aisyah and Lyn Parker
Asian Studies Review, volume 38, issue 2 (June 2014) pp. 205–223

Chapter 5
Ohitorisama, Singlehood and Agency in Japan
Laura Dales
Asian Studies Review, volume 38, issue 2 (June 2014) pp. 224–242

Chapter 6
Masculinities in Asia: A Review Essay
Chie Ikeya
Asian Studies Review, volume 38, issue 2 (June 2014) pp. 243–252

CITATION INFORMATION

Chapter 7
A Collision of Masculinities: Men, Modernity and Urban Transportation in American-Colonial Manila
Michael D. Pante
Asian Studies Review, volume 38, issue 2 (June 2014) pp. 253–273

Chapter 8
Obscenity, Moral Contagion and Masculinity: Hijras *in Public Space in Colonial North India*
Jessica Hinchy
Asian Studies Review, volume 38, issue 2 (June 2014) pp. 274–294

Please direct any queries you may have about the citations to
clsuk.permissions@cengage.com

Notes on Contributors

Siti Aisyah is a Lecturer and Director of Gender Mainstreaming and Children's Studies at the Alauddin State Islamic University of Makassar, Indonesia. Her research focus is on gender and Islam, particularly in the Muhammadan Tradition (Hadith). Her research projects have included domestic violence in Makassar, Indonesia; trafficking and local wisdom in South Sulawesi, Indonesia; gender bias in Islamic schools' curricula in South Sulawesi; and Muslim understanding of Islamic teaching on gender relations. She is the author of *Rereading of Qur'anic Understanding on Domestic Violence: In Search of Domestic Violence in Makassar Indonesia* (2012).

Laura Dales is Assistant Professor in the Discipline of Asian Studies at The University of Western Australia, Perth, Australia. Her research interests include women's groups, feminism, sexuality, singlehood and marriage in Japan and Asia. She is the author of the monograph *Feminist Movements in Contemporary Japan* (Routledge, 2009). Her interest in singlehood and marriage flows from research conducted through a Japan Society for the Promotion of Science Postdoctoral Fellowship taken up at Osaka University, Japan (2009–10). This study provoked her current research focus, an Australian Research Council DECRA project examining intimacy beyond the family in contemporary Japan.

Jessica Hinchy is Assistant Professor in the School of Humanities and Social Sciences at Nanyang Technological University, Singapore. Her research focuses on late eighteenth- and nineteenth-century north India and examines the historical experiences of groups marginalized due to their social, domestic and gendered practices. Her work also analyzes broader questions about the nature of colonial governance at the local level in north India. Her additional areas of interest in South Asian history include: colonial criminology and law; slavery; historical concepts of childhood; and medical knowledge of gender and sexuality.

Chie Ikeya is Associate Professor in the Department of History at Rutgers University, New Jersey, USA. She maintains an active interest in the fields of Asian history/studies, women's and gender history, race, gender and sexuality studies, and colonial and postcolonial studies. Her recent publications include *Refiguring Women, Colonialism, and Modernity in Burma* (2011), "Colonial Intimacies in Comparative Perspective: Intermarriage, Law, and Cultural Difference in British Burma" (*Journal of Colonialism and Colonial History* 14(1), Spring 2013) and "The Life and Writings of a Patriotic Feminist: Independent Daw San of Burma" (in *Women in Southeast Asian Nationalist Movements*, ed. Susan Blackburn and Helen Ting, 2013).

NOTES ON CONTRIBUTORS

Tamara Jacka is a Senior Fellow in the Department of Political and Social Change in the College of Asia and the Pacific at The Australian National University, Canberra, Australia. Her research interests are in gender and social change in contemporary China. Her publications include *Women's Work in Rural China: Change and Continuity in an Era of Reform* (1997); *On the Move: Women and Rural-to-Urban Migration in Contemporary China* (co-edited with Arianne Gaetano, 2004); *Rural Women in Urban China: Gender, Migration and Social Change* (2006); *Women, Gender and Development in Rural China* (co-edited with Sally Sargeson, 2011); and *Contemporary China: Society and Social Change* (co-authored with Andrew Kipnis and Sally Sargeson, 2013).

Michael D. Pante is an instructor in the Department of History at Ateneo de Manila University, Philippines. He obtained his MA in History from the same university and is currently pursuing a PhD in Philippine Studies from The University of the Philippines. He is also associate editor of *Philippine Studies: Historical and Ethnographic Viewpoints*. His research interests are transportation history and urban studies.

Lyn Parker is an anthropologist and Professor in Asian Studies at The University of Western Australia, Perth, Australia. She has specialized in the anthropology of Indonesia and has conducted fieldwork mainly in West Sumatra and Bali. Her published work includes *From Subjects to Citizens: Balinese Villagers in the Indonesian Nation-State* (2003), *The Agency of Women in Asia* (2005), and *Women and Work in Indonesia* (with Michelle Ford, 2008). Her most recent book, co-authored with Pam Nilan, is *Adolescents in Contemporary Indonesia* (2013). She is currently conducting research on women, education, citizenship, multiculturalism and religion, environmentalism and education for sustainability in Indonesia.

Wanning Sun is Professor of Chinese Media and Cultural Studies in the China Research Centre at the University of Technology Sydney, Australia. Her most recent publications are *Maid in China: Media, Morality and the Cultural Politics of Boundaries* (Routledge, 2009), and (as editor) *Media and the Chinese Diaspora: Community, Communications and Commerce* (Routledge, 2006). She is a member of the editorial board of Media International Australia, and a member of the executive advisory board of the *Asian Journal of Communication*. She is currently completing a monograph on the media and cultural practices of China's rural migrant workers.

Introduction: The Everyday Agency of Women in Asia

LYN PARKER and LAURA DALES

The University of Western Australia

This issue of *Asian Studies Review* includes a themed section that addresses agency in relation to women's everyday lives and experiences in Asia. Four papers follow this Introduction: Siti Aisyah and Lyn Parker (2014) study domestic violence in Makassar, Sulawesi, Indonesia; Laura Dales (2014) explores singlehood for women in Japan; Tamara Jacka (2014) challenges stereotypes around older rural women in China; and Wanning Sun (2014) examines literary representations of rural migrant women in southern China.

Building on a discussion begun in the edited collection, *The Agency of Women in Asia* (Parker, 2005), this collection revisits theoretical questions and explores some of the issues posed in that volume, but with a special focus on ordinary, everyday social practice in contexts of work, marriage, singlehood and maternity. In particular the papers in this collection contribute to the theorisation of agency, exploring not only the ways in which women express agency, but also feminist expectations of agency, the repercussions of the exercise of agency, the effect of negative representations of women on women's agency, and the ways in which scholars can understand and assess agency.

Acknowledging the important theoretical work that already exists on agency (e.g. Comaroff and Comaroff, 1997; Mahmood, 2001 and 2005; Ortner, 2001 and 2006), and the minor spate of edited books on women's public activism in Asia recently (e.g. Burghoorn et al., 2008; Iwanaga, 2008; Roces and Edwards, 2010), this collection takes a different tack. Women's everyday lives, on the ground in lived situations, have been neglected in this new scholarship. In this collection, we focus on women's relational and emotional lives, their experience of domestic practices and daily social and sexual interactions, on the way they build relationships, and their involvement in forms of interdependence and mutual aid. Some pictures are intimate and intensely personal; others are of public behaviour – of women shouting out, or publishing on the internet. Some agency is transient, as when women are carried along with the ebb and flow of family relationships or economic ups-and-downs; some is more permanent in its effects, as when the agency of women enacts legislation against domestic violence, or when new literary forms effect new images of working-class migrant women.

The focus on women in Asia addresses the continuing marginality of women as subjects in disciplines outside feminist studies, and the marginality of Asia within feminist studies. We aim to contribute to the study of the "Other" – that is, the study of "Asia" and of "women", of subalterns and of alternatives to the hegemony of the West. Ahearn (2001) posited that agency is culturally mediated. In grounding our collection in Asian cultures, we are testing the concept of agency in non-Western cultural environments. This position raises many theoretical challenges, such as ideas of personhood cross-culturally, different understandings of the value of personal autonomy, the nature of ideal femininity and the meaning of family. These are significant themes not just because they demand re-thinking of the subject, her personhood and profile, but also because of movements in the social and political landscape. Asian societies are undergoing rapid social change, which includes phenomena such as shifts from arranged marriages to love marriages, a decline and delay in marriage in some countries, the emergence of new forms of intimacy, as well as new patterns of work and mobility, that impact on women's everyday lives.

This selection of articles provides the opportunity to explore the ramifications of such transformations and to assess their significance for women. The papers challenge the assumption that globalisation, greater mobility and autonomy automatically enhance women's agency, or that women's increased agency is uniformly evaluated as a social good. The papers, taken together, show the enduring strength of local cultures, and the need to always take into account the specificity of local histories, while never presuming an unchanging essence.

There is no doubt that agency has become an "indispensable theoretical category" (Ortner, 2001, p. 77) – arguably the keyword of both practice theory in anthropology and feminist anthropology and sociology. A focus on agency enables us to see that in the face of dominant power and discourses, subordinated and marginalised groups and individuals make room to move. They are not passive recipients, captives of dominant discourses. Agency is this capacity to negotiate with power in whatever form – as complicity, compromise, deviance or resistance – and with whatever motivation – whether it be intentional or unintentional, voluntary or involuntary, self-expression, self-interest or group interest. Women exercise agency in the interstices of power, and for this reason a focus on women's agency in everyday life seems particularly apposite.

The papers' focus on the minutiae of everyday life does not mean that the authors are blind to the dominant discourses, politics and economic forces that shape the contemporary world. In fact, it is these broader structures that delimit the discussions of the everyday. But these dominant forces do not just trickle down to the level of the individual and determine her social relations. Rather, the papers show how relations of power and wider discourses interplay with individual subjectivities, how women make their everyday lives meaningful through discursive practices, how women's agency feeds back, shaping the contexts of family, friendship, courtship or community. The papers also show, at a higher level, the importance of interrogating how women's agency is represented: who defines agency, to what end, and with what motivation?

For readers who might not normally read feminist work, we want to point out that these papers are not just about women. Women almost always exist in the real everyday world within gendered social relations; because of this, the authors attend to gender relations, not just to women. It is not tenable to only focus on women: mature single women in Japan who want to marry are thinking about marriage to a man; grandmothers in China are embedded within families; women getting beaten at home in Indonesia are getting beaten up by men. The point is therefore that these papers might be for women, but that the issues need to be addressed with men, and the construction of masculinities, in mind.

In this collection, the category of "women" is diverse. The subjects of our papers are old women, grandmothers, singles in their 30s and 40s, married women, poor rural women, comfortable middle-class women, and urban women. These different ages, life stages, marital statuses, socioeconomic classes and geographic, ethnic and religious identities bear in different ways on the construction of women. The intersections are many and complex, but almost always these non-gender characteristics of women shape their identity as women, just as gender characteristics shape other identities. It is useful to remember that well-worn feminist image of who we see in the mirror: is it "just" a woman? Or is it a woman who has just been bashed up by her husband? Or is it an old woman, whose body bears witness to the hard life of farming in north-west China? While it is obvious that different sorts of inequalities (e.g. of class and race) cannot be treated in the same way, and it is probably impossible to design a study that captures this complexity, a focus on the agency of women certainly serves to highlight more than just gender inequality. The papers in this issue reveal a great deal about social conditions in China, Japan and Indonesia – particularly issues of class, ethnicity, geographic location, age and marriage.

The first article is by Wanning Sun (2014) and it examines agency in the context of literary representations of rural migrant women in southern China. Sun proposes that the semi-autobiographical or self-ethnographic literary works that detail the lives of northern migrant women effect agency in the form of cultural politics. These works offer a re-configuration of the term "northern girl", a label that typically ascribes promiscuity and moral abjectness, depicting women instead as pragmatic and sexually autonomous actors. Sun argues that migrant subaltern literature provides an alternative avenue to understanding women's experiences as sexual agents, and challenges dominant constructions of migrant women that ignore the interrelation of gender, class and geography.

The paper by Tamara Jacka (2014) on "left-behind" older women in rural China demonstrates that a discourse of vulnerability does not encapsulate older women's capability. Jacka notes that the construction of a "vulnerable group" can undermine women's agency by diminishing the contribution of older women as social actors. Furthermore, the categorisation "masks a great deal of diversity among older women in the ways in which their lives are shaped by a range of practices, relationships, norms and institutions". In this case, the strategic promotion of older women's special needs for welfare benefits can ultimately erode the self-esteem of women, and reinscribe their marginality as perceived non-productive social actors.

Siti Aisyah and Lyn Parker (2014) show that women's expressions of agency can come at a high price. In their examination of domestic violence in Makassar, Indonesia, Aisyah and Parker note that wives' transgressive behaviour, resistance and criticism of their husbands can provoke domestic violence, and furthermore these acts can be construed as justification for violence by the broader society. Thus, within the unequal power relationship of marriage in Indonesia, women's expressions of agency do not necessarily and always serve women well. On the other hand, it was through a careful expression of women's agency that the Law on Domestic Violence was passed in 2004; and since then women's groups have been working to change the discourse on domestic violence.

Laura Dales (2014) addresses the possibilities of agency in singlehood for Japanese women. Within the context of demographic changes, discourses of singlehood such as the *ohitorisama* (the single woman or "singleton") remain tied to the ideal of marriage. The potential for this discourse to engender agency is delimited by factors beyond marital status, including the health, economic capacity and familial support available to the single woman. Shifts in the discursive construction of singlehood may assist in the creation of a legitimate social space for women, but women's agency requires structural as well as symbolic foundations.

These papers all advocate a re-examination of agency that is sensitive to factors beyond individual control and personal impact. The conceptualisation of agency as relational empowerment, cultural practice or capability allows us to consider the meanings of a variety of micro-level practices, beliefs and interpersonal engagements. These discussions note the marginalising effects of ageing, rurality, singlehood, domestic violence and economic dependence on women's lives, but do not necessarily see agency as the cure-all for these issues. Rather, the authors advocate care in the construction and evaluation of agency. A cautious approach recognises both the limitations of the term – what it can mean for women's lives concretely, to exercise agency – and the limitations of existing definitions of agency that attract the attention of scholars, states and communities. If agency is multifarious, it is also not unlimited. This collection explores the boundaries of agency, specifically looking to map the areas that women traverse in their daily lives.

References

Ahearn, Laura (2001) Language and agency. *Annual Review of Anthropology* 30 [accessed through ProQuest].
Aisyah, Siti and Lyn Parker (2014) Problematic conjugations: Women's agency, marriage and domestic violence in Indonesia. *Asian Studies Review* 38(2), pp. 205–23.
Burghoorn, Wil, Kazuki Iwanaga, Cecilia Milwertz and Qi Wang, eds. (2008) *Gender politics in Asia: Women manoeuvring within dominant gender orders* (Copenhagen: NIAS Press).
Comaroff, John L. and Jean Comaroff (1997) *The dialectics of modernity on a South African frontier.* Volume II of *Of revelation and revolution* (Chicago: University of Chicago Press).
Dales, Laura (2014) *Ohitorisama*, singlehood and agency in Japan. *Asian Studies Review* 38(2), pp. 224–42.
Iwanaga, Kazuki, ed. (2008) *Women's political participation and representation in Asia: Obstacles and challenges* (Copenhagen: NIAS Press).
Jacka, Tamara (2014) Left-behind and vulnerable? Conceptualising development and older women's agency in rural China. *Asian Studies Review* 38(2), pp. 186–204.
Mahmood, Saba (2001) Feminist theory, embodiment, and the docile agent: Some reflections on the Egyptian Islamic revival. *Cultural Anthropology* 16(2), pp. 202–36.
Mahmood, Saba (2005) *Politics of piety: The Islamic revival and the feminist subject* (Princeton: Princeton University Press).
Ortner, Sherry (2001) Specifying agency: The Comaroffs and their critics. *Interventions* 3(1), pp. 76–84.
Ortner, Sherry (2006) *Anthropology and social theory: Culture, power and the acting subject* (Durham and London: Duke University Press).
Parker, Lyn, ed. (2005) *The agency of women in Asia* (Singapore: Marshall Cavendish).
Roces, Mina and Louise Edwards, eds. (2010) *Women's movements in Asia: Feminisms and transnational activism* (Abingdon and New York: Routledge).
Sun, Wanning (2014) "Northern girls": Cultural politics of agency and South China's migrant literature. *Asian Studies Review* 38(2), pp. 168–85.

"Northern Girls": Cultural Politics of Agency and South China's Migrant Literature

WANNING SUN

University of Technology Sydney

Abstract: *This paper is concerned with the cultural politics of agency, and explores the relationship between cultural form, migrant experience and social change. It traces the emergence of a range of literary forms in south China and how these new cultural forms provide hitherto unavailable space to contest the state- and market-driven narratives, which tend to link* dagongmei's *(rural migrant women's) sexuality with inexperience and vulnerability on the one hand, and criminality, immorality and incivility on the other. The paper suggests that these newly emerging cultural forms present alternative perspectives on the practical circumstances, moral rationalities and emotional consequences that condition and shape migrant women's sexual experience, and for this reason, they constitute important points of intervention.*

Introduction

Quite a few girls in my factory have a moonlighting job earning money that way. But we do not call them *er nai* (mistress) or *xiao jie* (bar girl); we call them *an chang* (undercover hooker). More lenient requirements apply with undercover hookers, in terms of age and looks, and of course, they earn less than mistresses or bar girls. I did not sell myself in the hard times, and I am even less inclined to do so now, especially given that my life has improved a bit. What's more, there is another pathway – finding a man who is prepared to help me pay for my brother's education. For suitable candidates, I have to rule out any ordinary worker on the assembly lines; with what little wages they earn, he can hardly feed himself, let alone provide a stipend to his future brother-in-law. So my thoughts turn to Wang Lei again. As an assistant manager in the Technical Unit 1 of my factory, his monthly salary must be at least 15,000 yuan – more than enough to pay for my brother's study. Unfortunately, he hasn't shown any interest in me. In fact, having worked in the factory for five years, the handsome-looking Wang Lei has not attracted any gossip of any romantic liaisons, which is quite intriguing. Could he have some biological defects? I know so little about him, and have few chances to get close to him. But there are quite a few boys in the Technical Units 2 and 3, and they are mostly my age. Their salaries range from 3,000 yuan to 20,000 yuan. If I manage to catch one of them, my brother's education will be taken care of. From now on, I must look out for more excuses to go to technical units (Fang, 2008).

The above excerpt is taken from *I Am a Floating Flower* (*Woshi yiduo piaolin de hua*), a book written by Fang Yimeng, a rural migrant from Sichuan Province, about her life as a factory worker in Dongguan, the Pearl River Delta, south China. Using the pen name Wang Haiyan, the book starts with a mining incident, which kills Haiyan's father, wiping out her plan to go to university. Desperately trying to pay off family debt and support her brother's education, Haiyan comes to Dongguan and becomes a factory worker. She falls in love with a married man, gets pregnant, and has an abortion. She then gets involved with Wang Lei, a technical staffer in the factory, but Wang Lei ends the affair without giving her a reason. Wang Haiyan's dream of a better life in the city, romance, and earning enough money to support her family back in the village becomes increasingly remote, as the grim reality of a rural migrant woman surviving at the margins sinks in. Haiyan realises that people like herself are nothing but "*bei mei*" (northern girls) or "*dagongmei*" (migrant woman workers) and are the objects of contempt and prejudice. In the preamble, she describes her book as a "self-narrative" (*zi shu*), and explains her motivation for writing down her experience:

> I have come across many media reports of *dagong* people like us. For some reason, they give more attention to migrant women than men. In these reports, migrant women are either fallen women now living as mistresses, bar girls, hookers trying to satisfy their vanity and material needs, or they are barely able to eke out a depressing and miserable life, which is less dignified than dogs and pigs. As a girl who has worked in Dongguan for many years, I always get really angry when I read these reports (Fang, 2008).

For this reason, Fang says that her autobiographical account is intended to present a comprehensive picture of the life of migrant workers by bearing witness to the enormous contribution people like herself have made to China's economic prosperity. She hopes that many years from now, when people praise the Pearl River Delta and China for its economic miracles, they will not forget that China's global factory runs on the blood, sweat and tears of countless people like herself.

I Am a Floating Flower has been described as an "autobiographical account", a documentary novel (*jishi xiaoshuo*), and a type of internet literature (*wangluo wenxue*). Fang resolved to put her own experience into words in 2006, but she did not think of publishing the material online until much later. Once she started to upload instalments of her writing to Tianya, a website that publishes internet literature, her frank and unadorned account of migrant women's lives soon attracted an enormous following, with readers posting messages of endorsement and offering supportive comments. In fact, her writing became so popular that it had to be taken down a number of times due to the perceived risk of it being too "candid". Fang's online writings caught the attention of book publishers, and she was soon offered a book contract on the condition that she stop uploading any new instalments. Abiding by the agreement, Fang stopped publishing her writing online, and the book was launched in 2008, but the earlier instalments of Fang's book are still available online, and readers continue to post messages. Fang now writes her own blogs, and works in the human resources department of a real estate company in Shenzhen. When the Nanfang Dushi Bao (Nanfang Metropolitan News) interviewed her, she said that she had given up all hope of finding romance in her life, was emotionally not attached to anyone, and thought that people like her "do not have the means and resources to experience romance" (Liu, 2008).

The migrant women's experiences as narrated in *I Am a Floating Flower*, together with the story of Fang's endeavours as a writer, help make a number of points about agency, class, gender and sexuality, and the role of public culture in negotiating the relationship between them. The excerpt that begins this paper, containing the ruminations of a rural migrant factory worker considering her options in the marriage market, sounds like the honest thoughts of a practical young woman with few means, who nevertheless wishes to make the best of her ordinary life. What makes this rationalisation of an ordinary woman extraordinary is not the logic of her thought; it is the fact that such thought is in fact presented as if it were ordinary, sensible and common sense. In other words, the main protagonist Wang's rationalisation, which seems logical to her and the multitude of rural migrant women in a similar situation, is anything but acceptable "common sense" when measured against the parameters of the moral-sexual economy promoted by and informing most narratives in the realm of public culture.

If agency is defined as the "socioculturally mediated capacity to act" (Ahearn, 2001, p. 112) and analysis of agency entails looking at the "interested practices of real people" (Ortner, 1998, p. 16), then it is abundantly clear from anthropological literature, as well as the narratives presented above, that there is no shortage of agency in the *dagongmei* community. Furthermore, it is also clear that there are diverse modalities of agency at work. In her critique and analysis of the Comaroffs' ethnography, feminist anthropologist Sherry Ortner makes a distinction between two forms of agency. The first form manifests itself as a kind of power, referring to those who have the power to dominate and those who are dominated but may have the power to resist. This form of agency, according to Ortner, is contrasted with the agency of intention, referring to "projects, purposes and desires" of not only individual actors but, more importantly, "a variety of culturally constituted desires, purposes, and projects that emerge from and of course reproduce different socially constituted positions and subjectivities" (2001, p. 79). The two forms of agency, stresses Ortner, are not mutually exclusive; nor do they exhaust the entire category of agency. The "I" in Fang's book obviously consciously engages in the personal project of finding a suitable marriage partner – one that is commensurate with the intention and desire of her position as a socioeconomically disadvantaged woman who nevertheless has familial obligations to fulfil. At the same time, Fang's decision to record her own experience is motivated by a political desire both to contest the state- and market-dominated public culture that misrepresents migrant women like herself and to produce an alternative and more "authentic" ethnography of the *dagongmei* experience. In doing so, she is exercising agency to resist symbolic as well as material domination.

The experience narrated in *I Am a Floating Flower*, along with the narrative of Fang's experience as a writer, points to the analytical purchase of agency as an "indispensable theoretical category" (Ortner, 2001, p. 77). At the same time it alerts us to the fact that unless we are aware of and have the means to describe and analyse the language in which these multiple modalities of agency are constructed in public culture, we run the risk of not registering, recognising and understanding them. These literary constructions are particularly valuable given that, for cultural reasons, first-hand anthropological material on how rural migrant women exercise sexual agency is often difficult to obtain.[1] While rural migrant women's capacity to pursue individual projects, desires and purposes is never in doubt, their capacity to insert themselves into the symbolic order and undertake moral and political interventions in the field of public culture is little understood. Analysing these literary constructions may prove to be instructive in this sense, given that, whether in the first person or the third person, these narratives enable readers to experience the world through the eyes of rural migrant women traversing urban life. Readers therefore come to make sense of urban life from the *dagongmei* perspective and understand their decisions and behaviours as being grounded in the constraints and limitations imposed on the *dagongmei*'s moral and material world.

In other words, the challenge we are confronted with – both theoretically and empirically – is not so much whether or how rural migrant women exercise various modalities of agency. Rather, it is understanding what kind of signifying practices are commonly deployed to make space for the "diverse politics of agency, involving the dense web of relations between coercion, negotiation, complicity, refusal, dissembling, mimicry, compromise, affiliation, and revolt" (McClintock, 1995, p. 15). Drawing on insights from feminist anthropology but aiming to take it further, I conceptualise agency as *cultural politics* and seek to demonstrate its analytical and empirical usefulness. Who has the power to name, define and give expression to agency? What is necessary to gain the means of producing, shaping and perpetuating the political lingua franca, media and cultural forms and dominant discursive practices? From where does the power to define the parameters with which the sexual experience of migrant women can be talked about originate? What is the process by which private and personal longings, dreams and desires turn into "public allegories" (Rofel, 2007) that mark certain social groups' projects, purposes and desires as more legitimate than others?

Given the dramatic speed with which Chinese society is becoming stratified in terms of gender, class and the rural-urban divide, addressing the question of inequality, public culture and power has become a matter of intellectual and empirical urgency. A cultural-political approach to agency means asking about the uneven capacity among various actors to shape the meanings of cultural products and to distribute the resources of cultural production, as well as the variegated capacity to deploy "new languages by which to describe oneself in the belief that they have desirable social consequences"

(Barker, 2000, p. 383). Concerned with the questions raised above, in this paper I examine the agency of *dagongmei* as it is constructed in a range of state, market, NGO, media, popular culture and academic discourses. I then trace the development of a subaltern literary genre, and through this, consider the relationship between new media/cultural forms and the emergence of a new language with which to express migrant women's sexual agency. Finally, in the last section, I present evidence from some works from this genre, with a view to identifying expressions of alternative sexual-moral economy, which both draws on and further informs the sexual experience of *dagongmei*.

Caged Agency?

Much has been said about the complex and fraught nature of the *dagongmei* as a social identity. *"Dagong"* is a Cantonese expression that means "working for the boss". In her ground-breaking study of factory workers in south China, Pun Ngai argues that *dagongmei* (migrant women workers) is a "specific Chinese subaltern" (Pun, 2005, p. 15), and as such "is a specific cultural-symbolic artefact as well as a worker-subject, constituted at the particular moment when transnational capital came to China in the postsocialist period" (Pun, 2005, p. 18). Although the term *dagongmei* was originally associated exclusively with assembly line production – conjuring associations with "docility", "nimble fingers" and a "pure and productive body" (Pun, 2005) – it has since evolved to become a general term describing *all* rural migrant women offering their cheap labour in a wide range of occupations in exchange for monetary and other material gains and, as such, has become an "element of popular culture in China" (Cartier, 2001, p. 193).

In south China, *dagongmei* are often referred to as *bei mei* (northern girls), but who is a northern girl depends on the person using the term and, more importantly, where the term is used. In Hong Kong, a *bei mei* is a migrant woman worker from mainland China, often engaged in the sex industry. To local residents in Guangdong Province, *bei mei* refers to any Chinese woman who is north of Guangdong. Similar geocentric and sexist logic works in terms such as *wailaimei* (women from outside) used in Shanghai, and *dalumei* (women from the mainland) used in Taiwan. But the configuration of *bei mei*, which is almost always derogatory in use, is not just geographical. It is also moral-sexual. In Hong Kong, it is often used to describe prostitutes working in either Hong Kong (like the woman in the film *Durian Durian*) or southern cities such as Shenzhen (Cartier, 2001, p. 193). In *Bei Mei*, a novel by Sheng Keyi, the term "*bei mei*" describes women who practise a new moral economy of sex regardless of their occupation – the northern girls in the novel include cleaners, hotel room attendants, waitresses, domestic servants, company receptionists, as well as sex workers. In other words, although *bei mei* are indelibly associated with sexual transgression, they are not necessarily synonymous with sex workers.

The state, capital, international NGOs and transnational cultural elites all jostle to speak for and on behalf of China's rural migrant workers, and the sexuality of rural migrant women is an integral dimension of the constructed *dagongmei* identity. For instance, the sexuality of *dagong* individuals – men and women – is portrayed in policy and academic discourses as a source of social instability and moral disorder.

Likewise, mobility is felt to pose serious challenges to the implementation of birth control (Zou, 2007). Chinese scholars have also noted the difficulty of managing long-term and stable relationships among rural migrant workers (Zhang, 2007; Zou, 2007; Cai, 2008). We know from this literature that casual sex is rife among migrant workers, and around 11 per cent of male workers visit prostitutes (Zhang, 2007, p. 125). These works have also identified a widespread issue of "sexual repression" (*xin yayi*), especially among male workers, due to a number of factors, including single-sex dormitory systems in many forms of employment, the difficulty of finding and maintaining long-term relationships due to high levels of mobility, and a growing tendency to see sex as an exchange of commodities. While these findings acknowledge workers' sexual urges as natural, they simultaneously express an anxiety about the danger of not being able to control or contain the problem, from the point of view of social stability and order, moral standards and public health. Much of the state's advice to migrant workers is in the form of handbooks and guidelines on how to behave in the city. Often this advice is overly simplistic, ineffectual and/or impractical. For instance, workers are advised simply to avoid extra-marital sex and to adopt healthy hobbies rather than watch pornography (Wemheuer, 2008). These perspectives seldom frame workers' sexual repression in terms of citizens' sexual human rights; nor do they reveal much about the range of sexual subject positions that are taken up by rural migrant workers, or what kind of cultural or emotional resources are available to resolve, make sense of and cope with this issue.

Narratives in the state media often portray women in a binary manner. On the one hand, the *lienü* (defiant woman) discourse, which typifies the normative subject position often promoted in official narratives, urges rural migrants to engage in ceaseless self-improvement and develop a strong sense of self-respect, self-reliance and self-strength, all of which are essential to, and crucial manifestations of, achieving good *suzhi* (quality) (Jacka, 2006; Yan, 2008; Sun, 2009a). Narrative accounts of individual migrant women informed by this discourse portray women risking their own lives to protect themselves from sexual violence and harassment, implying that one's sexual purity is more important than one's life and that failure to act heroically is morally questionable. For instance, the Women's Federation's endorsement of *lienü* – a woman who prefers suicide to being sexually violated – betrays a patriarchal order of sexual morality and is felt to do more damage than good to the sexual dignity of migrant women (Sun, 2004; Jacka, 2006).

On the other hand, some migrant women are often chastised in official narratives for having easily succumbed to the lure of easy money and shamelessly selling their bodies instead of doing "respectable" work, or for being naïve enough to fall prey to predatory men (Sun, 2004). Rural migrant women are often shown in these narratives to be willing to use sex for favours, opportunities and monetary gain, and because of this, they are cast as being uneducated, morally questionable, and lacking in civility, thus needing self-improvement and self-development (Jacka, 1998; 2006; Davin, 1999; Dutton, 1998; Sun, 2004; Yan, 2008). Yet these narratives are usually reluctant to acknowledge that the sexual decisions made by rural migrant women in order to lend assistance to their families and friends could in fact be acts of bravery, selflessness, if not heroism. The discourse of self-improvement also informs the position of certain migrant advocacy groups, such as the Rural Migrant Women's Home, whose discourses on gender are sometimes accepted but sometimes rejected by migrant women (Jacka, 2006). Diana

Fu (2009) observes that the Rural Migrant Women's Home encourages women to become *nü qiangren* (strong women) and gives them discursive space to speak about themselves, thus achieving a certain degree of empowerment. In the process of "hailing" their member migrant women into the "ideal" *dagongmei* subjectivity, the Home ends up reproducing the state discourse of economic reform and becomes an agent in disciplining these women into a docile, cheap labour force. Here we see a paradoxical scenario. While both certain migrant advocacy groups and subaltern migrant writings may share a common goal of improving the lives of rural migrant women, migrant women's self-writings, which highlight sexual strategies, could be used as potential evidence of migrant women's moral abjectness, and if so, have the adverse effect of reproducing rather than ameliorating their exclusion from the mainstream moral order.[2]

Profit-driven media narratives often reinforce this sexualised image of the *dagongmei* and construct them as morally loose and sexually out of control (Sun, 2004; Zheng, 2009). In addition, *dagongmei* as desiring subjects have been largely discussed within the context of their relationship to consumer goods, including fashions and cosmetics, which are supposed to make them look sexually desirable, or "sexy" (Pun, 2005; Jacka, 2006; Yan, 2008). In the meantime, a sizeable and still growing body of findings points to the commodification of their bodies and the emergence of an unstable, female working-class subject (Jacka, 2006; Gaetano and Jacka, 2004; Pun, 2005; Yan, 2008; Sun, 2009a; Fu, 2009). These works also comment on the tension confronting migrant women between traditional values and urban modern lifestyles (Gaetano, 2004; Jacka, 2006; Gaetano and Jacka, 2004). For instance, evidence from Beijing suggests that sexual harassment of domestic workers occurs frequently in urban homes, but for a range of reasons, most victims find themselves unable to complain, let alone to seek justice (Sun, 2009a). Among migrant women in Beijing, premarital sexual activity has increased, often involving unprotected sex and unplanned pregnancies. And when sexual activity is an issue, women are more subject to censure than men (Jacka, 2006, p. 221).

Dagongmei have the added difficulty of having far fewer outlets than other social groups – such as male migrants – for pursuing their desires, and often live in much more circumscribed, deprived and scrutinised spatial arrangements. Some new data that has emerged from a recent large-scale survey conducted by a Shenzhen-based team on the sexuality of rural migrant women in Shenzhen finds that a considerable number of migrant workers admit that they feel sexually repressed, and while only 17.5 per cent of the women surveyed have experience of sexual intercourse, the great majority of women resort to "self-pleasure" and "self-adjustment" as ways of coping with sexual desire. They do not pay for sex; nor do they provide sexual services for monetary gain (Cai, 2008).

Shifting from one end of the spectrum of moral purity occupied by *dagongmei* to the other end are rural women who enter the sex industry and work as prostitutes. Zheng Tiantian's ethnography of bar hostesses in Dalian in northern China (Zheng, 2004; 2009) reminds us that alongside the factory assembly line, brothels, bars, entertainment centres and hair salons are also the workplaces of these migrant women. In contrast to factory workers, sex workers – often referred to in popular idioms as "*ji*" (chickens) – are seen to have patently "menacing and contaminating" bodies (Zheng, 2004, p. 88) and are portrayed in popular representations as sources of urban desire, anxiety, fascination and fear (Sun, 2004; 2009b; Zhao, 2002; Zheng, 2009). In both cases, however, there is clearly a process of commodification of the body – the *dagongmei* selling labour to capital and prostitutes selling sex to clients. As Zheng Tiantian points out, sex workers defy the state's opposition to prostitution and market their bodies for "independent, autonomous, and instrumental uses". At the same time, however, Zheng argues that sex workers' strategies are manifested through, rather than outside, the constraining and enabling masculine state structure, and "their very agency paradoxically binds and limits them by reinscribing and reproducing the hegemonic state discourse that legitimises and naturalises the docile virgin/promiscuous whore split image". As a result, "their agency becomes what is held against them and reinforces their marginality and low status" (Zheng, 2009, p. 241).

Southern Migrant Literature and Subaltern Genre

The development of Shenzhen, Dongguan and other cities in the Pearl River Delta as the sites for China's global factories in the past three decades has given rise to a distinct regional culture featuring migration and industrialisation. It must be noted that from its onset the so-called "*dagong* culture" (*dagong wenhua*) has been the child of both market imperative and the Shenzhen local government's initiative to foster local literature and culture. As early as the late 1980s and early 1990s, life on the factory assembly line and dormitory regimes in south China gave rise to "*dagong* literature" (*dagong wenxue*), consisting of songs, poems, a myriad of self-funded publications, online forums, and fiction and non-fiction writing, all depicting *dagong* experience. Keen to exploit literary talents to foster a sense of belonging to Shenzhen, promote social harmony, and ensure social stability, the Shenzhen government actively pursued a number of experiments whereby business and the Party-state joined forces to produce local culture. In 1984, *Special Zone Literature* (*Tequ Wenxue*) started to publish works focusing on the experience of migrants in Shenzhen; in 1988, *Dapengwan*, a local Shenzhen magazine, declared that "reflecting the lives of the *dagong* community" would be its main editorial ambit. In addition, several literary and public culture journals, such as *Huacheng*, *Guangzhou Wenyin*, and *Fushan Wenyin*, also started to create new columns, set up special prizes, and hold essay writing competitions in order to promote writings on *dagong* experience.

These local initiatives not only went a long way towards legitimising *dagong* as a literary genre and mobility as a literary theme, but also presented invaluable space for the vast amount of migrant experience to become part of what Lisa Rofel calls "public allegories", and thus became crucial in the "remaking of public spaces and stories through which human nature discovers itself" (2007, p. 6). In 1988, *Special Zone Literature* published 'Report from the Kingdom of Women', a fictional piece by Chen Bing'an (Chen, 1988) documenting the yearnings and aspirations of 200,000 casual *dagongmei* in Shenzhen. In 1991, *dagongmei* An Zi's debut, an uplifting literary reportage titled 'Rites of Youthful Passage' (*Qingchun yizhai*), was published in *Shenzhen Special Zone Daily* and subsequently as a book (An Zi, 1992). It is considered the first literary work on the transformation of China's *dagongmei* written by a *dagongmei*. It bears mentioning that of all the subaltern writers, An Zi, later often dubbed the "queen of the *dagong* community", is often singled out in the mainstream perspective as representative of the *dagongmei* spirit, since her book tells a story of social mobility – the journey of a rural migrant woman to become a spectacularly successful entrepreneur. In comparison to An Zi, Zheng Xiaoqiong, a migrant woman poet whose poems project a chilling but compelling vision of the alienation and dehumanisation experienced on the assembly line, has had a much more ambiguous reception.

Much of *dagong* literature in more recent years has started as online writing. For instance, Fang Yimeng's novel *I Am a Floating Flower: A Dagongmei in Dongguan* (*Wo shi yiduo piaolin de hua*) was only published after it became immensely popular online. All episodes of Sheng Keyi's novel *Northern Girls* (*Bei mei*), together with her other titles, to be discussed below, are easily available on the internet. In other words, political economy aside, it is impossible to conceive of the rise of *dagong* literature without considering the growing presence of new media and communication technologies. Individuals in the *dagong* community have been enthusiastic adopters of mobile phones and the internet (Qiu, 2009), and the emergence of spaces for blogging, microblogging, online publishing and social media interactions – mostly via the mobile phone – among factory workers in south China has led to a certain degree of democratisation in the world of publishing. Anyone who has the technical literacy to harness these technologies can publish online – material that would otherwise not be able to pass the reviewing process of conventional publishing – and anyone with a mobile phone and a monthly subscription to QQ can read material online or download material to their phone. In a way, this has revolutionised the world of publishing. Increasingly, publishers decide to publish in book form material that is already available online and, judging by the number of hits and the volume of download traffic, has proven to be popular. Many of the *dagong* literary works are published via this pathway.

Due to the diffuse modes of publishing and consumption, it is hard to be precise about the scale and composition of the readership of *dagong* literature. While it is safe to speculate that these books are mostly purchased by urban and educated readers in cultural institutions, including academic, media and literary associations who are interested in the lives of migrant workers, the diversification of the modes of circulation makes it difficult to gauge the size of the actual readership. In my fieldwork, I have talked to many young migrant workers who regularly download reading material from online sources, often onto their mobile phones.[3] A former migrant worker, who is now working for a migrant advocacy group and is writing a novel about *dagong* life, told me that the more literary-inclined sector of the migrant worker community would like to record their experience by writing it down, but they are too busy or too tired to do so. In a way, reading other people's writing about a life that is familiar to them is a way of vicariously expressing themselves.[4]

Although not all migrant writings are concerned with sexuality, it is safe to say that many are. One often finds expressions of rural migrants' sexual desire as well as documentation of sexual repression and frustrations. They are also narratives of, on the one hand, libidinous, opportunistic and strategic sexual activity engaged in by migrant individuals, and, on the other hand, exploitative, predatory and sometimes violent sex imposed on them. Stories range from sexual deprivation, marital crises and family break-ups brought on by mobility, and the difficulty – if not impossibility – of finding romance and emotional intimacy in sex, through to feelings of confusion surrounding the appropriate level of sexual intimacy one should negotiate with one's lover once both have left the village and moved to the city where sexual mores are more liberal.

Migrant stories often unfold against the background of the rural migrant's place of work, daily life and social interactions in the city. This includes the industrial assembly lines, factory dormitories, rented rooms, companies, business premises, and various other places of interaction between unequal social groups, such as hotels, restaurants and spaces providing services and hospitality. Even though migrants have left home to come to the city, their place of origin – rural, northern or inland – still counts against them. Not only are sexuality and mobility the twin engines of these narratives; sex is often both the metaphor and embodiment of the social and economic activities pursued by migrants in these places. In fact, many of these writings foreground the interplay between sexuality and migrant experience, rather than simply using it as the backdrop of an unfolding story. In other words, these works, written to register the dramatic change in social relations and moral economy, are marked by a distinct and deliberate narrative technique of sexualising social-economic inequalities, between the urban and rural, the north and south, and the poor and the wealthy. In this sense, they are strangely reminiscent of the Restoration drama in England, as well as the fiction of Richardson and Fielding, in which themes of love are narrated with increasing frankness and cynicism about marriage as a means of income and property transaction (Williams, 1973).

In researching the history of prostitution in early twentieth-century Shanghai, Gail Hershatter observes that prostitutes in pre-revolutionary China were "subaltern several times over" (1993, p. 108). Since it is difficult to find historical records in which prostitutes represent themselves directly, historians resort to a wide range of sources – from cautionary guidebooks to prostitutes' accounts and legal documents – to find traces of subaltern voices. This approach uncovers multiple, relational degrees of subalternity, proving that subaltern perspectives emerge only when discourses are seen "in relation to each other" (Hershatter, 1993, p. 126). Hershatter's point regarding subalternity as a relational concept that needs to be examined through specific categories is crucial to the analysis here. After all, not all migrant writings are concerned with the lives of rural migrants, and not all of them focus on the survival of the "people at the bottom". For this reason, it is important to realise that southern migrant literature is sharply stratified, with much of it unconcerned with the everyday struggles of low-skilled, rural migrant labourers. Thus, it is only half-jokingly that a literary critic in China comments that *Shenzhen: A Passionate Night* was written for readers who earn 10,000 yuan, *Shenzhen Lovers* was written for readers who earn 100,000 yuan, and *Shenzhen to the Left, Paradise to the Right* was written for readers whose annual income is 1 million yuan (Chen, 2007, p. 40).

For this reason, what many Chinese literary critics refer to as the "subaltern migrant writings" (*dicing yimin wenxue*) on sexuality should be distinguished from two other genres that feature sex and sexual desire as the main motifs. The first genre is produced by a group of urban, middle-class female writers, often referred to as "beauty writers" (*meinu zuojia*), well known for their explicit and erotic depictions of female sexuality. Mian Mian's collection of short stories, *Sugar* (*Tang*, 2000), and Wei Hui's *Shanghai Baby* (*Shanghai baobei*, 1999) fall into this category. To be read as a battle cry against the patriarchal order of female objectification, these works posit individual women as desiring subjects, whose sexual agency lies in full and explicit expressions of sensations of the female body in ambiguous response to the desire machine of the metropolis (Wang, 2007, p. 163). Middle-class, urban, and unapologetically introspective on the body and the carnal experience of the private self, these writings are nevertheless decidedly uninterested in the wider issues of social inequality, gender, class and the rural-urban disparity, despite the fact that they may share with subaltern female writings a conviction to write from the perspective of women as desiring subjects. The second genre is comprised of pornographic writings in magazines and fictional works that "are meant to satisfy the sexual desire of travellers and city men and to provide economic benefits". These publications are typically sold in public spaces such as train stations, book vendors and street corner newsstands under the guise of "legal education" materials, and they often portray rural women as objects of rape, abuse and crime (Zheng, 2008, p. 11).

A compounding factor to bear in mind is that rural migrant men themselves, often a social group with the scantest cultural capital, resources and consumption power, are often the targeted readers of what Tani Barlow (2005) refers to as the "smut" literature of urban China, which eroticises and objectifies women. At the same time, genuine attempts to represent the sexual experience of migrant men and women as part of their daily power struggle, and as an integral aspect of social experience and economic activity, may often be too salubrious for this group of readers and instead appeal mainly to the more literary-minded sector of the rural migrant population, as well as urban readers who are either curious about, or genuinely interested in, the lives of China's socially disadvantaged groups. In other words, since sex sells, as the saying goes, its slippage and spill across genres and social identities as a subject matter is worth bearing in mind. This is especially the case since some publications, while originally intended to express subaltern social issues confronting rural migrants, are either seduced by profit or driven by the need to survive and start catering to the tastes of the lowest common denominator. The transformation of *Da Peng Wai*, which started as a literary magazine publishing migrant writers on the experience of migration, into a popular magazine featuring scantily dressed women, erotica and sexual crime attests to this (Nie, 2008, p. 93). The intricacy and complexity of China's popular cultural landscape, in which sex figures centrally, cautions us against any attempt to limit our search for a truly subaltern perspective within a singular, clean-edged domain of representation. This is particularly the case when what does and does not qualify as *dagong* literature remains a slippery issue (Yang, 2007).

Northern Girls: Self-Ethnography of Migrant Women

Against the hegemony of "grand narratives" of modernisation promulgated in these mainstream discourses, and juxtaposed to the widespread practice of eroticising rural migrant women, some literary-inclined individuals within the migrant community in south China have produced some perspectives on mobility and sexuality that turn these hegemonic representations on their heads. An integral part of the so-called *dagong* culture, this genre is showing promising signs of providing much needed alternative perspectives in the post-Mao Chinese cultural landscape. *Northern Girls* is one of them. As its title indicates, the novel narrates the lives of a number of young rural migrant women in S City in Hunan Province, one of the biggest sending zones of outbound rural migrants in China. Author Sheng Keyi is herself a migrant, whose survival in the south was initially marked by poverty, deprivation and humiliation. Sheng is now described as a "flower of subaltern literature" (*diceng zhihua*) (Yang, 2007, p. 131), and *Northern Girls* has been translated into English.[5] In the novel, these northern girls try to eke out a living working as waitresses, cleaners, maids and masseuses. They find themselves entangled in myriad insalubrious sexual liaisons, including sleeping with married men and then being abandoned after getting pregnant, selling sex for cash or temporary residential permits, being rounded up by local police while dating boyfriends in public, being sterilised by force on suspicion of being guilty of evading the family planning scheme, renting their bodies for surrogacy, and being brutally raped and murdered when sexual liaisons go awry. These experiences are narrated in a realistic, almost documentary style that is confronting, unflinching and gritty, driving home the message that brutal and tragic as these experiences are, they are in fact quite familiar to many *dagongmei*, who live out, on a daily basis, the "culture of survival".

Xiao Hong, the main protagonist in the novel, warrants special and separate consideration, not necessarily because her characterisation is a closer depiction of the sexual experience of *dagongmei*, but because it points to the possibility of an alternative sexual *dagongmei* agency, as well as the limit beyond which such possibility cannot be entertained. Growing up in rural Hunan, Xiao Hong becomes sexually precocious because she is forced to have sexual intercourse with her brother-in-law at the age of 14 and acquires a reputation as a village "slut" for sleeping around. Yet even though Xiao Hong is sexually uninhibited and promiscuous, she refuses to sell her body for money when she arrives in S City at the age of 16. Xiao Hong has conspicuously larger breasts than other girls and therefore becomes an object of desire in S City, a city awash with libidinal urges and sex for sale. Living under the impression that she has finally escaped her brother-in-law, Xiao Hong sets out to pursue her own freedom to have sex with whomever she wants, when she wants, and on her own terms and conditions, and finally, to have the freedom to refuse to sell her body.

Xiao Hong does succeed in achieving a certain degree of sexual autonomy and freedom, without guilt. Although disappointed that the only man with whom she forms some emotional attachment is engaged to someone else, she tries her best to have a fulfilling sex life as a single woman. Furthermore, she negotiates with men on her own terms and according to her own sense of justice. While working as a hotel room attendant, Xiao Hong finds herself alone in a room occupied by a government official in his 50s. Like everyone else, the government official assumes Xiao Hong is available for sex.

> Eyeing Xiao Hong, the man hands over a 50-yuan note for the beer he has ordered through room service, and says, "I know how it goes: for 10 bucks, I'd have to bring my own tissue; for 100 bucks, I can have you in whatever positions; for 1,000 bucks, I can have you for the whole day; for 10,000 bucks, I can do you till you are dead. So which deal are you offering?" Xiao Hong hears him, thinks for a second, and goes over to him, taking off his vest, stripping him of his underwear, and says, "Let me take a good look at you first". She walks around this man, who now looks like a skinned toad, with a flabby bottom and a thing between his legs that resembles a newly sprouted seedling just planted into the rice paddy. After that, Xiao Hong feigns seriousness and says, "Uncle, I am sorry. I am still a virgin. I am only curious about your body. I have stripped you bare. Now you have to get dressed again. So here is 50 yuan for your trouble. It's my tip for you". She throws the 50-yuan note which she has been holding in

her hand, and she walks out of the door... This government official has apparently suffered a heavy blow from this encounter, and each time he walks past the reception at the entrance, he never dares to look the girls in the eye (Sheng, 2004, p. 154).

Xiao Hong does not understand why sex should have any value in market economic terms. At the same time, she does not understand why wanting sexual gratification is often considered to be an exclusively male desire. Equally importantly, although Xiao Hong's quest for sexual freedom often dovetails with the eroticisation of the *dagongmei* body, resulting in easily available sex for Xiao Hong, love and affection, which she equally craves, are far more difficult to obtain. In other words, much as she enjoys her new found sexual freedom in S City, Xiao Hong soon realises that her status as a lowly *dagongmei* often stands in the way of obtaining the sexual and emotional equality she desires. While working as an assistant in a hair salon, Xiao Hong attracts the attention of, and is attracted to, a handsome young man from a local organised crime gang. While in bed, she realises, much to her disappointment, that her partner is not interested in pleasuring her. After he finishes his "business" in bed, he gets dressed and tosses a ring to an apparently unfulfilled Xiao Hong, saying calmly, "I only sleep with a woman once".

Unlike their male counterparts, *dagongmei* not only have to cope with sexual frustration in the city, but also have to manage these frustrations vis-à-vis the patriarchal order and traditional expectations surrounding marriage, norms of gender propriety, and popular stereotypes associated with mobility and immorality (Gaetano, 2004, p. 5). Despite her obvious "sexiness", Xiao Hong refuses to sell her body for money or other gains, but when she returns to the village, saddled with gifts for families and neighbours, she realises that almost everyone at home, including her own sister and father, assumes that she has been working as a sex worker. The assumption is that Xiao Hong cannot possibly have money to buy these presents in the city unless she has sold her body. Upon this realisation, Xiao Hong blurts out, "Damn it! When I go back to S city, I will do precisely that – sell my body. At least I would deserve the reputation I have here!" (Sheng, 2004, p. 144).

Misunderstanding and social prejudice against mobile women aside, the greatest moral dilemma confronting the *dagongmei* is the competing and contradictory messages directed towards her regarding the value of her body. While families back at home question her sexual propriety due to her mobility, the moral economy of the market is predicated on the easy and ready availability of sex from promiscuous rural migrant women (Zheng, 2009). Relatively successfully, Xiao Hong manages the underlying tension of freedom and autonomy, on the one hand, and constraint and subjugation, on the other, armed with an optimism and naiveté typical of her youth. This tension finally reaches breaking point towards the end of the book, which shifts abruptly from a realist mode of storytelling to that of fantasy. Xiao Hong's breasts start to take on a phantasmagorical dimension. After an unplanned pregnancy, Xiao Hong finds, much to her horror, that her breasts, so far the source of her sexual pleasure and source of men's attraction to her, are diseased with the "proliferation of mammary glands". They start to grow uncontrollably, until they get as heavy as "two bags of rice", making it difficult for Xiao Hong to move around the city. She has become not only an unsightly spectacle but also miserably trapped in this newly transfigured body.

Xiao Hong's friend, Li Sijiang, is another *bei mei* from Hunan, who realises, on arriving on the outskirts of Guangzhou, that unless she has a temporary residential permit she is not free to go anywhere or to look for work. And she is also told by her distant cousin, a migrant and fellow traveller, that the easiest and quickest way to secure a permit is for her to sleep with the local district chief, the man who has the authority to issue a temporary residential permit. Since Li is a virgin, her chances are even better, as "they are always prepared to pay a higher price to have sex with a virgin". Fearing arrest for unlawful residence, and eager to find work, Li sleeps with the district chief. After that, she says calmly, "What is a hymen? I don't think I have lost anything. Just think: starting from tomorrow, we will be free" (Sheng, 2004, p. 33), indicating that trading her virginity for the freedom to work and live in a new city without police harassment is both logical and justifiable.

Loach (*Ni Qiu*, 2002), by You Fenwei, is another novel-length fictional work that focuses on the sexuality of rural migrants. Although the novel centres on the sexual adventures of Guei, a rural young man who now works as a removalist, casual labourer, kitchen hand, cleaner and construction worker, the narration of the sexual experiences of the *bei mei* who appear in Guei's orbit of everyday life is equally revealing of a new cultural politics of sexual agency. Guei has a girlfriend, Tao Feng, from the village, who comes to join him in the city. Constrained by the traditional rural values of chastity and female modesty, she refuses to give her body to Guei until they marry, much as he wants her. In the meantime, Guei, through the arrangement of a friend, becomes the housekeeper for a middle-aged woman, Gong Yu, with whom he has a passionate affair. The wife of a rich and powerful property developer with extensive connections with the city government, Gong is an extremely unhappy "kept woman" until she meets Guei. While Guei's girlfriend Tao Feng insists on no sex before marriage, Kou Lan, another migrant woman, is deeply in love with Guei, unbeknownst to Guei himself, and is prepared to do anything for him. Although not a girlfriend, Kou Lan is grateful to Guei, who previously rescued her from her abusive boyfriend, and regards him as both a saviour and a friend worth dying for. When Guei, though innocent, gets into trouble with the police and is wrongfully detained, Kou Lan learns that the only way to rescue her object of desire is for her to sleep with the policeman. Without hesitation, she pays her dues in kind, and a week later, Guei is released. Kou Lan would be considered by many to be a "loose" and "easy" woman, but she clearly acts out of a deep-seated conviction that given the powerless position she is in, rescuing her friend in exchange for a one-off sexual exchange makes good moral-economic sense. The narrative account of the circumstances in which these women make sexual decisions is in sharp contrast to the normative *lienü* discourse often promoted in official narratives.

These women's decisions and choices are expressions of agency, which exist in the "mediation between conscious intention and embodied habituses, and between conscious motives and unexpected outcomes" (Ortner, 2001, p. 77). They also stand in contrast to another strand of narrative, particularly in the state television drama series, which tends to construct migrant women's sexuality as a metaphor for social mobility. There, migrant women are represented as working hard to improve their *suzhi* level, and end up being rewarded with the love and sexual desire of urban men with superior social status (Lee, 2006; Sun, 2009a). In contrast to such "morally uplifting" narratives are the perennial media stories of the "gold-digger" – the migrant domestic worker marrying or offering sex to her geriatric employer in order to get her hands on his money, property and entitlement to urban privileges (Sun, 2010). In comparison to these top-down perspectives, subaltern migrant literary writings do not so much narrate sexual experiences that are more "typical" of rural migrant women as a group; rather, they function to reinstall a range of subject positions that are either unavailable in popular narratives, or unacceptable against the criteria of the ideal woman narratives promoted in the official discourses.

Conclusion: Agency as Cultural Politics

Following cultural studies' concern with the question of who has the power to name, to represent common sense, to create "official versions" of history, and to represent the legitimate social world (Jordan and Weedon, 1995, p. 13), a cultural politics of agency can be pursued in three (related) directions. The first proceeds from understanding how the desires and actions of each of these actors – the state, capital, NGOs, transnational elites and rural migrant workers themselves – work to reinforce, accommodate, contradict or undermine one another as they exist in an articulated and mutually impacting structure. The second involves constructing a cultural politics of agency that foregrounds the very categories through which the "desires, purposes and projects" of actors are narrated. Building on these and taking these further, the third direction seeks to unravel the fraught process through which certain specific media forms and cultural practices emerge and develop in response to the negotiations and contestations between various actors. I suggest that insofar as women and agency in China is concerned, feminist scholarship has done reasonably well in the pursuit of the first two directions, but it has yet to develop an analytical language to pursue the third direction. A picture of the cultural politics of agency in relation to women, especially women from socioeconomically disadvantaged backgrounds, remains somewhat opaque. This paper is an attempt to fill this gap.

Pursuing agency as cultural politics, as this paper does, produces some useful clues to the question of whose sexual practices are transgressive enough to deserve the label of "northern girl" in social exchanges, popular culture or literary works. It also draws our attention to the question of whose signifying practices are put in place to perpetuate, negotiate or contest the hegemonic imagination of the northern girl. Finally, and most importantly, it helps us to gain a conceptual and empirical understanding, however preliminary and inchoate, of an alternative sexual moral economy, according to which we can hope to recast the northern girl, not as a singular group marked with sexual perversity, but as having, like most other social groups, a complex and often contradictory set of sexual-moral agencies.

In dominant public cultural narratives, the term northern girl evokes a distinct spatial, as well as a moral, dimension: the label potently inscribes moral abjectness onto people from northern and inland China, who trade sex for monetary or other material gains in proliferating forms of exchanges in southern coastal cities. There, the "semiotic potential of the migrant body" (Cartier, 2006, p. 142) seems to be mined to the advantage of those who benefit from the naming and exploitation of northern girls, and not to that of the northern girl herself. In light of the new cultural politics of sexual agency proposed here, however, the northern girl is no longer associated with moral abjectness; instead, she is assigned to a new analytical role. In this new configuration, the northern girl is defined not so much by the specificity of her occupation or her sexual behaviour, but by her sexual agency, which defies, challenges and redraws the sexual moral parameters of the powers that be. At the same time, more than the constructed identity of the *dagongmei* (in its "purest" form, as Pun Ngai's factory workers imagine themselves to be) or the prostitute, the northern girl helps collapse the image split between a pure, hard-working woman and a girl with loose sexual morality. For those who are concerned with the cultural politics of power, the body of the northern girl signifies, as well as trades in, a range of inequalities – gender, class, as well as geography – thus forcing us to view her body as a site of unequal exchange between the north and south, men and women, and urban elites and rural migrants.

The literary works discussed here provide an alternative perspective on the practical circumstances, moral rationalities and emotional consequences – what Ortner calls "the agency of intentions" – consisting of desires, purposes and projects. Reading these accounts against those normative ones promulgated in state-controlled media, in "authoritative" genres such as news and current affairs programs and "serious" high-brow literature, we are able to see the working of what Ortner calls "agency as power" and the contestation between the dominant and the dominated. And looking at how the two forms of agency interact reminds us to take seriously "the categories through which historical subjects make meaning of their own experience, the degree to which subalterns both legitimate and subvert hegemonic categories" (Hershatter, 1993, p. 106). Writers of this genre often describe their writings – whether written in the first person narrative (e.g. *I Am a Floating Flower*) or the third-person narrative (e.g. *Northern Girls*) – as "true accounts" and, thus, declare their political desires and purposes, and engage in projects that contest dominant cultural constructions in the domain of public culture. For this reason, claims made about the ethnographic nature of their writings are best taken to mean that these narratives should be read more as accounts of the collective experience of *dagongmei* or *bei mei* as a socially marginalised cohort, and less as strictly autobiographical writings about individuals. As Sheng Keyi writes in the Preface to *Northern Girls*, "the lived experience of *bei mei* is much more real and meaningful than the novel itself" (Sheng, 2004, p. 1).

Furthermore, these claims also suggest that ethnographies are "genres, as much as other literary forms" and are also socially constructed (Karp, 1986, p. 132). In doing so, migrant subaltern literature has the likely impact of de-authorising scholarly ethnographic accounts that, despite their best intentions, often end up missing vitally important clues to the diversity and complexity of their sexual agency.[6] These writings constitute important moral interventions, not so much because they present a more authentic or truthful account of the sexual experience of rural migrant women than mainstream public narratives, but because they offer a competing – and more compelling – interpretation of their sexual-moral agency.

Acknowledgments

The author would like to thank the two reviewers for their insightful comments and helpful suggestions for future work.

Notes

1. The exception to this observation is ethnographies of migrant women as sex workers. See Zheng (2004; 2009).
2. I am grateful to a reviewer for pointing out this complicating factor.
3. Although this paper is not ethnographic in nature, it is informed by my extensive fieldwork on the work and lives of China's rural migrants, which took place in Shenzhen, Dongguan and Suzhou from 2009 to 2011.
4. Repeated conversations with Xiao Quan took place in Suzhou on several trips in 2009 and 2010. He is now heading an NGO that advocates for rural migrant workers in Suzhou.
5. Sheng is now becoming internationally recognised for her work. She was, for instance, invited to speak at the 2012 Sydney Writers' Festival.
6. I have been encouraged by a reviewer to pursue this point further in my future work, particularly by engaging with feminist philosophical debates on "experience" and "standpoint". I will certainly take it up in my future work.

References

Ahearn, Lauren (2001) Language and agency. *Annual Review of Anthropology* 30, pp. 109–37.
An Zi (1992) *Qingchun yizhan: Shenzhen dagongmei xiezheng* (Haikou: Haitian Press).
Barker, Chris (2000) *Cultural studies: Theory and practice* (London: Sage).
Barlow, Tani (2005) Pornographic city, in Jing Wang (ed.), *Locating China: Space, place and popular culture*, pp. 190–209 (London: Routledge).
Cai Li, ed. (2008) *Shenzhen nu laowu gong hunlian zhuangkuang yanjiu* (Beijing: Social Sciences Academic Press).
Cartier, Carolyn (2001) *Globalizing south China* (Oxford: Blackwell).
Cartier, Carolyn (2006) Symbolic city/regions and gendered identity formation in south China, in Tim Oakes and Louisa Schein (eds), *Translocal China: Linkages, identities, and the reimagining of space*, pp. 139–54 (London: Routledge).
Chen Bing'an (1988) Laizi nu'er guo de badao. Available at http://www.baike.com/wiki/陈秉安, accessed December 2013.
Chen Xiaomin (2007) Chengshi wenxue: wufa xiansheng de "da ta zhe", in Yang Honghai (ed.), *Quangqiu yujin xia de dangdai dushi wenxue*, pp. 1–41 (Beijing: Social Sciences Academic Press).
Davin, Delia (1999) *Internal migration in China* (London: Macmillan).
Dutton, Michael (1998) *Streetlife China* (Cambridge, UK: Cambridge University Press).
Fang Yimeng (2008) *Woshi yiduo piaolin de hua* (Beijing: Xiandan chubanshe).
Fu, Diana (2009) A cage of voices: Producing and doing *dagongmei* in contemporary China. *Modern China* 35(5), pp. 527–61.
Gaetano, Arianne M. (2004) Filial daughters, modern women: Migrant domestic workers in post-Mao Beijing, in Arianne M. Gaetano and Tamara Jacka (eds), *On the move: Women in rural-to-urban migration in contemporary China*, pp. 41–79 (New York: Columbia University Press).
Gaetano, Arianne M. and Tamara Jacka, eds. (2004) *On the move: Women in rural-to-urban migration in contemporary China* (New York: Columbia University Press).
Hershatter, Gail (1993) The subaltern talks back: Reflections on subaltern theory and Chinese history. *Positions: East Asia Cultures Critique* 1(1), pp. 103–30.
Jacka, Tamara (1998) Working sisters answer back: Representation and self-representation of women in China's floating population. *China Information* 13(1), pp. 43–75.
Jacka, Tamara (2006) *Rural women in urban China: Gender, migration, and social change* (Armonk, NY: M.E. Sharpe).
Jordan, Glenn and Chris Weedon (1995) *Cultural politics: Class, gender, race, and the postmodern world* (Oxford: Blackwell).
Karp, Ivan (1986) Agency and social theory: A review of Anthony Giddons. *American Ethnologist* 13(1), pp. 131–37.
Lee, Haiyan (2006) Nannies for foreigners: The enchantment of Chinese womanhood in the age of millennial capitalism. *Public Culture* 18(3), pp. 507–29.

Liu Dingguo (2008) Zuoping tai xieshi, haipa lu zhengrong. *Nanfang Dushi Bao*, 22 January, p. DA 42.
McClintock, Anne (1995) *Imperial leather: Race, gender and sexuality in the colonial contest* (New York: Routledge).
Mian Mian (2000) *Tang* (Beijing: China Theatre Press).
Nie Wei (2008) *Wenxue dushi yu xinyxiang minjian* (Guilin, Guangxi: Guang Normal University Press).
Ortner, Sherry (1998) Generation X: Anthropology in a media-saturated world. *Cultural Anthropology* 13(3), pp. 414–40.
Ortner, Sherry (2001) Specifying agency: The Comaroffs and their critics. *Interventions* 3(1), pp. 76–84.
Pun, Ngai (2005) *Made in China: Women factory workers in a global workplace* (Durham, NC: Duke University Press).
Qiu, Jack Linchuan (2009) *Working-class network society: Communications technology and the information have-less in urban China* (Cambridge, MA: The MIT Press).
Rofel, Lisa (2007) *Desiring China: Experiments in neoliberalism, sexuality, and public culture* (Durham, NC: Duke University Press).
Sheng Keyi (2004) *Bei mei* (Wuhan: Changjiang wenyi chuban she).
Sun, Wanning (2004) Indoctrination, fetishization, and compassion: Media constructions of the migrant woman, in Arianne M. Gaetano and Tamara Jacka (eds), *On the move: Women in rural-to-urban migration in contemporary China*, pp. 109–28 (New York: Columbia University Press).
Sun, Wanning (2009a) *Maid in China: Media, morality, and the cultural politics of boundaries* (London: Routledge).
Sun, Wanning (2009b) Making space for the maid: Metropolitan gaze, peripheral vision and subaltern spectatorship in urban China. *Feminist Media Studies* 9(1), pp. 57–71.
Sun, Wanning (2010) Sex, city, and the maid: Between socialist fantasies and neoliberal parables. *Journal of Current Chinese Affairs* 39(4), pp. 53–69.
Wang Suxia (2007) Cuangru, jiudu, yu youdang, chuanyue, in *Quangqiong hua yujin xia de dangdai dushi wenxue*, pp. 158–70 (Beijing: Social Sciences Academic Press).
Wei Hui (1999) *Shanghai baobei* (Shengyang: Chunfeng Arts and Literature Press).
Wemheuer, Felix (2008) Governing the body of the peasant worker in China's cities: Dangerous sexual desires of the "other" in the official discourse. Available at http://public.univie.ac.at/fileadmin/user_upload/proj_faminesoc/wemheuerchina.pdf, accessed December 2012.
Williams, Raymond (1973) *The country and the city* (London: Chatto and Windus).
Yan, Hairong (2008) *New masters, new servants: Development, migration, and women workers* (Durham, NC: Duke University Press).
Yang Honghai (2007) Shenzhen wenxue: xin dushi xinlin beiwang lu, in *Quangqiong hua yujin xia de dangdai dushi wenxue*, pp. 125–31 (Beijing: Social Sciences Academic Press).
Zhang Yuejin (2007) *Zhongguo nongmingong wenti jiedu* (Beijing: Guangming Ribao chubanshe).
Zhao, Yuezhi (2002) The rich, the laid-off, and the criminal in tabloid tales: Read all about it!, in Perry Link, Richard P. Madsen and Paul G. Pickowicz (eds), *Popular China: Unofficial culture in a globalising society*, pp. 111–35 (Lanham, MD: Rowman & Littlefield).
Zheng, Tiantian (2004) From peasant women to bar hostesses: Gender and modernity in post-Mao Dalian, in Arianne M. Gaetano and Tamara Jacka (eds), *On the move: Women in rural-to-urban migration in contemporary China*, pp. 80–108 (New York: Columbia University Press).
Zheng, Tiantian (2008) Performing media-constructed images for first-class citizenship: Political struggles of rural migrant hostesses in Dalian, in Rachel Murphy and Vanessa L. Fong (eds), *Media, identity, and struggle in twenty-first-century China* (London: Routledge).
Zheng, Tiantian (2009) *Red light: The lives of sex workers in postsocialist China* (Minneapolis: University of Minnesota Press).
Zou Xinshu (2007) *Zhongguo chengshi nongmingong wenti* (Beijing: Qunyang chubanshe).

Left-behind and Vulnerable? Conceptualising Development and Older Women's Agency in Rural China

TAMARA JACKA

The Australian National University

> **Abstract:** *Concern has been growing recently in China about the well-being of children, women and the elderly "left behind" on the farm when family members leave the village in search of waged work. Increasingly, the left-behind are portrayed in academic and policy discourse as a "vulnerable group" of passive dependants, sidelined by modernisation and abandoned by their families. This paper challenges this discourse, arguing that while attention to the well-being of the left-behind is vital, there is an urgent need for a shift in focus from their vulnerability to their agency. The paper focuses on the agency of left-behind women between the ages of 50 and 80. It aims, first of all, to point the way toward an empirically richer understanding of the social construction of older women's agency and well-being. The second aim of the paper is to suggest how different conceptualisations of "agency" and "older women" might contribute to more ethical and politically effective strategies for development and the improvement of women's well-being. To further these two aims, the paper draws on fieldwork conducted in rural Ningxia, north-western China, and on critiques of the "capability approach" to development expounded by Amartya Sen and Martha Nussbaum.*

In the last few decades, policymaking and scholarship relating to development in China has been dominated by an urbanist teleology and a corresponding marginalisation of the countryside and the people "left behind" there when family members migrate out. Since the 1980s, growing rural-urban disparities, combined with a thirst among burgeoning capitalist enterprises for cheap, manual labour, have led to hundreds of millions of rural workers moving off the land and out of the countryside, toward urban centres and export-oriented industrial processing zones. All the same, migrants constitute only a minority of the rural population. Most are young and middle-aged men and young, single women, who leave family members in the village and return months or years later. Until the early twenty-first century, however, little attention was paid to those back on the farm. All eyes were on the young migrants. The left-behind were referred to disparagingly as the "386199" or "women-children-elderly" work team, the numbers referring respectively to 8 March, International Women's Day, 1 June, Children's Day, and 9 September, which is a traditional festival often referred to as Seniors' Day (*laoren jie*). The supposed "low quality" (*suzhi di*) of the 386199 work team was seen to be causing declines in rural economic growth (see, for example, Guo, 2008). The problems faced by rural women, children and the elderly themselves were rarely accorded attention by policymakers or scholars, either inside or outside China, until the twenty-first century.

Since then, however, there has been a shift in Chinese state discourse and the emergence of policy oriented toward achieving a "harmonious society" (*hexie shehui*), "people-centred" (*yi ren wei ben*) development and "construction of the new countryside" (*xin nongcun jianshe*). These initiatives have partly been a reaction to the growth in social unrest and protest generated as a response to huge and increasing rural-urban inequalities and rural disadvantage, but they are also driven by the belief that the next stage of capitalist growth will require a boost in domestic – especially rural – consumption. Consequently, the state has begun focusing less on how to extract capital accumulation from agriculture and more on ways to "give back" to the rural population and improve their incomes, buying power, living standards and quality of life.

Against this backdrop, since the mid-2000s a new scholarly literature has emerged about the difficulties and lack of welfare faced by the 386199 work team, now given the less obviously derogatory tag "left-behind" (*liushou*) women, children and the elderly. This literature is sympathetic to the left-behind and gravely concerned about their situation, but it does not overturn the urbanist telos: a telos that is at once also ageist and sexist. The agents of development continue to be perceived primarily as young men and women heading for the city. Left-behind women, children and the elderly are depicted not as agents, but rather as "vulnerable groups" (*ruoshi qunti*) who suffer insecurity, stress, loneliness, depression and ill-health as a result of their abandonment. As one leading researcher of left-behind women puts it:

> With ever increasing numbers of male labourers leaving the countryside for work in the city, the problem of the left-behind woman has attracted growing concern from society... As a vulnerable group, [left-behind women] ... face security issues and bear a heavy physical and psychological burden. Consequently, the academic community has an important responsibility to strengthen research on this vulnerable social group, and to propose reliable and feasible measures to address their predicament (Xu, 2009, p. 55; see also Xu, 2010; Ye and Lu, 2011; Ye and He, 2008; Li and He, 2010).

One left-behind "vulnerable group" – the rural elderly – has become the object of particular concern, largely because the image of the elderly person as being frail and dependent on others is so strong, and because population control policies have contributed to a rapidly ageing population, such that the proportion of the population aged over 60 is predicted to rise from 10 per cent in 2006 to around 30 per cent in 2050 (UNFPA, 2006, p. 3). The fact that the majority of elderly people live in rural areas where they have extremely limited access to pensions or other state support, combined with the perception that the exodus of young people from the countryside is threatening family support for the elderly, is resulting in a pervasive sense of crisis in elderly care.

This paper runs against the grain of recent elite discourse on the vulnerability of the left-behind. It draws on qualitative and quantitative fieldwork research conducted in Snow County (a pseudonym), a poor rural county in Ningxia, north-western China, and focuses on left-behind women's exercise of agency and the contributions they make to development. I am particularly interested in the agency and activities of women between the ages of about 50 and 80.[1] The paper is motivated by two concerns, both of which relate to the social construction of (lack of) agency. On the one hand, the vulnerable group discourse reproduces a stereotype of left-behind older rural women as abandoned, dependent, passive and weak; unable to look after themselves, let alone make a contribution to development. Like all stereotypes, there is a grain of truth here – some women, especially those who have been incapacitated by illness or extreme old age, do fit this picture, but as a general description of older left-behind women, it is empirically inaccurate and misleading. The first aim of this paper is, then, to highlight the gaps between elite vulnerable group discourse and the realities of most older women's lives in Snow County. On the other hand, elite discourse can play a powerful part in the social construction of development. In the case of the vulnerable group discourse, this may be a problem. The term "vulnerable group" was first promoted in the 1980s by the Commonwealth Expert Group on Women and Structural Adjustment in an effort to draw attention to the harm done to women and other disadvantaged groups by the World Bank's structural adjustment policies (Parpart, 1995, p. 228). Since then it has been taken up by the United Nations (UN) and its agencies and by activists everywhere, the rationale being that an emphasis on the vulnerability and neediness of a group can help to strengthen that group's claim to resources. As Jane Parpart notes, however, one effect has been a further entrenchment of a divide between First World, modern "experts" and Third World pre-modern, helpless female "victims" (Parpart, 1995, p. 229).

I argue that even as a short-term strategy for gaining resources, emphasising vulnerability is politically dangerous. Rather than leading to a more equal distribution of the resources needed for well-being, such a strategy risks inviting individualised, paternalistic welfare benefits that are likely to lead to a loss of self-esteem and an increase of passivity in recipients. Such welfare benefits may reinforce a perception that recipients are a costly burden, and generate a widespread sense that, rather than being enhanced, social support for such people should be kept to a minimum.[2] The second aim of this paper, then, is to highlight the potentially limiting effects of the vulnerable group discourse on left-behind older women, and to suggest how different conceptualisations of "agency" and "older women" might contribute to more desirable forms of development. To further these two aims, the paper draws on and critiques the "capability approach" to well-being and development expounded by Amartya Sen and Martha Nussbaum. This approach provides a broad, normative framework for conceptualising, evaluating and assessing individuals' well-being and social arrangements and policies relating to well-being and development (Robeyns, 2005, p. 94). Sen and Nussbaum reject understandings of "well-being" that emphasise economic growth, income, consumption or living standards, and those that concentrate on people's happiness or desire-fulfilment. Instead, they argue that an individual's well-being should be assessed in terms of her achievement of "functionings", defined as the ways of "being and doing" that she has reason to value, and her "capabilities": that is, the potential and opportunities she has for achieving "functionings" (Sen, 1984; Robeyns, 2005). Nussbaum and Sen equate well-being, broadly speaking, with "human flourishing" and "a life worthy of human dignity". Both see a close connection between dignity and agency. Nussbaum writes, for example, that "human dignity, from the start, is equal in all who are agents in the first place" and that "in a wide range of areas, ... a focus on dignity will dictate policy choices that protect and support agency, rather than choices that infantilise people and treat them as passive recipients of benefit" (Nussbaum, 2011, p. 30). Agency here is understood as the ability and power to identify and choose goals and act upon those choices. It is an important functioning in its own right, as well as being necessary for the achievement of many, though not all, other functionings (Kabeer, 1999, p. 438; Sen, 1984).[3]

The capability approach is useful, first of all, because it pulls together several important ideas from the work of feminists and others coming out of and critiquing liberal political philosophy. Secondly, Sen's version of the approach forms the theoretical underpinning of the UN's advocacy of human development and its human development index, and as a consequence, has already become highly influential globally, including in China. There, the government's new discourse on "people-centred development" has been partially inspired or at any rate legitimised by the UN's human development discourse, as well as by the Confucian ideal of "(the good of) the people as the foundation (for governance)" (*minben*) (Jacka and Sargeson, 2011, p. 6). In this paper, therefore, I take the capability approach and critique of that approach as my theoretical starting point, in the hope that in so doing I might contribute to efforts to add value to "people-centred" development discourse.

Nussbaum (e.g. 2011, pp. 2–14) has used stories about individuals to shift attention from economic growth to human dignity and agency. In the next part of this paper I follow Nussbaum's example by recounting a story about a 63 year-old woman in Snow County, Yang Yulan.[4] In terms of vulnerability and agency, Yang is, as I will show, typical of left-behind older women in this area. The remainder of the paper draws on Yang's story to challenge the notion that such women are a vulnerable group, to highlight their activities and agency, and to explore both the potential benefits and limitations of a capability approach to development that seeks to expand the agency and capabilities of older rural women, such as Yang, as opposed to dwelling on their vulnerability.

Yang Yulan's Story[5]

Yang Yulan lives in a village in the mountains, about 2,900m above sea level. She has two adult sons and two adult daughters, all of them married with children of their own. She and her husband, Li Jianguo, share a courtyard housing compound with their youngest son, Hou Yinshi, his wife Zhang Zhaoxiong, and their 2 year-old son. Yang's older son and his wife and two young children have set up a separate household in another courtyard next door. Her daughters married into two different villages nearby.

Yang and her husband and Hou and his family share the same budget and eat together when they are at home, but Hou spends most of the year away from home. He works in Guyuan, a town two hours' drive away, for about seven months each year, coming home in July for the wheat harvest and again for the New Year festival in January, and staying through till April to help with the ploughing and crop planting. When they first married, Zhang was also a migrant worker, but since she gave birth, she has mostly stayed at home with her son. Twice she has left her son with Yang for a few months, so that she could find casual work in Guyuan. She also visits her own parents for a few days each month, sometimes taking her son and otherwise leaving him with Yang. Later this year, she plans to join her husband in Guyuan and from then on to stay there for most of each year, leaving her son in Yang's care.

Both Yang and her husband, Li, are in poor health. Yang has suffered from daily back pain, stomach pains, headaches and dizziness for several years and for the last three years arthritis has been giving her pain in her hands and legs. She hasn't been to the doctor because she feels her problems are not serious enough to warrant the cost and bother. Despite her health problems, Yang does most of the cooking and shares the other housework and care of her grandson with Zhang, and she is the main farmer in the household. When the weather is fine, she usually works for a few hours in the fields. Li helps her, but usually works for a shorter period. He does most of the heavy work: ploughing, planting the wheat, potatoes and linseed, and harvesting the wheat. In this, he is helped by his younger brother, who lives in the same village, as well as by Yang and Li's sons. Yang harvests the potatoes, with help from her sons. Last year, her sister's two sons also helped her in return for some potatoes. In addition, Yang raises a couple of chickens and a pig. Soon they will kill the pig for the New Year festival. Until recently, she was also raising two cows, but she sold them because her worsening arthritis has made climbing the hills to cut grass for the cows every day too painful.

The wheat and linseed that Yang and Li grew last year will provide them with their staple diet for the next twelve months. Last August, Yang sold 1,000 yuan worth of potatoes, and earned nearly 2,000 yuan from selling the cows. She also grows onions and other vegetables in the courtyard, and sells them on a seasonal basis at the local township market. As a result, Yang and Li can partially cover their grandson's needs as well as their own, and as long as they do not incur any large hospital costs, they need little money from Hou and Zhang.

This is just as well, because Hou only earns a net cash income of a few thousand yuan a year, and is still paying back relatives for the 50,000 yuan he borrowed a few years ago to pay a bride price to Zhang's parents. For her part, Zhang is loath to give her parents-in-law any more money than is absolutely necessary. There is a great deal of conflict between Yang and Zhang. Yang says that her daughter-in-law complains bitterly about her marital family's poverty and refuses to eat with her because she's "dirty". Previously, Yang responded by threatening repeatedly that she and her husband would move out and live by themselves, leaving Zhang to do the farm work and look after her son on her own. Hou tells us he avoided calling home so that he wouldn't have to listen to his wife's complaints. But Yang has now stopped talking about moving out. Her sister has advised her to stay put and be more conciliatory, because as she gets older she will need more support from her daughter-in-law.

Challenging the View of Left-behind Older Women as Abandoned

Yang Yulan, like other older women in Snow County, has a hard life, but her difficulties are mainly caused by interrelated problems of poverty, ill-health and a lack of affordable medical care, gender inequalities and family conflict, rather than by being abandoned and lacking care or support. In fact, not only is she supported by her son and daughter-in-law, however grudgingly, she and her husband are able to draw on extensive kin networks for help with work and for emotional support. This is typical.

Living arrangements give some indication of the family support available to older women in Snow County. The vast majority of older women whom we surveyed belonged to households that also included other adults. Around 43 per cent lived with one or more sons, daughters-in-law and grandchildren, with or without their husband. The rate of outmigration among household members was high. As shown in Table 1, 329, or 45.6 per cent, of older women lived in households in which one or more adults had worked away from home for six months or more of the preceding year.[6] However, only 101 (14.0 per cent) had *all* other adult household members working away from home for six months or more.[7] The well-being of the small number of older women living for most of the year alone or just with young children is of concern. Yet, most people have kin living close by, in the same village or a neighbouring village, and as illustrated in Yang's story, a great deal of mutual assistance occurs between such kin. Contrary to common concerns about an attenuation of kinship ties and abandonment of the elderly (Yan, 2003, pp. 162–89), various forms of interdependence and mutual aid between older people and their kin are alive and well in Snow County.

Challenging the View of Left-behind Older Women as Passive Dependants

Contrary to the stereotypical image of the elderly as being primarily "dependants", the story above shows that Yang Yulan is an active, able worker who makes a major contribution to her family. In fact, her son and daughter-in-law are as dependent upon Yang as she is upon them. Across rural China, a large proportion of agriculture and care work is undertaken by older left-behind women. Their work is crucial to their families, because it provides food security, as well as maintaining usage rights to land, which are important as a fall-back position when migrants lose their waged jobs or

Table 1. Women's Living Arrangements during the Preceding Year (July 2009–July 2010)

Household Living Arrangements	Age Cohort (Years)			
	51–60	61–70	71–80	Total
Lived alone for entire period	1	4	1	7
One or more (but not all) other adult household members away from home for 6 months or more	175	101	53	329
All other adult household members away from home for 6 months or more	61	24	16	101
Other living arrangements	128	102	55	284
Total	365	231	125	721

Source: Author survey, Ningxia (2010).

become too ill or frail to continue working as waged labourers. The women also provide childcare services that are otherwise unavailable or too costly for rural families, and this enables younger adults in the family to seek employment away from the village, which can bring in more cash income.

Declines in physical health meant that some women in their 50s with whom we talked undertook much less work than Yang, but we also talked with one couple in their late 70s who continued to spend several hours a day tilling their fields. As shown in Table 2, on average among the women we surveyed the heaviest workloads were borne by those aged between 21 and 60, but the workloads of those over the age of 60 were also substantial.[8]

Many older women gain a great deal of respect, self-esteem and informal power within the family from their work. Yang Yulan, for example, is proud of the contribution she makes through her farm work and the childcare she provides, and derives considerable bargaining power from her son and daughter-in-law's dependence on this contribution.[9] In addition, rural women, including older women, commonly have a greater say in decision-making than either they or their men folk usually care to admit. In Yang's household, her son made himself out to be the main decision-maker, but Zhang said that when her husband came home for the New Year festival, he handed over his earnings to her and she decided how much would go toward paying off debts, how much would be given to her parents-in-law and how much she would keep for herself. It was also clear that Yang had a large hand in deciding how much fertiliser to put on the crops and what proportion of the potato crop to sell each year, as well as deciding whether or not to sell their cattle. She also determined how to spend the money from that sale and controlled the money that she earned through the year from selling the vegetables she grew. I have insufficient data to be certain, but it is probable that Yang's agency has increased as a result of being "left-behind" in the sense that, in

Table 2. Women's Workloads: Mean Hours per Day, during the Preceding Month (June–July 2010)

Type of Work	Age Cohort (Years)					
	16–20 N=26	21–35 N=373	36–50 N=893	51–60 N=365	61–70 N=231	71–80 N=125
Crop farming	2.5	3.9	5.1	4.5	2.8	0.6
Animal husbandry	0.1	0.3	0.4	0.4	0.4	0.3
Waged work	0.6	0.4	0.2	0.0	0.0	0.0
Other income-earning work	0.2	0.1	0.3	0.1	0.0	0.0
Cooking	1.2	1.2	1.3	1.3	1.2	1.0
Childcare	0.2	2.6	0.6	0.9	1.0	0.7
Elderly care	0.2	0.2	0.2	0.1	0.0	0.0
Washing clothes	0.7	0.6	0.6	0.4	0.4	0.2
Sweeping	0.3	0.3	0.3	0.4	0.4	0.3
Other domestic work	0.3	0.0	0.0	0.0	0.0	0.1
Total	6.4	9.8	9.1	8.2	6.3	3.3

Source: Author survey, Ningxia (2010).

her son's absence from farm production, she has taken a greater role in making decisions in that area, as well as doing more of the work. This may also be the case for other left-behind older women.

In crucial ways, however, the agency of both Yang Yulan and her daughter-in-law, and that of other rural women in China, is severely constrained by the gendered nature of some of the key institutions shaping their everyday lives. This is illustrated by the story of Xie Fenzhu, another woman whom we interviewed in Snow County. Xie – just a few years younger than Yang – is the main farmer in her household, but has only a small cash income of her own. Her husband used to work as a construction labourer, and still earns some money doing casual work around the village. As the head of the household, he has an account with the local rural credit cooperative into which the government pays an allowance for farm land that the household relinquished for reforestation. When their adult children give their parents money, they give it to their father. Like the vast majority of women in Snow County, Xie has no bank account of her own and cannot take out a loan. In most cases, the rural credit cooperative lends money to the male head of a household, and only very rarely lends to women.[10]

Xie's husband beats her frequently and has caused serious injuries. On several occasions she and her adult daughters have asked village government leaders to stop her husband's violent behaviour, but the officials have usually said that they cannot intervene in a private family matter. Xie cannot pay to have her injuries treated and her husband refuses to pay for her. He has agreed to the divorce that Xie requested. But Xie feels that she cannot go through with it because that would leave her without any land to farm. Under the virilocal marriage system which dominates rural China, a woman's land usage-rights are vested in her husband's household after marriage. Following divorce, it is usual in most parts of rural China for the woman to lose rights to land in her husband's village, but not to regain such rights in her natal village.

Re-conceptualising Agency and Well-being among Left-behind Older Women

Why is it important for theories and strategies aimed at improving well-being among older left-behind women to recognise their agency and the importance of their contributions to society? What can be achieved by this discursive move and what are its limitations? The answers to these questions are connected to understandings about citizenship. Despite very different political histories, in contemporary China, as in Western liberal and neoliberal societies, key social institutions have been built upon an implicit social contract. Moreover, the post-socialist Chinese state, like Western liberal and neoliberal states, has been reproducing a hierarchical distinction between some people considered model citizens and parties to the social contract who "deserve" or "earn" respect, power, autonomy and social entitlements, and others considered less deserving. Broadly speaking, in today's China as in the West, the model citizen is an able-bodied male adult, who earns an independent income and contributes to society through employment or self-employment in "productive" work. Those who do not or cannot earn an income and contribute to society through paid work have been marginalised, disadvantaged and regarded as inferior because they are deemed to be "dependent", "unproductive" and lacking in abilities and agency.

People seen to belong in this latter category are, first of all, commonly considered less suitable for political life, and therefore their power to shape social and political institutions in ways that might improve their own and others' well-being is constrained. Secondly, any social support they receive is commonly not considered an entitlement, but rather a form of "charity", welfare "handout" or special help or protection. As Nancy Fraser and Linda Gordon write, a contract-versus-charity dichotomy can be seen in many contemporary Western countries in the opposition between social insurance and public assistance programs (Fraser and Gordon, 1992). Both forms of social provision, they point out, are financed through "contributions", differing only in terms of where and how these are collected – through sales taxes or wage deductions, for example. But advocates of social insurance programs designed them

> to appear "contributory", seemingly embodying the principle of exchange; recipients, originally intended to be exclusively white, male, and relatively privileged members of the working class, are defined as "entitled". Public assistance, in contrast, continued the "noncontributory" charity tradition, so that its recipients appear to get something for nothing, in violation of contractual norms (Fraser and Gordon, 1992, p. 61).

Today in the US, public assistance or welfare is highly stigmatising and deprives people of autonomy. As Iris Young (2002, p. 46) puts it:

> Those who need help and support from others do not deserve equal respect, nor can they expect to be able to decide how they will conduct their lives. If you are dependent, then those on whom you depend have some say over the goals you set for yourself and how you will enact them.

Several scholars have referred to a "social contract" in Maoist China, with the state providing a range of welfare entitlements to citizens in return for their political compliance (Tang and Parish, 2000, p. 3). Yet this was not a contract involving some citizens "earning" entitlements by "contributing" to society and excluding others who were not "productive" or did not "contribute". All citizens were organised into state or collective work units or rural collectives, and, in theory, the means of production was owned by "the people", and goods distributed evenly among them. In practice, of course, there were inequalities both between work units and collectives and within them, but these inequalities were not a matter of exclusion from a social contract, or of individuals being seen not to "deserve" entitlements or respect because they were not "productive".

In rural areas, older people benefited from collectivisation in three respects. First, production teams guaranteed remunerated work to all those who needed it and could contribute minimal labour. This meant a significant increase in economic security for older people who previously would have lost employment in competition with younger workers. Second, production teams distributed grain according to need as well as work. Each year, most teams first distributed 30–40 per cent of the harvest as subsistence grain to all team members, and only then divided the remainder, in the form of grain and cash, according to the number of workdays people had undertaken in collective labour. The cost of the grain distributed in the first phase was charged against the number of workdays earned by each household, but if a household was unable to pay for the grain they needed, the charge could be carried over until they were able to pay. Of particular importance to the frail elderly who could no longer work, debts could be carried over for many years and were cancelled at death (Davis-Friedmann, 1991, pp. 19–20).

The third benefit of collectivisation for older people, especially women, relates to the fact that unlike younger adults who were required to work full time for the production team, men over the age of 60 and women over 50 in households with at least two other adults working for the team were allowed to "retire" to the private, "inside sphere" to do domestic work, grow vegetables on their household's private plot and raise domestic livestock, which they could then sell for cash. Once they had grandchildren, most women withdrew from collective labour to work full time in the inside sphere. As remains the case today, the amount of work they did was often not recognised, but their contribution was nevertheless valued by other household members because it made it possible for daughters-in-law, in particular, to earn more by working longer hours for the production team. In addition, the work that older women, especially, put into tending the private plot and rearing a few domestic livestock commonly brought in a sizable amount of cash, amounting to 20–30 per cent of a household's income (Davis-Friedmann, 1991, pp. 20–21).

In the 1980s, marketisation of the economy, destruction of the "iron rice bowl" of lifelong employment and welfare in urban work units, and the return to a household-based rural economy all contributed to rapid economic growth. However, they also led to heightened social inequalities, sharp declines in the provision of collective welfare and increases in the number of people without access to such welfare, and a greater reliance on families, and in particular, women's unpaid care work, in place of social welfare provision. In rural areas, the status and well-being of older people, in particular, suffered with the removal of the "safety net" of collectively provided subsistence grain, as well as collectively-subsidised healthcare. In addition, older people's (and women's) ability to earn a cash income greatly diminished, due to heightened competition for the few opportunities for waged labour in and around the village, and because the profits to be earned from agriculture and agricultural sidelines, such as raising domestic livestock, declined sharply relative to the incomes to be earned in off-farm wage labour.

In the 1990s and 2000s, there have been improvements in the provision of social welfare by the state. Simultaneously, however, a dichotomy similar to that critiqued by Fraser and Gordon in the US has emerged in China between "noncontributory" welfare programs and "contributory" social insurance. With regard to the former, in the Maoist period, the urban "three withouts" (*sanwu*) and the rural "five guarantee household" (*wubaohu*) programs provided for the basic needs of a small number of destitute citizens without family support. Rural family values were such that to receive *wubaohu* payments was shameful, as it indicated a lack of descendants. The stigma may also have been associated with the fact that costs were borne by the local community – that is, the production team or brigade and its members. In the post-Mao period, the *wubaohu* program remains, but the "three withouts" program has been superseded by the means-tested minimum livelihood guarantee program (*dibao*), established in urban areas from the early 1990s and in rural areas from the mid-2000s. The *dibao* today is received by more people than the "three withouts" payments were previously, but still only by a small minority of the population. Furthermore, despite the fact that the programs are now funded by the state, receipt of *dibao*, as well as *wubaohu*, appears to be as stigmatising now as the *wubaohu* was previously. In Snow County in 2010–11, some very poor households, including *dibao* recipients and non-recipients, were looked down upon by neighbours and local officials who saw their poverty as being caused by the laziness, incompetence and irresponsibility of household members. Some poor villagers complained, though, that they had been cheated out of *dibao* payments by corrupt local officials who had ignored their repeated efforts to have their entitlements recognised. Dorothy Solinger (2011) reports that, in the city of Wuhan, those who did receive *dibao* frequently complained that their allowances were not enough to pull them out of destitution, they were subjected to invasive and complex monitoring and verification procedures, and their continued receipt of even the most pitiful payments was uncertain.

With regard to "contributory" programs, the state has been developing and extending insurance schemes, to which employers as well as employees contribute, to help cover the costs of health and provide old-age pensions for wage earners and their family dependants. Today, rural migrant workers are legally entitled to participate in such programs, but flaws in the system mean that the vast majority do not. In rural areas, a program of collective medical insurance has been established and most rural residents now contribute, but the scheme only covers a fraction of their medical costs. As yet, only a small minority of rural residents participate in contributory elderly pension schemes; most households considering the costs of contribution too high and the benefits too low and uncertain. In the last few years, pilot schemes combining the contributory elderly pension with a flat, universal pension provided to all rural elderly by local governments have been rolled out in some areas (Cai et al., 2012, pp. 98–105). In future years, coverage of these schemes is likely to increase, but their viability and sustainability may be undermined by two factors: first individuals and families may consider buying into insurance an unnecessary expenditure, given the government's provision of a basic pension and second, governments may be unwilling to increase the size of the basic pension to cover living costs. Both problems are likely to be exacerbated if the vulnerable group discourse continues to influence understandings about older people in rural areas. This is because it fails to recognise such people as workers, who contributed to society in the past and continue to do so in the present. It therefore makes rural elderly pension schemes seem less like "contributory" social insurance, and more like "noncontributory" welfare, similar to *dibao*, and potentially with similar consequences for recipients' well-being.

In short, despite advances in social welfare provision as well as impressive economic growth and improvements in average living standards, contemporary Chinese policy makers, scholars and activists are faced with the same serious question as those in the US and elsewhere: How can one ensure that well-being, including agency, autonomy and respect, is maintained for people who fall outside the social contract because they do not earn an income or "contribute" to society through "productive" paid work? Feminists have sought to address this problem and specifically to enhance the well-being of women and increase both the entitlements and respect that is accorded them, primarily by advocating three approaches, each of which is apparent in Sen and Nussbaum's work. First, they have promoted women's involvement in "productive" work (Sen, 1990; Sen, 1999, pp. 189–203; Nussbaum, 2000, pp. 285–86). Second, they have challenged the notion that only work that is paid and "productive" counts as a contribution to society, and have highlighted other contributions made by women in unpaid "reproductive" work (Sen, 1990; Nussbaum, 2002). Third, Nussbaum and others have challenged dichotomous notions of "independence" and "dependence", arguing that *all* human beings are dependent on others in different ways at different times during the course of our lives, and that interdependence and mutual care must be recognised as the necessary grounds on which people build lives of autonomy and respect. From here, Nussbaum suggests a rethinking of social contract theory (Nussbaum, 2002; Nussbaum, 2006).

How might these three approaches operate and what could they achieve in the rural Chinese context? To address this question, it is necessary to first explain some shifts that have occurred in rural gender divisions of labour and gendered power relations in the post-Mao era. When possibilities for waged labour outside the village opened up, they were taken up first and foremost by men and young, single women. Meanwhile, there was a feminisation as well as an ageing of the population working in less profitable agriculture. Once considered predominantly masculine, productive "outside" work, agriculture, including both crop farming and the raising of domestic livestock, came to be seen as "inside" work, associated and done in close conjunction with women's other "inside", "unproductive" work, cooking and cleaning, and caring for children and the frail elderly (Jacka, 1997, pp. 128–42).

This gender division of labour, combined with a marked withdrawal of the state from efforts to directly promote gender equality, contributed to a disempowerment of women in both the "inside" and "outside" spheres. Thus, in villages across China, government bodies are dominated by men and by patriarchal interests. Women are very rarely elected to positions of leadership in village government because it is assumed that their "low quality" makes them unsuitable for the task, they are too busy with their "inside" work, and in any case, "good" women devote their energy to caring for their family and do not interact with people outside the family, especially men. Within the family, also, villagers and officials alike assume that men should be the decision-makers with respect to agricultural production and large financial investments and expenditures, both because it is believed that they are more capable and knowledgeable than women, and because they are the main breadwinners. In practice, as I have noted, women *are* decision-makers as well as capable workers in the family, but the assumption that they are not underpins institutions and practices that discriminate against women and limit their agency – for example by providing bank loans almost exclusively to men, and not to women such as Yang Yulan and Xie Fenzhu, whatever their needs or abilities.

A strategy of trying to enhance the well-being of women by increasing their involvement in waged work will do little to improve the situation of older women such as Xie and Yang. For one thing, the majority of industrial and service-sector enterprises do not employ women over the age of 40. Some older rural women work as manual labourers in road works and on construction sites, but the work and conditions are harsh, pay is low, and it is considered demeaning for women to have to do such jobs. For older rural women, then, a more realistic strategy for improving well-being might be to highlight the contributions they make in the "inside" sphere, including income-earning and subsistence farming, and domestic work. For example, organising older women into production cooperatives and providing microcredit would enable women to turn their work in animal husbandry or growing vegetables into more profitable, status-enhancing projects.[11] In addition, if Yang Yulan and other grandparents were to be paid by the local government for providing childcare services, this might enhance their economic standing and their agency, self-esteem and sense of self-efficacy more effectively than a welfare payment. Enhanced self-esteem might in turn contribute to further improvements in their status and power in the family. As Sen and others have argued, a greater sense of self-esteem and a sense that she can achieve change make it more likely that a person will stand up for herself (Sen, 1990, p. 136; Nussbaum, 2000, p. 288; Bandura, 1997).

Greater appreciation of their agency might also enable older women to play a more active role in village government or in community groups. This might then enable individual women to work with others, not just to help themselves, but also to address gender inequalities, for example in land usage-rights, and thereby improve gender equality and the well-being of women generally (Nussbaum, 2000, p. 289). The potential significance of such an approach is suggested by the active role played by older women in several recent campaigns protesting against land expropriation and government leaders who pocket the proceeds from land development, rather than distributing them to poor villagers (Woodman, 2011; Sargeson and Song, 2010). Efforts that highlight and enhance agency and contributions to society *might*, then, enable women to improve their well-being, but on their own they may not be enough. Without more direct moves to challenge power relations, and without a transformative redistribution of resources, efforts that highlight and enhance older women's agency are likely, in fact, to result in their co-optation and exploitation rather than improvements in well-being. The case of older women protesting land expropriation in the village of Taishi in the Pearl River Delta provides a warning about this. Some accounts indicate that the women were primarily concerned about gendered poverty. Having lost their land, most of the village's men and young women had left in search of waged labour. Some of the middle-aged women left behind were able to find poorly-paid jobs doing farm labour, while other older women were forced into the highly demeaning work of sorting and hauling garbage to earn enough to live on (Woodman, 2011, pp. 199–202). Sophia Woodman (2011, p. 205) writes, however, that these women's protests were "translated" by younger, male activists outside the village into a struggle for rights and democracy and a campaign to recall the elected village leader, which ultimately failed. Paradoxically, the village contention "became a struggle for democratic rights in which the holders of those rights were largely rendered incapable of representing themselves – except in casting ballots – and others who spoke for them were transformed into the de facto leaders of the action". Woodman (2011, p. 206) argues that "creating a counter-hegemonic movement based on rights depends on transforming the identities of participants into rights-bearing subjects" and cites Merry as arguing that "poor women think of themselves as having rights only when powerful institutions treat them as if they do" (Woodman, 2011, p. 207). Evidently, she writes, this did not happen in Taishi (Woodman, 2011, p. 207).

Another kind of warning about the limitations of efforts to improve women's well-being by enhancing their agency without directly challenging power relations is provided by "participatory" community development projects. Elsewhere, I have discussed research that I undertook at the site of an overseas-funded participatory environmental protection and community development project implemented in Shaanxi by a leading domestic women's NGO. The project greatly increased the workloads of village women selected to be members of a new local Environmental Protection Association (EPA). Despite the project's aim of empowering women, it had no significant effect on gendered divisions of labour or control over the distribution of key resources in the village. Instead, members of the EPA found themselves responsible for cleaning and picking up garbage around the village. Their other main task, overseeing a microcredit scheme, also did little to improve their own authority in the village or to empower other village women. The loans that were given out were largely appropriated by men, but in any case were too small to be met with anything other than complaints from villagers. Overall, the potential significance of this project was entirely overshadowed by the opportunities provided by the establishment of a mine and processing plant in the area, control of which was held by male village leaders in cahoots with the male mine managers. When a delegation from a Chinese charity organisation visited the village to determine the community's needs for funds, they were wined and dined by the male village Party secretary and the mine boss. The head of the EPA, an older woman, had no chance to talk to the visitors – she was too busy in the kitchen cooking their meal (Jacka, 2010, p. 109).

What, if anything, does the capability approach have to offer in the way of guarding against this type of co-optation and exploitation of women's agency and work? Both Sen and Nussbaum emphasise various aspects of the social constructedness of agency, capabilities and well-being. They give particular attention to the ways in which the institution of the family and gender divisions of labour constrain women's agency and capabilities and erode gender equality (Sen, 1990; Nussbaum, 2000, pp. 241–97), but they do not advocate any particular institutions or institutional change that might overcome these problems. Their capability approach provides a normative framework, but must be supplemented by deliberative processes to determine the institutions most likely to enhance well-being in different contexts.

It is instructive to compare the capability approach with human rights based approaches to development. Kate Carroll suggests that human rights based approaches, on their own, have generally been ineffectual in tackling structural inequalities, for they tend to focus on supporting individuals to achieve their rights, or on achieving legislative change rather than on the real attainment of equal rights or social justice. Focusing on the individual obscures questions about what others need to do to ensure that person's rights, while "legislation alone cannot tackle structural inequalities… Organisations must recognise that unless power relations have changed so that laws can be applied equally for all people, then the change will not impact on the majority" (Carroll, 2009, p. 2). Much the same challenges are likely to be faced by those attempting to implement a capability approach to well-being and development. To address these concerns, Carroll (2009, p. 2) argues, development policy makers and practitioners need first of all "a vision of a just society". Arguably, this is one of the strengths of the capability approach. They also need to ensure that people's agency is increased, enabling "a critical mass of individuals [to] mobilise to hold duty bearers to account for policies which perpetuate injustice" (Carroll, 2009, p. 2). Again, this is a key emphasis in the capability approach. In addition, however, redistributive policies are required. To be effective, such policies must transform power relations: "Aid giving, intended to redistribute, may not address long term inequality if it is targeted towards short term 'safety net' measures" (Carroll, 2009, p. 3). To fully realise either human rights or capabilities, therefore, there needs to be a fundamental, long-term shift in the distribution of assets, access and power.

There is a second set of limitations associated with a strategy to improve people's well-being by highlighting and enhancing their agency and contributions to society, rather than dwelling on their "vulnerability" and dependence on others. This relates to the fact that, however much we try to redefine and enlarge concepts of independence, productiveness and contributions to society, there are always likely to be some, such as small children, the severely disabled, and the frail elderly, who are extremely dependent on others. How does one ensure that such people can "live a life worthy of human dignity"? Nussbaum, like other feminists, critical gerontologists and those working with the disabled, emphasises that the dichotomy commonly drawn between those who are "independent" and "productive" and those who are "dependent" and "unproductive" is ideological. All human beings, she notes, are dependent on the care of others in different ways at different times over the course of their life-span (Nussbaum, 2002, pp. 188–89). Taking this into account, one might argue that small children and the frail elderly have a claim to respect as well as support, despite their dependence, because they will in the future be independent, productive members of society, or because they were in the past. In practice, this is a common approach, underpinning, for example, social investment in children and the provision of pensions to retirees. As Nussbaum notes, though, it seems a poor substitute for an ethics that respects and supports individuals as ends in themselves, rather than for their contribution to society in the past, present or future (Nussbaum, 2002, pp. 191–92).[12] Consequently, Nussbaum challenges the very notion of a social contract that necessitates individuals' "productive" contribution to society. The capability approach, she suggests, provides a more ethical and politically desirable conception of personhood and social cooperation. It uses "an account of cooperation that treats justice and inclusiveness as ends of intrinsic value from the beginning and that views human beings as held together by many altruistic ties as well as by ties of mutual advantage" (Nussbaum, 2006, p. 158). Furthermore, it acknowledges "many types of dignity in the world including the dignity of mentally disabled children and adults, the dignity of the senile demented elderly, and the dignity of babies at the breast (Nussbaum, 2002, p. 193). With the capability approach, Nussbaum (2006, p. 160) concludes,

> we do not have to win the respect of others by being productive. We have a claim to support in the dignity of our human need itself. Society is held together by a wide range of attachments and concerns, only some of which concern productivity. Productivity is necessary, and even good; but it is not the main end of social life.

Conclusion

Is this approach hopelessly unrealistic? Nussbaum (2006, p. 410) herself poses this question and responds that "only time and effort" will tell. Given the global dominance of capitalism and neoliberal ideology, it will take a great deal of effort to achieve a social order that meets all individuals' needs for respect as well as other capabilities as ends in themselves, regardless of their productivity. Such a social order must be a core goal for development. For the time being, however, it also is strategically important for those concerned with the well-being of elderly rural women – or any other "unproductive" disadvantaged or "vulnerable" people – to retain the link between the claim to respect and "productivity", but broaden understandings of what it means to contribute productively to society. Emphasising and enhancing the agency of "vulnerable groups" is crucial both to their own well-being and to broader development toward a just social order. This seems to be the thinking underpinning the UN's (2002) Madrid International Plan of Action on Ageing, the aim of which is "to ensure that persons everywhere are able to age with security and dignity and to continue to participate in their societies as citizens with full rights" (UN, 2002, p. 7). The Plan states that "[o]lder persons should be treated fairly and with dignity, regardless of disability or other status, and should be valued independently of their economic contribution" (UN, 2002, p. 10). In a few places it mentions the vulnerability of older people to poverty, natural disasters and humanitarian emergencies, but its overriding emphasis is on the agency and contributions of older people, especially the work that older women do in caring for family members, subsistence production, household maintenance and volunteer work in the community (UN, 2002, p. 9). Article 12 of the Plan reads:

> The expectations of older persons and the economic needs of society demand that older persons be able to participate in the economic, political, social and cultural life of their societies. Older persons should have the opportunity to work for as long as they wish and are able to, in satisfying and productive work, continuing to have access to education and training programmes. The empowerment of older persons and the promotion of their full participation are essential elements for active ageing. For older persons, appropriate sustainable social support should be provided (UN, 2002, p. 3).

With its socialist heritage and recent commitment to "people-centred" development, China is well placed to achieve the aims of the Madrid Plan, and specifically, to further development and well-being among older women in rural areas. I suggest that to meet these aims, policy makers, activists and scholars need to find an approach that incorporates three elements emphasised in this paper: an appreciation and enhancement of older women's agency; attention to the structural underpinnings of gender and age inequalities, the constraints these put on older women's agency, and the dangers of exploitation they pose; and a vision of justice that builds equality of agency and respect, as well as the fulfilment of other basic needs, into a conceptualisation of development.

Acknowledgments

The author is grateful to Jonathan Unger, Sophia Woodman, members of the Anthropology Department at Peking University, and two anonymous referees, for their critical feedback on earlier versions of this paper. Thank you also to Chen Wei for his assistance with data analysis. The paper draws on research funded by the Australian Research Council (DP0985775).

Notes

1. One reason for focusing on women aged 50 and over, rather than employing the more conventional definition of "the elderly" as aged 60 or 65 and above, is that the former approach is more in line with rural Chinese understandings of old age. For further discussion, see Pang, de Brauw and Rozelle (2004, p. 75). The well-being of rural women aged 50–60 is also neglected in recent literature on the "left-behind" because most of them fall in the gaps between the categories "left-behind women" and "left-behind elderly". They are too young to belong to the latter category, which is

usually defined as women aged 60 or more, whose adult children have migrated out of the village. Yet most do not belong to the former category, which is defined as married women aged 60 or less, whose husbands have migrated out. Few women aged over 50 have migrant husbands, but many have migrant children.
2. Iris Young describes how this has occurred in the US (Young, 2002).
3. This is my own interpretation and condensation of conceptualisations of agency articulated in different ways in a range of writings about the capability approach, especially by Sen. There are some differences in the ways in which Nussbaum and Sen conceptualise "agency" and "well-being" and the relationship between them. For discussion, see Crocker (2008) and Nussbaum (2011, pp. 197–202). These differences are not important for this paper.
4. All names in this account are pseudonyms.
5. This account draws on semi-structured interviews conducted by myself and two research assistants. Over three trips, in July 2010 and January and April 2011, we conducted a total of six separate interviews with Yang Yulan, her son and her daughter-in-law. These formed part of a total of around 147 interviews, conducted with 54 rural women in Snow County, as well as some of their household members and a small number of non-related returning migrants and village officials.
6. The findings in Tables 1 and 2 come from a questionnaire survey conducted in July 2010, with assistance from the Snow County Bureau of Public Health. We surveyed a total of 2,013 women in seven villages across two townships. In each township, we selected villages closest to the township centre and surveyed every woman aged 16–80 in each village who was available and willing to participate, until we reached our target of around 1,000 women in each township.
7. The figures in Table 1 for "All other adult household members away from home for 6 months or more" probably overestimate the number of older women in multiple-member households living alone for most of the year, as there are likely to be some households in which the adults migrating out did so at different times. The figures for "Other living arrangements" point to the variety of living arrangements among older women. They include those living in households in which one or more adults are away from home for 1–5 months of the year, as well as those whose adult children have established separate households elsewhere but whose young grandchildren live with them.
8. The total workloads indicated in the Table are likely to be underestimates for three main reasons. First, these figures are the sum of hours worked in the various tasks listed in this Table, but some tasks are not listed. These include collecting dry grass and twigs for fuel, and cutting grass for domestic livestock (the government prohibits the grazing of domestic livestock on mountain slopes). Second, women tend to underestimate the number of hours they spend in domestic work, especially childcare and elderly care, in part because much of it is conducted at the same time as other work. Third, it rained unusually heavily in the month preceding this survey. This meant that women did less field work than they would normally do in the summer months. In the winter months, much less time is spent in the fields, but more time is spent on indoor tasks, such as preparing for weddings, which are often held around the time of the New Year festival in January or February.
9. Gender divisions of labour tend to mean that in old age, lack of authority, respect and self-esteem are greater problems for men than for women: Even after they have become too frail to work in the fields, women continue to be appreciated for their domestic work and childcare, whereas men, once they are no longer able to work either in waged labour or on the farm, lose their respected role as breadwinner.
10. Among the 54 women with whom we conducted semi-structured interviews in Snow County, all lived in households in which a loan had been made from the rural credit cooperative, but only one had taken out a loan in her own name.
11. These are common elements in poverty alleviation and participatory development projects in China and elsewhere across the developing world. However, they are usually targeted at younger women and men, and to date have very rarely included older people (Ewing, 1999, p. 39).
12. This approach also gets us no further in enabling "a life worthy of dignity" for those who are severely and permanently disabled.

References

Bandura, Albert (1997) *Self-efficacy: The exercise of control* (New York: Freeman).
Cai, Fang, John Giles, Philip O'Keefe and Dewen Wang (2012) *The elderly and old age support in rural China: Challenges and prospects* (Washington, DC: The World Bank).
Carroll, Kate (2009) Reinvigorating human rights based approaches with redistribution. IDS in Focus Policy Briefing, Issue 11: Redistribution and beyond: Exploring the basics. Available at www.ids.ac.uk, accessed 2 October 2011.
Crocker, David A. (2008) *Ethics of global development: Agency, capability, and deliberative democracy* (Cambridge: Cambridge University Press).
Davis-Friedmann, Deborah (1991) *Long lives: Chinese elderly and the Communist revolution* (Stanford, CA: Stanford University Press).
Ewing, Deborah (1999) Gender and ageing, in Judith Randel, Tony German and Deborah Ewing (eds), *The ageing and development report: Poverty, independence and the world's older people*, pp. 33–45 (London: Earthscan and HelpAge International).
Fraser, Nancy and Linda Gordon (1992) Contract vs charity: Why is there no social citizenship in the United States? *Socialist Review* 22, pp. 45–68.
Guo Yali (2008) Ninxia nongcun funü renli ziyuan xianzhuang dui nongcun jingji fazhan de yingxiang. *Sheke Zongheng* 23(6), pp. 20–26.
Jacka, Tamara (1997) *Women's work in rural China: Change and continuity in an era of reform* (Cambridge: Cambridge University Press).
Jacka, Tamara (2010) Women's activism, overseas-funded participatory development, and governance: A case study from China. *Women's Studies International Forum* 33(2), pp. 99–112.
Jacka, Tamara and Sally Sargeson (2011) Introduction: Conceptualizing women, gender and rural development in China, in Tamara Jacka and Sally Sargeson (eds), *Women, gender and rural development in China*, pp. 1–24 (Cheltenham, UK and Northampton, MA: Edward Elgar).
Kabeer, Naila (1999) Resources, agency, achievements: Reflections on the measurement of women's empowerment. *Development and Change* 30, pp. 435–64.
Li Chunyan and He Congzhi (2010) Nongcun liushou laoren de zhengfu zhichi yanjiu. *Zhongguo Nongye Daxue Xuebao (Shehui Kexue Ban)* 27(1), pp. 113–20.
Nussbaum, Martha C. (2000) *Women and human development: The capabilities approach* (Cambridge: Cambridge University Press).
Nussbaum, Martha C. (2002) The future of feminist liberalism, in Eva Feder Kittay and Ellen K. Feder (eds), *The subject of care: Feminist perspectives on dependency*, pp. 186–214 (Lanham: Rowman and Littlefield).
Nussbaum, Martha C. (2006) *Frontiers of justice* (Cambridge, MA: The Belknap Press of Harvard University Press).
Nussbaum, Martha C. (2011) *Creating capabilities: The human development approach* (Cambridge, MA: The Belknap Press of Harvard University Press).
Pang, Lihua, Alan de Brauw and Scott Rozelle (2004) Working until you drop: The elderly of rural China. *The China Journal* 52, pp. 73–94.
Parpart, Jane (1995) Deconstructing the development "expert": Gender, development and the "vulnerable groups", in Marianne H. Marchand and Jane L. Parpart (eds), *Feminism/postmodernism/development*, pp. 221–43 (London: Routledge).
Robeyns, Ingrid (2005) The capability approach: A theoretical survey. *Journal of Human Development* 6(1), pp. 93–114.
Sargeson, Sally and Yu Song (2010) Land expropriation and the gender politics of citizenship in the urban frontier. *The China Journal* 64, pp. 19–46.
Sen, Amartya (1984) Well-being, agency and freedom: The Dewey lectures 1984. *The Journal of Philosophy* 82(4), pp. 169–221.
Sen, Amartya (1990) Gender and cooperative conflicts, in Irene Tinker (ed.), *Persistent inequalities: Women and world development*, pp. 123–49 (New York and Oxford: Oxford University Press).
Sen, Amartya (1999) *Development as freedom* (New York, NY: Anchor Books).
Solinger, Dorothy (2011) *Dibaohu* in distress: The meager minimum livelihood guarantee system in Wuhan, in Beatriz Carrillo and Jane Duckett (eds), *China's changing welfare mix: Local perspectives*, pp. 36–63 (London and New York: Routledge).

Tang, Wenfang and William L. Parish (2000) *Chinese urban life under reform: The changing social contract* (Cambridge: Cambridge University Press).

UN (2002) Report of the second world assembly on ageing, Madrid, 8–12 April (New York: UN). Available at http://www.c-fam.org/docLib/20080625_Madrid_Ageing_Conference.pdf, accessed 7 October 2011.

UNFPA (2006) Population ageing in China – facts and figures (Beijing: UNFPA). Available at http://www.un.org.cn/public/resource/e7102d15216f85e5c2e4d2e33784b72f.pdf, accessed 13 October 2011.

Woodman, Sophia (2011) Law, translation, and voice: Transformation of a struggle for social justice in a Chinese village. *Critical Asian Studies* 43(2), pp. 185–210.

Xu Chuanxin (2009) Nongcun liushou funü yanjiu: huigu yu qianzhan. *Renkou yu Fazhan* 15(6), pp. 54–73.

Xu Chuanxin (2010) Xibu nongcun liushou funü jiating yali ji yingxiang yisu fenxi. *Renkou yu Jingji* 178(1), pp. 73–78.

Yan, Yunxiang (2003) *Private life under socialism: Love, intimacy, and family change in a Chinese village 1949–1999* (Stanford, CA: Stanford University Press).

Ye Jingzhong and He Congzhi (2008) *Jingmo xiyang: Zongguo nongcun liushou laoren* (Beijing: Shehui Kexue Wenxian Chubanshe).

Ye, Jingzhong and Lu Pan (2011) Differentiated childhoods: Impacts of rural labor migration on left-behind children in China. *Journal of Peasant Studies* 38(2), pp. 355–77.

Young, Iris Marion (2002) Autonomy, welfare reform, and meaningful work, in Eva Feder Kittay and Ellen K. Feder (eds), *The subject of care: Feminist perspectives on dependency*, pp. 40–60 (Lanham: Rowman and Littlefield).

Problematic Conjugations: Women's Agency, Marriage and Domestic Violence in Indonesia

SITI AISYAH

Universitas Islam Negeri Alauddin Makassar

LYN PARKER

The University of Western Australia

Abstract: *This paper examines women's experience of domestic violence within marriage in Makassar, South Sulawesi. It analyses the meaning of marriage for men and women, the roles of men and women within marriage, shifts in marriage practices – particularly the shift from arranged to "love" marriage – and unequal gender positions within marriage. We discuss some salient issues in the "margins of marriage" in Indonesia: polygyny and constructions of masculinity that condone the practice of polygyny/affairs, and attitudes towards divorce, particularly for women. We then examine women's perception of the causes and triggers of domestic violence as revealed by fieldwork data, using the lens of women's agency. Our findings are that women perceive that their expressions of agency – for instance in challenging men's authority, moral righteousness and adequacy as breadwinners – are the most common triggers for male violence within marriage. Finally, we discuss the difficulty for women of escaping domestic violence, thereby getting some purchase on the relative capacity of women to resist, deflect or deal with the violence.*

Introduction

Most studies of domestic violence are about violence that occurs within marriage. In Indonesia, the construction of marriage is quite distinctive and this paper explores the connections between the nature of marriage and the occurrence of domestic violence.

Since the vast majority of women in Indonesia are married and most domestic violence occurs within marriage, there is a need to examine this important and enduring social institution through a domestic violence lens, and *vice versa*, to examine domestic violence as an aspect of marriage.[1]

This paper has four aims: to contribute empirical information about domestic violence in Indonesia to the slim body of literature on this subject; to use this information to enhance our understanding of the ways in which domestic violence can be culturally constructed; to develop a stronger consciousness of the gendering of marriage in Indonesia; and to use the data on domestic violence to better understand women's agency within marriage in Indonesia. The "problematic conjugations" in the title refer to three couplings: the unequal union of husband and wife in marriage; the articulation of marriage and domestic violence; and the connections between women's agency in marriage and the occurrence of domestic violence in Indonesia.

Agency

We are interested in linking two bodies of literature on domestic violence that seem theoretically incompatible. On the one hand, we have many feminist works that position women's experience of domestic violence as central to their analyses (e.g. Allen, 2011; Bambang, 2006; Harding, 1991; Skinner et al., 2005). The feminist focus on women's personal experience of domestic violence has resulted in the dominant representation of battered women as victims. On the other hand, we have many feminist works that analyse the formative, discursive power of patriarchy, of gender-unequal social institutions such as marriage, and of ideologies, such as the gender system, as responsible for domestic violence, such that "patriarchy" is now central to domestic violence policy worldwide (e.g. Dobash, 1980; WHO, 2011). In this paper we want to use great depth of field: to keep women's experience sharp and in-focus in the centre of the picture, and to keep the discursive and institutional background also in focus.

The decision to write about women's agency in a paper on domestic violence might seem strange. Given that domestic violence is a destructive, everyday and inescapable experience for many women, one might well ask if agency is possible. In relation to domestic violence, it might be assumed that a paper on agency would focus on the work of supporting or protecting victims, or on the establishment of mechanisms within the criminal justice system to deal with offenders. While we do mention some of these measures, our focus is on the agency of women in abusive situations and it grew out of the evidence – notably, interviews with abused women who identified their expressions of agency as triggers for their husband's violence. This paper is thus a "dark" paper: it highlights instances where women's expression of agency prompts violence. We stress that we are not saying that women's agency causes domestic violence: we are only pointing to women's agency as a trigger for their husband's violence. The deeper causes, and the condoning, lie elsewhere, not least in the construction of marriage and masculinity in Indonesia.

In the literature on domestic violence, the emphasis has long been on women as victims. This focus has shifted somewhat to conceptualisations that transcend the victim/agent dichotomy: the more recent term, "survivors", encapsulates this shift (Dunn, 2005; Picart, 2003). The shift is partly a response to the fact that there is more research on "women who stay" – i.e. in abusive relationships. Nevertheless, the dominant discourse about battered women remains one of victimisation. "[C]entral to this vocabulary is the removal of agency" (Dunn and Powell-Williams, 2007, p. 982). The concomitant is that women who leave abusive marriages are considered to have exercised agency, while women who stay remain victims.

This paper takes agency as arising from within social discourses, norms and structures, and as the capacity to move, literally or figuratively, in self- or group-interest, in the gap between hegemonic discourses and authority structures on one side and everyday practice on the other. We expect expressions of agency to be diverse because different societies and groups have different norms and differently value particular actions – e.g. speaking one's opinion might be positively valued in one context or society but regarded as poor form in another. In this way agency is culturally embedded (Korteweg, 2008) and "always occurs within social relations and cultural practice" (Parker, 2005, p. 20). Agency might be manifest in transgressive thinking, in challenging talk, in literary expression, in identity construction and in meaning-making. In our case, women's agency in marriage is exercised when, for example, women challenge or criticise their husbands verbally, a challenge that is simultaneously a challenge of gender norms and husbandly power. In the domestic violence literature, however, the meaning of agency is usually "free will" or the making of choices (Dunn and Powell-Williams, 2007, p. 980). In this literature, scholars, social workers and advocates alike struggle to come to terms with "women who stay", because of the discursive strength of this idea of agency in Western liberal democratic cultures. It seems unbelievable that women who are bashed by their husbands would choose to stay in such relationships (Loseke, 2003). Nevertheless, following the path laid out by postcolonial feminist scholars, we argue against the classic Western formulations of agency – especially liberal notions of autonomous rational choice – as necessarily implying the exercise of free will, opening the way to empowerment for women (e.g. Mahmood, 2001; Ram, 2007). Ram (2007, p. 139) critiques the

> liberal construction of agency as consent between free, knowing individuals. In this construction, the clear light of reason and free choice guides the agency of individuated, contracted adults, unburdened by myth, tradition, and such irrational authorities inherited from the past.

In such formulations, "culture", "religion" and "tradition" are assumed to hold women back; what they need is liberation (Abu-Lughod, 2002).

Feminism's twin goals have been to identify the subordinating structures and relations within which women live and to change the situation for women who are oppressed, marginalised or subordinated. As Parker (2005, p. 6) has written elsewhere, "…a central objective of feminist scholarship has been to represent women…, wherever possible giving voice to subaltern women who might not otherwise be heard. In this discursive context, the search for women's 'agency' is prefigured in any feminist scholarship". Such ideas, however, can lead to the "romanticization of resistance" (Abu-Lughod, 1990), with "the teleology of emancipation underwriting many accounts of women's agency" (Mahmood, 2001, p. 210). Mahmood critiques the assumption of Western feminism that women universally desire to be free from relations of subordination. Ortner (2001) usefully advances the arguments over agency, identifying two modalities: agency related to power and agency related to intention.

For this paper on domestic violence in Indonesia, we argue that "agency is mainly an issue of power" (Parker, 2005, p. 16). In framing domestic violence within marriage, we are really examining power relations within marriage. In turn, we are examining a society, a religion and a nation-state that can be described as patriarchal. Patriarchy alone, however, is not an adequate explanation of domestic violence. Clearly most husbands in Indonesia are not violent towards their wives. Also relevant is the unit or frame of analysis. Butt and Munro (2007) examined pre-marital pregnancies of young women in Papua. In literature on youth, the free expression of sexual desires has often been seen as the exercise of personal agency. They challenge this interpretation for their field site, arguing that if the analytical frame includes pregnancy and childbirth, and the ways pre-marital childbirth disempowers young women, agency turns into constraint. Similarly, we argue that the framing of domestic violence within marriage is significant in any adjudication of agency.

Domestic violence in Indonesia

Domestic violence has only recently been named in Indonesia, and the most common terms used to describe it are *kekerasan terhadap perempuan* (violence towards women) and the acronym KDRT (*Kekerasan Dalam Rumah Tangga* – violence in the household). *Kekerasan Dalam Rumah Tangga* was the official term used in ground-breaking legislation in 2004: Law 23/2004 has the title *Penghapusan Kekerasan Dalam Rumah Tangga* (The Abolition of Violence in the Household). KDRT has become a common acronym in daily newspapers.

After the resignation of President Suharto in May 1998, Indonesia moved rapidly towards democratisation: the press, bridled under Suharto's New Order, was freed, women's groups flourished and many topics, formerly proscribed, were given free rein. Domestic violence was one, and it was a tremendous achievement for feminist activists to get this Law up and running so quickly.[2] Law No. 23/2004 defines domestic violence as:

> any act against anyone, particularly women, bringing about physical, sexual or psychological misery or suffering, and/or negligence in the household, including threats to commit acts, the use of force, or constraint of freedom in a manner against the law within the scope of the household (ROI, 2004, our translation).

The Law is inclusive in its definition, and much work on implementation and training, service provision and reporting has been done by women's groups and government agencies. Most people in Indonesia now know the concept of "domestic violence". For each of the last three years, more than 100,000 cases of violence against women have been reported; in 2011, 113,878 cases of domestic violence were reported, 97 per cent being violence towards wives (KOMNAS Perempuan, 2012, p. 1). Yet there remain serious problems of victim blaming and compliance with the Law, and there is now some feeling of stagnation in activist circles (KOMNAS Perempuan, 2012). One of the most intransigent problems is the norm that conflict within the family is not a public matter. Scholars have begun the enormous task of researching domestic violence in Indonesia (e.g. Aisyah, 2007; Baso et al., 2002; Bennett et al., 2011; Djanna, 2007; Hakimi et al., 2001; Idrus, 1999; Idrus and Bennett, 2003; Imawan et al., 2006; Prasetyo and Marzuni, 1997; Rowe et al., 2006; Suhandjati, 2002).

Outline of paper

Our depth of field in this paper ranges from women's perception and understanding of the everyday violence of their husbands towards them to Indonesia's legislative framework and socio-cultural norms. After outlining our methodology, we examine the institution of marriage in Indonesia and in our field site in South Sulawesi: the meaning of marriage for men and women, the roles and unequal positions of men and women within marriage, polygyny, and attitudes towards divorce. We then examine women's perceptions of the triggers of domestic violence as revealed through fieldwork data. Finally, we discuss the difficulty for women of escaping domestic violence, thereby getting some purchase on the relative capacity of women to resist or deal with the violence.

Methodology

The fieldwork to collect the data used in this paper was undertaken in Makassar, the capital city of the province of South Sulawesi, Indonesia, in 2004.[3] Hereafter, participants will be referred to as S (survivors of domestic violence), WA (women activists), GO (government officials) and RS (religious scholars). Makassar has a population of 1.3 million people (BPS, 2010). The majority of the population is Muslim. Makassar is dominated by the Makassarese, who are Muslim, but other ethnicities are well represented – notably the Bugis, but also the Javanese, Mandarese and Torajans. Interviews were conducted with 38 participants. The main group of informants consisted of 19 women who have experienced or are experiencing domestic violence. They were chosen in two ways: introduction by activists in Non-Government Organisations (NGOs), and through the first author's own contacts developed during monthly Islamic study groups (*pengajian*) that she led at a community centre. The participants had a variety of social and educational backgrounds, ranging from not having completed primary school to holding a postgraduate qualification. All were Makassarese or Buginese, all were Muslim and all had lived in Makassar for more than ten years. In addition, the first author interviewed 19 people who had some relevant expertise or experience in dealing with domestic violence. This second group consisted of government employees working in support services, NGO activists in support services, and religious scholars at Makassar State Islamic University.

The Gender Relations of Marriage in Indonesia

Here we present information on marriage and the gender system in Indonesia, where relevant noting local differences in emphasis from the national Indonesian pattern. "Local" here refers to the Bugis-Makassarese culture in South Sulawesi. While Bugis and Makassarese see themselves as distinct ethnic groups, both Bugis and Makassar *adat* (custom) are strongly influenced by Islam, such that it is almost impossible to disentangle them.

Ideal marriage in Indonesia – laws and roles

The law and practice of marriage received considerable attention in feminist work on women in Indonesia during the New Order under Suharto (1966–98) (e.g. Blackburn,

2004; Blackburn and Bessell, 1997; Robinson, 2009; Suryakusuma, 1996; see also Butt, 2008; Cammack et al., 2008). Because of this, here we only focus on those aspects of marriage that are relevant to our data on domestic violence.[4]

The 1974 Marriage Law states that husbands are the heads of families, and that wives are housewives (ROI, 1974, Article 31 (3)). Although the implementation of law is commonly weak in Indonesia, this statement, that husbands are the heads of families, is known and accepted throughout Indonesia and has everyday material effects. During the New Order, Indonesian authorities promulgated an ideal of the happy and harmonious family. The ideological base of the Indonesian nation-state is the "family foundation" (*azas kekeluargaan*). The "family foundation" ideology presumed harmonious affective ties among family members; it assigned to each family member a "natural" place and a role to play. The gender roles within the family were said to be equal and complementary, but actually the model was infused with hierarchical principles, particularly respect for age and maleness. The *azas kekeluargaan* provided a vision of an integrated nation and state: the nation-state was to be one big, happy family. The father at the apex enjoys a natural authority, and those subordinate to him – the wife and children in the new nuclear family – serve his interests, which are conflated with the interests of the family. There is unity of power and authority, the primacy of family needs over individual needs, and no legitimate opposition. Although this was said to suit the Indonesian national character, real-life Indonesian families tend to be much more extended and complicated than this.

Marriage in Bugis-Makassarese society

Marriage for the Bugis involves not just the bringing together of two individuals in marriage but also

> the joining of two families into one, whether or not the "actors" belong to the same kin group... [T]he Bugis term for marriage [*siala*] ... can be translated as "to take each other"... [T]here is an act of exchange in which the groom's side takes the bride's, and vice versa, in order to form a new social alliance which plays an important role in kinship (Idrus, 2004).

Similarly, for the Makassarese,

> marriage among close family members (endogamous marriage) occurs with the aim of maintaining and strengthening kinship ties. The main consideration for choosing a daughter's partner is social status and kinship or relatedness, and this practice remains predominant. In order to maintain family strength and privilege, arranged marriages often occur (Aisyah, 2007, p. 70).

The Bugis and Makassarese are strongly Islamic societies. Both have patrilineal kinship systems, with marriage cementing a strong tie between wider families or clans. Substantial payments are made to the bride's family at the time of the wedding. These payments are forfeited by the male side upon divorce. For these and other reasons, divorce is uncommon (Jones, 1994, p. 220).

In Islam, the main reason for marriage is procreation. Marriage "establishes the rights and duties for both husband and wife, and protects any children born from the marriage" (Idrus, 2004). Sex may only occur within marriage; sex before, outside or after marriage is a major sin (*zina*). While procreation is the primary function of marriage for both genders, there are significant gender differences in the meaning of marriage. For men, marriage is an announcement and confirmation of sexual potency and hence masculinity. For women, "the significance of marriage is connected to … marriageability … [which] is connected to her sexual purity and commodified value" (Idrus, 2004). Unlike men, women do not usually discuss marriage in terms of sexual needs, as this would render them morally suspect. For Bugis women, there is an economic motivation to get married: "As women commonly said: 'There is someone who looks for money for me'…, thus making explicit the husband's role as breadwinner" (Idrus, 2004).

A second important feature of marriage in Bugis-Makassarese society is honour (*siri'*). *Siri'* has multiple meanings: honour, shame, shyness, fear, humility, disgrace, envy, self-respect, and morality (Baso and Idrus, 2002, p. 207, n. 1). In Indonesia generally, marriage is both a marker of adulthood and a fundamental aspect of an adult's identity and social status. In Bugis society, which is strongly hierarchical, marriage is an arena that one can use to enhance or lower one's social status. Usually, a man and a woman who marry are of equal status. Women can marry "up" (i.e. by marrying a man whose family status is higher than their own), but women who marry down because of love are usually "thrown away" (Idrus, 2004) – they are no longer recognised by their families. The woman is thus "the symbol of family *siri'* (honour)… A woman determines or stabilises the degree of nobility of her family" (Idrus, 2004).

Gender roles and responsibilities in marriage

The Indonesian state prescribes gendered roles within the family and household. The Marriage Law of 1974 sets out the rights and responsibilities of husbands and wives. The economic role of the husband is clearly articulated: "husbands are responsible for protecting their wives and for providing all the necessities of life for the household, in keeping with their capability" (ROI, 1974, Article 34 (1)). Article 34 (2) clearly lays out the wife's territory: "Wives are obliged to organise the household as well as possible" (ROI, 1974). In Makassar, the gender division of labour is defined according to *adat*. The main duties of women are domestic chores and child care; men should provide for and maintain the safety and welfare of family members. In Makassar society, women's status is "highly respected" and women should be "protected" (Hamid, 1994, p. 33; Baso and Idrus, 2002, p. 199). There are a range of cultural and social expectations of women – e.g. women should avoid any act that may cause family dishonour, such as adultery and elopement. The accounts of participants in this study with respect to gender roles within marriage are consistent with these anthropologists' accounts. One activist stated:

> There are double responsibilities [for women], especially for career women. They work outside the home and have to be responsible for domestic chores including cooking and taking care of children. Their income is considered secondary. Women are sometimes asked to quit their jobs in order to raise children. Moreover, women have to be submissive and obedient and need to ask permission

from their husband if they want to go out. Men, on the other hand, only work in the public sphere and rarely undertake household tasks (WA1, 2 March 2004).

Another respondent explained gender roles as follows:

> Women are supposed to serve and take care of their husbands, be tolerant and submissive, respect them and never challenge them. Men, however, as family financial providers and heads of family, are maintainers of family honour and provide family guidance (WA2, 3 March 2004).

One religious scholar did contradict the idea that women should always be submissive towards husbands, saying "Submission is not appropriate in all circumstances, especially in things that go against religion" (RS2, 8 April 2004). In other words, submission is required only where the husband's will is put to good purpose; it follows that there is no requirement that women should submit to acts of violence. That is, men do not have absolute rights or power over women. Married women are often expected to take on the role of managing the family income and expenditure, organising the household and caring for elderly relatives. Women nevertheless have limited power within the family: the position of household manager does not entail rights to control the family economy.

The margins of marriage: Polgyny

The 1974 Marriage Law and associated regulations made early marriage, divorce and polygyny more difficult in Indonesia. The issue of polygyny has been a continuing sore spot for the women's movement throughout the twentieth century, not least because it has been impossible for activists to unite under an anti-polygyny banner (Blackburn, 2004). Nurmila's recent study of polygyny in Indonesia revealed that polygyny was consistently associated with "significant degrees of emotional and physical violence" for women (2009, p. 14). Even literalist Muslim women felt "shocked" and "heartbroken" when their husbands suddenly announced that they intended to take a second wife (Nurmila, 2009, p. 82). To read these women's stories is to read of suffering, of "dying while standing", of trauma and distress, social isolation, loneliness and maltreatment "under the guise of male religious piety" (Nurmila, 2009, p. xiv). While Indonesia's Law on Domestic Violence 2004 does recognise acts that cause "sexual or psychological misery or suffering" as domestic violence, this is not to say that Indonesia recognises polygyny as necessarily entailing domestic violence (ROI, 2004). However, there does seem to be a strong link between polygyny and female suffering, and between polygyny and divorce. For instance, Suhandjati (2002) examined the cases of 50 women who registered as having experienced domestic violence: 12 were women who filed for divorce because of violence toward them that involved polygyny or *selingkuh* (unofficial wives, mistresses or long-running affairs).

Arranged and "choice" marriages

As young women in Indonesia increasingly pursue education and careers, marriage increasingly occurs through the individual choice of marriage partners. The discourse of *cinta*, romantic love, has become dominant in Indonesia, mainly through the medium of popular culture. This trend has occurred in Makassar, where educated and employed women sometimes refuse a parent's choice of partner and choose a partner themselves (Aisyah, 2007, p. 73). Nevertheless, young people still generally seek parental approval and consent. Although arranged marriage has become less common in Indonesia, it has not been discarded. Arranged marriage continues to exist in certain places, particularly in rural areas around Makassar (Aisyah, 2007, p. 72).[5] Marriages that are not arranged can be elopements or abductions. After such a marriage, women in Makassar are not only restricted to socialising with their husband's family members, but also may, on rare occasions, face the risk of being killed if they have damaged family *siri'* (Aisyah, 2007, p. 72).

We turn now to our data on domestic violence, to see how this discursive environment shapes women's perception of the violence that their husbands mete out to them. We preface this section by saying that we cannot claim that our data are comprehensive for Makassar, let alone for Indonesia.

Domestic Violence in Makassar

The view that domestic violence is a private matter that does not require intervention from outsiders is held by many in Indonesia, including some women who have experienced it. In this view, conflict and disagreement within marital relationships are natural, and husbands and wives are expected to resolve their problems within the family. In Makassar it is commonly believed that speaking out about domestic violence causes a woman to feel *siri'* (shame), which undermines family honour. One woman stated that it was better to keep silent rather than seek help, because seeking help would cause humiliation, and anyway, for the most part, she believed that she deserved it (S4, 4 March 2004). This puzzling final comment led us to think deeply about the meaning of marriage for our respondents.

Domestic violence and women's agency: Challenging men's authority

Many women in our sample traced the act of violence to an expression of their own agency vis-à-vis their husband's authority. One woman noted, "My husband beats me if I interrupt or talk while he is speaking" (S1, 4 March 2004). This is not to say that in general women blame themselves for domestic violence – contra the statement of S4 above. Rather, when a woman challenges a man's authority, he finds this threatening and retaliates by striking her.[6] The violent response of men to the exercise of agency by wives is one of the strongest themes in the talk of women who experience domestic violence in Makassar. It clearly indicates the hegemony of the patriarchal gender ideology, as enshrined in the Marriage Law: men are the powerful heads of families, and women are rightly subordinate to men. Some women stated that they were always at risk of abuse if they advanced an opinion or made comments during confrontations. The husband wished them to keep silent and not challenge them. In such cases, violence was often used to end the argument.

Articles 31 and 34 of the 1974 Marriage Law clearly ascribe power asymmetry. In addition, Muslim women often accept that marriage entails presumed consent for sexual intercourse, whenever a husband demands it outside of menstruation. This was also reported by Idrus and Bennett (2003, p. 51):

> He believes that as a husband, he has the right to be sexually served by his wife whenever he pleases. If I refused him, he would throw me onto the bed, take off my clothes, and force me to have sex. He also forced me to make sounds to stimulate his passion. He treated me not like a wife, but like a whore. If I resisted him, he would become angrier and hit me without any thought or respect.

Again the woman's agency in the form of resistance was met with further violence. The language of "serving" is frequently used. While women generally accept that they should serve their husbands with food and drink, opinion is divided over sexual services. In the Criminal Code there is no concept of marital rape. In our sample, only two women mentioned sexual violence, detailing that their husbands had tried to force them to engage in sexual relations, including during menstruation (S2, 15 March 2004; S19, 27 April 2004).

Alcohol consumption is proscribed by Islam and drinking is not the common social problem in Makassar that it is in countries such as Australia. When violence occurred after a drinking episode, it was usually if the wife asked, "Where have you been?" or "Can you please stop drinking?" (S1, 4 March 2004). The husband's responses to such questions included violence and threats to kill her. Another man expected his wife and children to always be waiting at home for him, after he had been drinking:

> My husband always gets angry or physically abuses me if I or my children are not at home. He often kicks me when I ask him not to drink alcohol. This occurs almost every day and the most frightening is when he hits me with a piece of wood. Because of that, I have a permanently broken leg (S3, 4 March 2004).

Another survivor also revealed that she had been beaten for going out (S3, 4 March 2004). This indicates that women's agency is countered by male possessiveness and wish to control. One woman stated that her husband's abuse was a way of problem solving for him (S1, 2 March 2004). Thus, domestic violence was frequently triggered by the wife's questioning of the man's authority, supremacy, adequacy or morality, and the man's intolerance of criticism.

Domestic violence and gender roles within marriage

Acts of domestic violence are frequently traced by women to their husband's perception that they (the women) are not playing their gender role as household manager, when the women felt that the men were not adequately providing for the family. There is often a sense that the man is shifting the blame for economic difficulties on to the wife:

> I am not allowed to manage the family budget. My husband keeps questioning how I spent the money if there is not enough to cover bills or food (S1, 4 March 2004).

Something of the pressures of the husband's role can be discerned in the following woman's description of a confrontation over their roles in the household economy:

> I asked him to look for a job. He replied that I should not harass or ask him to find work because he was aware of that. He said, "I know ten times [better] than you, and I understand [the need to seek employment], and you as a wife do not need to tell me about that". He also suggested that I was not clever enough to pass judgment on him [by making that suggestion] (S6, 8 March 2004).

This man sounds quite sensitive about his unemployed status: his male pride is wounded when his wife points out his inadequacies as a provider. In a developing country such as Indonesia, it is clearly impossible for all men to provide adequately for their families. For this reason, the burden of responsibility on men is a heavy one. Many men in Indonesia do not get married until they are economically independent: in this way, marriage for men is a mark of successful masculinity. This statement shows that embedded in men's role as provider for the family is an assumption that he occupies the high ground when it comes to evaluating the success or otherwise of the family unit: he denies his wife the right to criticise, by denigrating her intellectual capacity.

Five women provided stories of economic abuse. One said that her husband restricted her spending on daily necessities (S1, 4 March 2004); another that she had never received any financial support from her husband because he had another wife (S3, 4 March 2004). Other women stated that their husbands were physically violent towards them if they asked for money (S5, 4 March 2004; S13, 15 March 2004). These accounts indicate not only men's attempts to restrict and control women's access to financial resources, but also men's refusal to take responsibility for economic shortfalls – implied when their wives had to ask them for money. One survivor (S6) revealed her polygynous husband's failure to provide for his families – see below. Men shifted their failure to carry out their responsibility for the economic wellbeing of the family on to women, at the same time as they attempted to silence women's verbal reminders of their failure through violence.

Women are also often blamed by their husbands for failing to fulfil their gender responsibilities. Wives are often chastised over domestic misdemeanours such as a child's bad behaviour, children's injuries, poor cooking, or for going out without their husband's knowledge. One woman related that her husband hit her because her child fell over. The husband accused her of failing to meet her child-caring responsibilities, and of not taking care of their child (S1 and S2, 4 March 2004; S10, 14 March 2004). Another woman noted that her husband became angry when she did not provide meals for him. He commented that it was not difficult to cook rice, which takes only a few minutes. By belittling domestic skills, the husband denigrated her as a woman (S9, 13 March 2004). Physical and emotional violence are often used when women are perceived as not complying with their prescribed gender roles or failing to undertake them in ways deemed appropriate by men. The effect of such criticism is often to damage the woman's self-identity and esteem: she is made to feel inadequate as a woman, a wife and a mother.

It is also the case that each woman's story is complicated. The following excerpt from an interview shows a woman's typically densely-woven narrative that combines many strands: challenges to male authority, conflict over gender roles, alcohol abuse, conflict over control of money, and finally, the hurt of having to compete with another woman:

> My husband beats me if I interrupt or talk while he is speaking, or if the children fall down, or after drinking alcohol or if I am looking for him at a drinking site… I cannot make decisions about family expenditure and when the money is insufficient he keeps asking "How has the money been spent?" My husband often hits me if I purchase something which he dislikes. Also, my husband is having an affair with another woman (S1, 4 March 2004).

Rowe et al. also reported that "[s]pousal abuse often followed a wife's complaint about her husband's affair" (Rowe et al., 2006, p. 44). We turn now to this final theme in women's stories about the violence they experience.

Domestic violence, men having affairs and polygyny

"Having cancer might be better than having a polygamous husband" (S13, 15 March 2004).

Many women who are the victims of violent abuse by their husbands have to put up with sexual infidelity – through their partners having affairs or through polygyny, which is sometimes kept secret. Six of the 19 survivors interviewed noted that their husbands were having affairs. One woman who divorced her husband for this reason claimed: "If he has a special girlfriend, it means that he does not love me any more… I divorced him because I prefer to enjoy and improve my life, not to be beaten and dishonoured" (S18, 12 April 2004). The issue for wives is not just one of love, sexual jealousy and competition: it is also about their self-identity and self-esteem as women and wives, their social status and family honour. Polygyny and mistresses frequently mean economic deprivation for the wives as well as for their children.

One woman stated that her husband became violent when she challenged him about his affair with another woman. He denied having an affair, but many people had witnessed it. She advised her husband that "having a mistress is socially unacceptable and that he should be aware of such a mistake" (simultaneous interviews with S1 and S16, 4 March and 14 April 2004). Comments that take the moral high ground and challenge male power and authority are a common precursor to domestic violence in Makassar. Advising men to adhere to religious and cultural values and norms, such as abstaining from alcohol and not having affairs, leads to arguments that often end in violence. Women's attempts to "guide" men or to negotiate with them undermine and threaten men's apical position in the family. In taking a mistress or having affairs, a man is contravening social and religious norms. One of our interviewees said: "I never complain or tell anyone when my husband physically abuses me, but when he engages in a sexual scandal, I let others know about that" (S1, 4 March 2004). While it is regrettable that the perpetrator of violence gets away with his crime, we can almost hear the wife's vengeful pleasure as she reveals her husband's sexual misdemeanours. The cultural logic that causes men who are having affairs to be violent to their wives, thereby inflicting a double pain, seems to be related to the fact that their wives can take this moral high ground. The men have no defence: such behaviour is not condoned by religious or social norms – and indeed is a major sin (*zina*) in Islam. Women suffer significant emotional turmoil due to a husband's polygyny/affairs. They identified this issue more overtly and more frequently than any other as a contributing factor to domestic violence. The virtuous wife, who perceives that she has been wronged by her polygynous husband, is herself perceived as a threat by the husband, so he lashes out in an attempt to deny his wrong-doing and impose his will on her virtue.

When a man takes on a second (third or fourth) wife, he is legally required to secure the signed consent of his first and former wives. Such marriages are rather suspect in Indonesia: as noted above, marriages are supposed to be smooth and harmonious. Taking a second, third or fourth wife seems to be stating that the early marriage/s were lacking. Under the New Order, there was a disapproving attitude towards polygyny, at least in public:

> A woman who was a second wife couldn't be out in the open because of the sense of shame and embarrassment arising out of her position. Society despised those involved in polygamous marriages (Minza, 2009, p. 25).

When a man takes a second wife, there is the suspicion that the first wife is inadequate as a wife, particularly "in bed" – that is, that she does not know how to "serve" her husband and satisfy his sexual demands (Idrus, 1999, p. 84). In addition to the personal hurt that the first wife might feel at being supplanted in her husband's affections by a (usually younger, prettier) second wife, the first wife must also contend with gossip and sexual innuendo that undermine her confidence in herself. One woman, whose husband practised polygyny without her consent, stated that she suffers permanent psychological distress. She said that it was not easy to recover from his insults or to forgive him, even though he had since divorced his second wife. He had been considerate and quiet when living the lie. When she realised that he had married another woman, she had felt humiliated. She could not trust him again when he was away from home, even for business (S13, 15 March 2004). In the Indonesian and Islamic context, women assume that their husbands are sexually faithful. Often they have not realised, or made explicit to themselves, the sexual double standard that prevails in Indonesian society: that women must be pure and monogamous, but men not only may be sexually promiscuous, but can also enhance their masculine status by having affairs and taking multiple wives.

The fact that domestic violence goes hand-in-hand with polygynous marriage is hardly surprising. The man is under considerable social pressure, not least because he is supposed to be economically and equally supporting two (or more) families. Many divorce cases instigated by wives have been successful because polygynous husbands have been economically negligent – i.e. they have not provided for the family of the first wife (O'Shaughnessy, 2009; Suhandjati, 2002).

Domestic violence and socioeconomic class

Women of all educational backgrounds and socioeconomic statuses experience domestic violence. Rowe et al.'s (2006) study of academic women in Medan who experienced domestic violence makes it clear that professional standing and high education do not protect women from violent husbands. Further, the "material wellbeing and presumed independence of [financially independent] wives actually contributes to the violence because it challenges cultural patriarchy" (Rowe et al., 2006, p. 46). Idrus' study of eight cases of marital rape in 1997 in Makassar revealed a wide range of education and socioeconomic statuses (1999, p. 11). Nevertheless, there are some classed patterns. For instance, Suhandjati found that women with higher education (senior high school or above) were more likely to express their feelings and to file for divorce than those with only primary or junior high school education (Suhandjati, 2002, pp. 96–97).

Our Makassar data do not reveal any class patterns in the type or frequency of violence, but education was a factor in some women's strategising. One survivor saw education as necessary for women "to prevent them from being underestimated by men, especially when they are abused" (S2, 4 March 2004). One highly-educated woman, the family's main economic provider, does not tell other people about her experience of violence. She conceals her husband's violence because she believes it is a private family matter and a personal problem. Disclosing abuse is very embarrassing, and she is worried about being ostracised by the community. She said that they might ask, "Why do educated people have such problems?" (S6, 8 March 2004). This reveals a presumption that domestic violence is the preserve of lower-class, ill-educated people, and a middle-class concern with keeping up the appearance of propriety and respectability.

Escaping Domestic Violence

Leaving a husband is a very big step to take in Indonesia. The single woman is strongly stigmatised in Indonesian society. The category of single, adult woman does not really exist in Indonesian society: the word for mother, *ibu*, is also the title for all adult women. In effect, adulthood for women equates with motherhood. Marriage leads quickly to parenthood; infertile couples are much pitied. In Indonesian, the term *janda* refers to both widows and divorced women. The stigmatisation of *janda* has to do with the fact that they are autonomous women, not under the control of a man; sexual desire (*nafsu*) in a divorced or widowed woman is thought to be alive and unsatisfied. As Wieringa said, "Non-married women such as widows or divorced women,... sex workers and lesbians are seen as deviant or abjected and face various kinds of harassment" (2009, pp. 21–22). "Cultural stereotypes that divorced women are considered to be 'bad' and 'shameful' may contribute to [the perpetuation of] domestic violence" (WA2, 3 March 2004).

Divorce is restricted by the state, not only through the Marriage Law but also through discourses of shame (O'Shaughnessy, 2009, Ch. 3). The state courts are embedded in a gender order which defines female-initiated divorce as shameful and sees divorce as an attack on men's superior social status. Women who want to escape marriage are constructed as transgressive: if they initiate divorce, they are exhibiting impropriety. Women bear the brunt of public humiliation and shame for failed marriages as well as for their husband's affairs. In Bugis society, where marriage is a matter of family honour, a failed marriage is a public disgrace, especially for the woman. Reddy has noted that shame "derives from thoughts about how one is seen by others... Thus, shame can lead to withdrawal coupled with action aimed at managing appearances" (1997, p. 347).

Both educated and uneducated women in our study wanted to conceal domestic abuse in order to present an image of family harmony. One woman whose husband frequently abused her said she really hates her husband but is traumatised by having run away after a violent episode (S2, 4 March 2004). Another, who had been attacked almost daily, and has a permanently broken knee, said she feels irritation and anger, but has no power to confront her husband. She fears that he might kill her. The only thing she can do is accept the abuse (S3, 4 March 2004). One woman was physically, emotionally and economically abused by her husband, but opted to keep silent and tolerate the violence. She often thought about running away from her violent husband but her parents refused to allow her to stay with them (S1, 4 March 2004). This introduces an interesting new finding from this study: women who have experienced domestic violence following a love or "choice" marriage, as opposed to an arranged marriage, find that they cannot go home to their birth family. Two of the 19 survivors interviewed stated that their parents were reluctant to let them return owing to the fact that their marriages were marriages of choice. One woman said that it was the shame of being subject to criticism by others that kept her silent. Her family would criticise her, asking, "Why did you not screen him more carefully before marriage?" (S1, 4 March 2004). Particularly for women who have exercised agency in choice of marriage partner, domestic violence is a private matter that should be resolved privately. The following quote shows that this abused woman, who had married for love, was equally as frightened by the threat of violence if she returned to her natal family as by more violence if she stayed with her abusive husband:

> [I] wanted to make a complaint about the violence but I could not do that. My parents disagreed with my choice of partner. It was frightening to go to my parents' home or to stay at my own home... I was emotionally shattered; my left eye was swollen and bruised. [I wanted] to apply for divorce, but what about my children and their education? The status of "divorced" is not socially approved of and has negative [connotations]. Divorced women are not allowed to go out, and if we do, it is assumed we do so to find a man. This brings about family dishonour (*siri'*)... A woman is always blamed for divorce (S6, 8 March 2004).

Leaving the marital home is a very serious step, especially for women who cannot access temporary accommodation and get support from their natal family. If a woman escapes briefly and is then forced to return to her husband, she may well experience further violence. Thus, feelings of hopelessness, vulnerability and isolation are reinforced. Many women have no experience of supporting themselves. There is also the possibility of having to leave children behind – depending on local *adat*.

In Indonesia, women who experience domestic violence often have nowhere to escape and feel there is no way to end the violence. Parents' failure to provide support and temporary accommodation is a major obstacle for women who suffer domestic violence. One government official stated:

> Men are socialised into a belief that wife abuse is permissible and that they can do whatever they wish because the wife is considered as their property. Women, on the other hand, are powerless and ... tend to conceal it... Women survivors ... have difficulties in achieving financial autonomy and their self-esteem deteriorates. Neither temporary accommodation nor emotional support is available from family, community and state. The family and the community often lack respect for the victims and claim they have provoked the violence (GO3, 9 March 2004).

Table 1. Nineteen Women's Responses to Domestic Violence*

Responses	Number of Cases	% Cases
Accepted Abuse	9	36
Left	3	12
Separated	1	4
Sought Divorce	3	12
Resorted to Violence	5	20
Sought External Intervention	4	16
Total	25	100

*Some women offered more than one response.

In the table below we have presented 19 women's responses to domestic violence. Given the social and economic problems outlined above, it is hardly surprising that the dominant response was to accept the abuse.

Conclusion

This study has shown that, in Indonesia, marriage is constructed as an unequal power relationship in which husbands can legitimately wield power over wives. Domestic violence is an abuse of this husbandly power. Our study has shown how women's agency, marriage and domestic violence are interconnected. It has identified three points within marriage where women exert agency to claim some equality, dignity and autonomy, and at each of these three points their agency can be met with violence. The first is when women have chosen to marry a partner for love. In doing this, they resist parental authority and the social convention of arranged marriage. This expression of agency can come back to bite them later on: if their husbands are violent, their natal families can refuse to provide shelter for their errant daughters. As in Butt and Munro's (2007) study, if we take a wider frame, and look not just at the autonomy of the "love" marriage but also at the violence in the marriage, we see a classic example of how agency at one time can bring about disempowerment later on, when their husbands hit them, their families decline to support them, and can even turn violent against the victim. Second, if abused women take the initiative, "go public" and seek a divorce to escape their husband's violence, their agency is seen as transgressive and they are blamed for the failure of the marriage. The third, and most important, finding of the study is that most instances of domestic violence were identified by women as retaliation for and/or attempts to control women's agentic actions. Women consistently identified their own expression of agency within marriage as the cue for their husband's violence. Sometimes it was when women verbally challenged their husband's authority or moral righteousness, for instance, if the man was having an affair, marrying polygynously or drinking; sometimes it was when women pointed out their husband's inadequacies as a provider; sometimes it was when women pushed against their husband's possessiveness by going out or visiting their families. Thus domestic violence indexes not only the cultural construction of power within marriage, but also, ironically, wifely agency. This study shows the truth of Ortner's claim that "the cultural construction of power is always, simultaneously, the cultural construction of forms of agency and effectiveness in dealing with powerful others" (1997, p. 146). Women's expression of agency within marriage triggers men's violence.

Our identification of culturally specific aspects of marriage, the aetiology of domestic violence, and the lack of options for women who experience domestic violence in Indonesia indicate the great need for feminists to respond in a locally sensitive way to the needs of women who experience domestic violence. In the years since fieldwork was conducted for this project, Indonesian feminists have had considerable success not only in legislating a Law against domestic violence but also in direct action such as setting up refuges, information and reporting desks in police offices, and other institutional supports for women who experience domestic violence. The gender ideology still instantiated in marriage in Indonesia, as revealed in the first half of this paper, also shows there is much to be done in building a public discourse against domestic violence in the mass media.

Notes

1. In Indonesia, the level of non-marital cohabitation is so low as not to register in censuses. The level of domestic violence outside marital domestic violence – for example, violence towards children, housemaids or the elderly – is not yet known.
2. The neglect of domestic violence and the transition to democracy are dealt with in Blackburn (1999 and 2004). Sciortino and Smyth (2002) analyse the reasons for the silence about domestic violence in Indonesia.
3. The fieldwork on which this paper is based was undertaken by the first author during her PhD program; she was funded by AusAid and Flinders University, Australia. The researcher initiated contact with respondents personally and explained the purpose of the study and related issues and made appointments for interviews. In a few cases, preliminary contact was only with coordinators of women's NGOs. Most women were interviewed at a Women's Centre to minimise their stress; some were interviewed at home.
4. As part of the raft of new legislation after Suharto, a Muslim feminist scholar, Musdah Mulia, worked with a team in the Ministry of Religion to complete a Counter Legal Draft (CLD), which was a revision of Indonesia's Islamic legal code. Among the revisions were a ban on polygyny and arranged marriages, and the raising of the age of marriage for girls from 16 to 19 years. Both changes, she said, would help to prevent domestic violence and child abuse. The revisions were deemed so inflammatory that the Draft has not gone to legislation.
5. Recently, there have been reports of a swing towards arranged marriage in Java, particularly among fervently Islamic university students (Nilan, 2008; Smith-Hefner, 2005).
6. We note that the violent response of a man to his wife's challenge is an acknowledgment of her resistance. Scott notes "The ability to choose to overlook or ignore an act of insubordination as if it never happened is a key exercise of power" (Scott, 1990, p. 89, n. 44). The fact that the men did not ignore the challenge suggests that the men felt vulnerable – perhaps because the women had right on their side.

References

Abu-Lughod, Lila (1990) The romance of resistance: Tracing transformations of power through Bedouin women. *American Ethnologist* 17(1), pp. 41–55.

Abu-Lughod, Lila (2002) Do Muslim women really need saving? Anthropological reflections on cultural relativism and its others. *American Anthropologist* 104(3), pp. 783–90.

Aisyah, Siti (2007) Breaking the silence: In search of domestic violence in Makassar, Indonesia. Unpublished PhD Dissertation. Flinders University, Australia.

Allen, Mary (2011) Violence and voice: Using a feminist constructivist grounded theory to explore women's resistance to abuse. *Qualitative Research* 11(1), pp. 23–45.

Bambang, E. UU KDRT Dorong Perempuan Mengungkap Kasus Kekerasan yang Dialaminya. Viewed 19 January 2006 at http://www.jurnalperempuan.com/yjp.jpo/?act=berita%7C-477%7CX [no longer accessible online].

Baso, Zohra Andi, D. Aries Tina, S. Haerani and Alwi Rahman (2002) *Kekerasan terhadap perempuan: Menghadang langkah perempuan* (Yogyakarta: Pusat Studi Kependudukan dan Kebijakan Universitas Gajah Mada).

Baso, Zohra Andi and Nurul Ilmi Idrus (2002) Women's activism against violence in South Sulawesi, in Kathryn Robinson and Sharon Bessell (eds), *Women in Indonesia: Gender, equity and development*, pp. 198–208 (Singapore: Institute of Southeast Asian Studies).

Bennett, Linda, Sari Andajani-Suthahjo and Nurul I. Idrus (2011) Domestic violence in Nusa Tenggara Barat, Indonesia: Married women's definitions and experiences of violence in the home. *The Asia Pacific Journal of Anthropology* 12(2), pp. 146–63.

Blackburn, Susan (1999) Gender violence and the Indonesian political transition. *Asian Studies Review* 23(4), pp. 433–48.

Blackburn, Susan (2004) *Women and the state in modern Indonesia* (Cambridge: Cambridge University Press).

Blackburn, S. and S. Bessell (1997) Marriageable age: Political debates on early marriage in twentieth century Indonesia. *Indonesia* 63, pp. 107–41.

BPS (Biro Pusat Statistik) (2010) Tabel Hasil Sensus Penduduk 2010 Provinsi Sulawesi Selatan. Available at http://www.bps.go.id/aboutus.php?sp=0&kota=73, accessed 11 October 2011.

Butt, Leslie and Jenny Munro (2007) Rebel girls? Unplanned pregnancy and colonialism in Highlands Papua, Indonesia. *Culture, Health and Sexuality* 9(6), pp. 585–98.

Butt, Simon (2008) Polygamy and mixed marriage in Indonesia: Islam and the Marriage Law in the courts, in Timothy Lindsey (ed.), *Indonesia: Law and society*, 2nd edition, pp. 266–87 (Sydney: The Federation Press).

Cammack, Mark, Lawrence A. Young and Tim Heaton (2008) Legislating social change in an Islamic society: Indonesia's Marriage Law, in Timothy Lindsey (ed.), *Indonesia: Law and society*, 2nd edition, pp. 288–312 (Sydney: The Federation Press).

Djanna, Fathul (2007) *Kekerasan terhadap istri* (Yogyakarta: LKiS Yogyakarta).

Dobash, R. Emmerson (1980) *Violence against wives: A case against the patriarchy* (London: Open Books).

Dunn, J.L. (2005) "Victims" and "survivors": Emerging vocabularies of motive for "battered women who stay". *Sociological Inquiry* 75(1), pp. 1–30.

Dunn, Jennifer L. and Melissa Powell-Williams (2007) "Everybody makes choices": Victim advocates and the social construction of battered women's victimization and agency. *Violence Against Women* 13(10), pp. 977–1001.

Hamid, A. (1994) *Syekh Yusuf Makassar: Seorang ulama, Sufi dan pejuang* (Jakarta: Yayasan Obor Indonesia).

Hakimi, Mohammad, Elli Nurhayati, V. Utari Marlinawati, Anna Winkvist and C. Mary Ellsberg (2001) *Membisu demi harmoni: Kekerasan terhadap isteri dan kesehatan perempuan di Jawa Tengah Indonesia* (Yokyakarta: LPKGM-FK-UGM).

Harding, S. (1991) *Whose science? Whose knowledge? Thinking from women's lives* (New York: Cornell University Press).

Idrus, Nurul Ilmi (1999) *Marital rape (Kekerasan seksual dalam perkawinan)* (Yogyakarta: Ford Foundation with Pusat Penelitian Kependudukan, Universitas Gajah Mada, Seri Laporan No. 88).

Idrus, Nurul Ilmi (2004) Behind the notion of *siala*: Marriage, *adat* and Islam among the Bugis in South Sulawesi. *Intersections: Gender, History and Culture in the Asian Context* 10. Available at http://intersections.anu.edu.au/issue10/idrus.html, accessed 2 May 2011.

Idrus, Nurul Ilmi and Linda Rae Bennett (2003) Presumed consent: Marital violence in Bugis society, in Linda Rae Bennett and Lenore Manderson (eds), *Violence against women in Asian societies*, pp. 41–60 (London and New York: RoutledgeCurzon).

Imawan, W., W. Kusdiatmono, N. Arniati, M. Suanta and E. Waryono (2006) *Fasilitasi penyusunan data kekerasan terhadap perempuan di daerah tahun 2006* (Jakarta: Kementerian Negara dan Pemberdayaan Perempuan and Badan Pusat Statistik).

Jones, Gavin W. (1994) *Marriage and divorce in Islamic South-East Asia* (Kuala Lumpur: Oxford University Press).

KOMNAS Perempuan (2012) Stagnansi sistem hukum: Menggantung asa perempuan korban. Catatan Tahunan tentang kekerasan terhadap perempuan 2011. Photocopied report.

Korteweg, Anna C. (2008) The Sharia debate in Ontario: Gender, Islam, and representations of Muslim women's agency. *Gender and Society* 22(4), pp. 434–54.

Loseke, D.R. (2003) *Thinking about social problems: An introduction to constructionist perspectives* (New York: Aldine).

Mahmood, Saba (2001) Feminist theory, embodiment, and the docile agent: Some reflections on the Egyptian Islamic revival. *Cultural Anthropology* 16(2), pp. 202–36.

Minza, Wenty Marina (2009) *Perspective on polygamy in post-reform Indonesia* (Chiangmai: Silkworm Books).

Nilan, Pam (2008) Youth transitions to urban, middle-class marriage in Indonesia: Faith, family and finances. *Journal of Youth Studies* 11(1), pp. 65–82.

Nurmila, Nina (2009) *Women, Islam and everyday life: Renegotiating polygamy in Indonesia* (London and New York: Routledge).

Ortner, Sherry B. (1997) Thick resistance: Death and the cultural construction of agency in Himalayan mountain climbing. *Representations* 59, pp. 135–62.

Ortner, Sherry B. (2001) Specifying agency: The Comaroffs and their critics. *interventions* 3(1), pp. 76–84.

O'Shaughnessy, Kate (2009) *Gender, state and power in contemporary Indonesia: Divorce and law* (London and New York: Routledge).

Parker, Lyn (2005) Introduction, in Lyn Parker (ed.), *The agency of women in Asia*, pp. 1–25 (Singapore: Marshall Cavendish International).

Picart, C.J.S. (2003) Rhetorically reconfiguring victimhood and agency: The Violence Against Women Act's civil rights clause. *Rhetoric and Public Affairs* 6, pp. 97–126.

Prasetyo, Eko and Suparman Marzuni, eds. (1997) *Perempuan dalam wacana perkosaan* (Yogyakarta: Perkumpulan Keluarga Berencana Indonesia, Daerah Istimewa Yogyakarta [PKBI-DIY]).

Ram, Kalpana (2007) Untimeliness as moral indictment: Tamil agricultural labouring women's use of lament as life narrative. *Australian Journal of Anthropology* 18(2), pp. 138–53.

Reddy, William M. (1997) Reply. *Current Anthropology* 38(3), pp. 346–48.

Robinson, Kathryn (2009) *Gender, Islam and democracy in Indonesia* (London and New York: Routledge).

ROI (Republic of Indonesia) (1974) Marriage Law No. 1/1974. Available at http://id.wikisource.org/wiki/Undang-Undang_Republik_Indonesia_Nomor_1_Tahun_1974, accessed 1 August 2011.

ROI (Republic of Indonesia) (2004) Law on the Abolition of Domestic Violence No. 23/2004. Available at http://www.djpp.depkumham.go.id/inc/buka.php?czoyNDoiZD0yMDAwKzQmZj11dTIzLTIwMDQuaHRtIjs=, accessed 1 August 2011.

Rowe, William S., F. Sutan Nurasiah and Iryna M. Dulkha (2006) A study of domestic violence against academic working wives in Medan. *International Social Work* 49(1), pp. 41–50.

Sciortino, Rosalia and Ines Smyth (2002) The myth of harmony: Domestic violence in Java, in Frans Hüsken and Huub de Jonge (eds), *Violence and vengeance: Discontent and conflict in New Order Indonesia*, pp. 95–115 (Saarbrücken: Verlag für Entwicklungspolitik Saarbrücken GmbH, Nijmegan Studies in Development and Cultural Change).

Scott, James C. (1990) *Domination and the arts of resistance: Hidden transcripts* (New Haven: Yale University Press).

Skinner, T., M. Hester and E. Malos (2005) Methodology, feminism and gender violence, in Tina Skinner, Marianne Hester and Ellen Malos (eds), *Researching gender violence: Feminist methodology in action*, pp. 1–22 (Cullompton, Devon: Willan Publishing).

Smith-Hefner, Nancy J. (2005) The new Muslim romance: Changing patterns of courtship and marriage among educated Javanese youth. *Journal of Southeast Asian Studies* 36(3), pp. 441–59.

Suhandjati, Sri (2002) *Kekerasan dalam rumah tangga terhadap perempuan (Studi kasus gugatan cerai di Pengadilan Agama Semarang)* (Semarang: Proyek PTA/IAIN Walisongo).

Suryakusuma, Julia (1996) The State and sexuality in New Order Indonesia, in Laurie J. Sears (ed.), *Fantasizing the feminine in Indonesia*, pp. 92–119 (Durham and London: Duke University Press).

WHO (World Health Organisation) (2011) *Violence against women* (Fact Sheet No 239: Intimate partner and sexual violence against women). Available at http://www.who.int/mediacentre/factsheets/fs239/en/, accessed 13 June 2012.

Wieringa, Saskia E. (2009) Women resisting creeping Islamic fundamentalism in Indonesia. *Asian Journal of Women's Studies*. Available at http://www.iiav.nl/epublications/iav_b00103571.pdf, accessed 10 October 2011.

Ohitorisama, Singlehood and Agency in Japan

LAURA DALES

The University of Western Australia

Abstract: *Postwar Japanese society has experienced significant demographic shifts. Of particular note are trends in marriage delay, increased divorce, increased rates of lifelong singlehood and an increased proportion of life spent unmarried. In this context, singlehood is increasingly experienced by women, for at least some period in their adult lives. Nonetheless, while greater numbers of Japanese are living as singles for a greater portion of their lives, marriage and childbearing remain key markers of contemporary Japanese womanhood. Living outside marriage – as a single, divorced or widowed person – suggests divergence from the ideal, even if it is just an unavoidable temporary state. This paper explores singlehood as a contested space of ideals and practices, and presents the notion of* ohitorisama *as one model of contemporary female singlehood.*

Postwar Japanese society has experienced significant demographic shifts. Of particular note are trends in marriage delay, increased divorce, increased rates of lifelong singlehood and an increased proportion of life spent unmarried. In 2009 the average age of first marriage was 28 years for women and 30 years for men, reflecting a steady increase over the last decades: in 1980 these figures were 25 years for women and 28 years for men (NIPSSR, 2011). Furthermore, in 1980, 4.45 per cent of women and 2.6 per cent of men remained unmarried at age 50, but by 2005 these figures had increased to 7.25 per cent of women and nearly 16 per cent of men (NIPSSR, 2010). Singlehood is an increasingly common and long-term experience for Japanese adults. The implications of these shifts have been well documented by academics and social commentators, both within Japan and beyond. Sociologist Yamada Masahiro addressed the unmarried in his 1999 book, *The era of the parasite single*, problematising the population of (largely) young women who live at home with their parents until they marry.

Yamada's simplification and feminisation of this trend reinscribes notions of unmarried women as selfish, irresponsible and materialistic (Dales, 2005).

In this context, being unmarried represents a challenge to dominant notions of the feminine life course, and offers an alternative course for women's lives. In this paper, I explore what being unmarried might mean for contemporary Japanese women and the place of agency in constructions of singlehood. I do this first with reference to a discursive model of singlehood called "*ohitorisama*", and secondly by drawing on interviews conducted with Japanese women aged 30 to 49. My aim is twofold: firstly, to clarify how discourses of singlehood contribute to an understanding of Japanese femininity and its contemporary realities; and more broadly, to examine the relationship between women's singlehood and agency. Drawing on interviews conducted during fieldwork in Japan, I argue that experiences of singlehood vary significantly with levels of family support, financial capacity and an individual's health, and that single women's agency is therefore subject to broad socioeconomic factors, as well as cultural factors. In the interests of a more focused discussion, the women introduced in this paper are never-married and divorced women, aged 30–46.

It is important to recognise that the English term "unmarried" is an umbrella for individuals in a number of different situations: those who have never married; divorcees; single mothers; lesbians; those who live in de facto relationships; and widows.[1] In Japan, as in other contexts, the specific categories of "unmarried" may represent differing degrees of separation from the feminine ideal – the married woman. For example, while the never-married woman is almost certain to have no children – because the level of extramarital fertility is negligible – the divorced woman and the widow may have "achieved" motherhood. The never-married mother is arguably a member of the most marginalised group under the "unmarried" umbrella (Hertog, 2009, p. 2). The meaning and experience of singlehood is therefore shaped by relationships beyond marriage, including motherhood. There are also differences among women that flow from class, age, place of living, education and income. Inevitably, a discourse of singlehood that does not account for this diversity is limited in its application. Similarly, the extent to which singlehood might represent resistance to social norms can only be gauged with reference to the multiple forms of unmarried life, as well as the individual's experiences of life as an unmarried woman.

Living outside marriage – as a never-married single, divorced or widowed person – suggests divergence from the ideal, but divergence from the mainstream, even marginality, does not necessarily equate to powerlessness (Scott, 1985). As Hilsdon observes, "where women who fall outside the parameters of dominant notions of womanhood are considered 'unstable', both resistance and constraint are possible" (2007, p. 127). Within the diverse category, "unmarried women", the possibilities for resistance and constraint are shaped by factors including but not limited to their singlehood.

For the purposes of this discussion, agency is understood to be "the socio-culturally mediated capacity to act" (Ahearn, 2001, p. 112). Agency for the individual under a liberal, Western, humanist discourse implies autonomy of the individual in relation to society (Davies, 1991, p. 42). The notion of pure agency, however, denies human sociality and the bonds of interdependence manifest in all societies, albeit in diverse ways. Agency is temporally and historically bounded and the question of agency is always one of degree rather than possibility (Jeffery, 1998, p. 223). Acts can be understood as agentive only "within social relations and cultural practice" (Parker, 2005a, p. 20). For the unmarried women in this study, agency is conceptualised as an effect not of marriage, but of economic capability, personal fulfilment, supportive relationships and/or professional achievement and stability. It is the absence of these supports that makes singlehood a marginal or difficult social location, but the exercise of women's agency rests upon discursive as well as structural foundations. Singlehood, as a temporarily or permanently inhabited space, is constituted in relation to normative ideals of marriage and motherhood. A positive discourse of singlehood can bolster the foundations of unmarried women's subjectivity, supporting everyday acts of resistance, independence and agency.

I posit two broad questions in relation to the single Japanese women in my research: where marriage is a dominant and idealised norm, does being single represent an act of agency? And what do discourses of singlehood contribute to an understanding of Japanese femininity and its contemporary realities? To address these questions, I turn first to one version of singlehood: the *ohitorisama*.

Ohitorisama

The term *ohitorisama*, variously translated as "singleton", "single woman" and "individual", was coined by journalist Iwashita Kumiko and popularised in writings on her website from 1999 and subsequently in print. Iwashita's prior work included books on communication, the problem of stalking (and Japan's anti-stalking law), and food culture. From February 1999 she published a website targeted at women who want to eat out or travel alone – the "Association for the Promotion of the Single" (*Ohitorisama no kōjō iinkai*). In 2001, Iwashita's web writings were summarised and published as the book *Ohitorisama*.

Iwashita drowned while holidaying in Thailand in 2001, but since her death the term "*ohitorisama*" has been appropriated by a number of authors and incorporated into popular commentary, nonfiction and journalism. The Association for the Promotion of the Single was taken over by food journalist Haishi Kaori, whose work includes gourmet guidebook *Kyoto for the ohitorisama*, and *Cool women are good at being single* (*Kakkōii onna wa ohitorisama ga jōzu*) (2004), as well as *Marriage in your 30s can be happy!* (*30dai kara no kekkon ga happī ni nareru*).

In her original text, Iwashita defines the term in five ways, most notably as: "an adult woman who is an established individual; the particular sense needed to allow coexistence with others; and a life philosophy one should use for succeeding in work and love" (2001). She notes, in this definition, that those who are "'ideologically single', advocates against marriage, separatists and egotists" are excluded from the *ohitorisama* category. Interestingly, this definition contradicts later popular interpretations of the term on two counts – by excluding those who eschew marriage and by including (implicitly) married women. It is interesting that both Iwashita and her successor, Haishi, are or were married women, but this aspect of the *ohitorisama* model has not been broadly adopted in media usage of the term.[2] Neither Iwashita nor Haishi distinguish between those never-married and those who have been married. Iwashita does not address the issue of dependants (children or the aged), although Haishi suggests that "it is essential to get your family's or partner's understanding" if adopting the *ohitorisama* "philosophy" (2004, p. 55).

While these discussions represent the early history of the term, the evolution of the term has seen it shift away from Iwashita and Haishi's conceptualisation. Significantly, the term *ohitorisama* only achieved mainstream currency – and its predominant implication of singlehood – through the work of feminist scholar Ueno Chizuko. Since 2007, Ueno has worked on the topic of the ageing and aged *ohitorisama*.[3] The popularity of Ueno's books – her first book *Living senior years alone* (*Ohitorisama no rōgo*) has sold more than 750,000 copies – suggests the currency of this topic in the public imaginary. It is Ueno's discussion of *ohitorisama* – a state that all (women) are likely to experience, if only at the end of their lives – that appears to resonate among many Japanese women. While more recent media depictions of *ohitorisama* discussed below focus on the never-married, Ueno's discussion widens the scope for the term to be embraced by widowed and divorced women. In Ueno's usage, I suggest that *ohitorisama* can perhaps best be understood as a gloss for the English term "single", insofar as it is used to connote independence (if not youth).

The term is not the first neologism to draw media and public attention to single women. In the 1980s Japanese women who remained unmarried beyond 25 were labelled "Christmas cakes" (that is, of less value after the 25th) and more recently they have been called "parasite singles" (Yamada, 1999) and *makeinu* ("losers") (critiqued in Sakai Junko's 2003 book, *The howl of the loser dog*) (Shoji, 2005). As media-pleasing buzzwords that direct attention to very specific groups, these terms may be understood as indicators of cultural trends, rather than as memes per se. The older terms remain dormant in media and public discourse – typically unused after their brief period of celebrity – except as historical referents for contemporary problems. The "Christmas cake" can therefore be understood as an earlier incarnation of the *ohitorisama*, the latter having been modified upwards to address women beyond 30 years. The discursive history of women's singlehood is signposted by such catch-phrases, which act as ambivalent markers of behaviour or lifestyle that challenge ideals of femininity. They may be appropriated in feminist critique – as in the case of Sakai's "loser dogs" – but they retain sufficient negative valence that most women are unlikely to adopt them seriously. Thus, while the term *ohitorisama* is not pejorative like "Christmas cake", it is not necessarily an identity taken up by all women within its margins. While individual women may not use the term to define themselves, it exists as a category with particular social meanings.

The impermanence of all of the above terms is fundamental – because the boundaries of the problematised group shift – and may represent the central limitation to their usefulness as sociological frames of reference: as at best etic, rather than emic, accounts of marginality. That is to say, these are terms used *about,* more than *by*, Japanese singles.[4] The significance of the term *ohitorisama* is not simply that it includes (or might include) a growing section of the population, but also that it marks the boundaries of a particular problematic of contemporary women's singlehood. Women need not identify personally with the term for it to have either positive or negative valence, because it operates as a category of social reference: it is potentially both an entry point into discussions of issues relevant to single women, and shorthand for the problems inherent in the trends associated with that group (namely delayed marriage, low fertility). The term operates as a discursive marker of one version of singlehood available to Japanese women, suggesting possibilities for agency through the performance of everyday tasks conducted at the margins of socially-defined feminine ideals. The term *ohitorisama* is therefore not a seamless synonym for singlehood, but rather a lens through which we can understand the possibilities and limitations of singlehood as it is constructed today. The questions of who identifies as *ohitorisama*, who aspires to be *ohitorisama*, and who feels excluded from being *ohitorisama*, sit beside the question of how it is possible to live as an unmarried woman in contemporary Japanese society. While I touch on the former two issues, in this paper I am primarily concerned with the latter question, addressing the intersections between singlehood and agency and the ways that the term *ohitorisama* operates discursively to open paths beyond the typical life course.

The significance of *ohitorisama* is notable firstly because it expands the category of "single" denoted by earlier pejorative terms. In an ageing, low-fertility Japan, Ueno (2007, p. 2) argues that life alone is an inescapable fate, particularly for women, since they will more than likely outlive their husbands.

> In a low birth-rate ageing population, the time that women spend "doing family" is contracting. Even if they have a spouse, given the average life expectancy, in most cases the husband will pass on first. At most there are one or two children, and at some point they will leave home.
>
> If that's the case, women need to prepare themselves, to obtain the know-how not just to "do family", but also to live alone. If everyone, at some point, ends up alone, the difference is just whether you start preparing for it earlier or later.

Thus singlehood can be seen as the common ultimate destination point – or more specifically the penultimate stop – before death. If family has thus far been considered a sufficient and lifelong *raison d'être* for women, Ueno's words suggest that this may no longer be the case.

Ueno's conceptualisation of the *ohitorisama* differs in focus from the earlier version proposed by Iwashita and Haishi. Reflecting upon singlehood at the end of life, Iwashita and Haishi's conceptualisations of *ohitorisama* focus on the skills involved in becoming a self-realised "woman on one's own". In this model, the *ohitorisama* can be of any age. Both Iwashita and Haishi divide their books into "lessons", with hints on living an "*ohitorisama* lifestyle", eating alone, finding and enjoying suitable bars, solo travel. Iwashita (2001) offers chapters on financial planning for the single, romance, tips for sensual sex and "personalised marriage" (that is, marriage tailored to the particular needs of the individual). Both Iwashita and Haishi conceptualise the *ohitorisama* as an advance on old social mores, and a move away from co-dependence and passive femininity. Iwashita (2001, p. 226) suggests that over-adherence to social norms, and the belief that "not being married means you are strange, not being married means you're not a real adult or have no sense of responsibility", represent a psychological version of the Japanese national isolation that ended in the nineteenth century. Individuality and self-expression are both natural and desirable for women, and the *ohitorisama* practises these ideals in her daily life.

Supporting the broad argument that individuality and independence – two keystones of selfhood as conceptualised in liberal Western thought – enable maturity and healthy interpersonal relations, Iwashita and Haishi present two key themes in their discourse. Firstly, the *ohitorisama* life is defined in relation to consumption. The state of being unmarried is framed primarily in terms of the ways it impedes consumption, because dining, drinking and travelling are activities for couples or groups.⁵ The *ohitorisama* model is a means of overcoming the taboo or discomfort impeding these solo activities, to allow one to consume comfortably while alone. The stigma of dining alone, for example, can be allayed through the proper choice of establishment – for example, a restaurant with a dining counter (for single seating), with few couples and small-sized tables (indicating the target clientele), with female service providers and a mature male host (in his 30s or older) (Iwashita, 2001, pp. 40–41). These hints address the psychological barriers to being a visibly single social presence, and the ways that single women are excluded from social spaces. The provision of these hints suggests that failure to attend to dominant norms of femininity demands particular strategies to increase resistance to shame. It also suggests that single women are (or should be) inclined to overcome these obstacles, to use agency to claim their legitimate social space. In another example, Iwashita suggests in Lesson 3 of *Ohitorisama* ('Get beautiful by staying in a hotel by yourself') that even women who live alone should consider an occasional stay in a luxury downtown hotel – she recommends the Four Seasons Chinzansō in Tokyo.⁶ As for the "new woman" of the early twentieth century, for the *ohitorisama* consumerism is a means of self-expression and a way of navigating social changes that destabilise feminine norms (Sato, 2003, p. 16–17). Consumption is both the means and the goal here – by consuming, women assert their economic capacity, and by consuming alone they challenge notions of appropriate conformity that discourage women's sole social engagement as "lonely" (*sabishii*). Furthermore, as Iwashita (2001, p. 6) suggests, the number of women who "use their money to buy 'me time' [is] increasing". Iwashita's book explicitly references Tokyo establishments for eating and drinking, evoking a metropolitan, able-bodied subject with considerable disposable income and the time (and social capital) to cultivate sophistication. The aspirational element of this model makes it attractive for dissemination as a snapshot of contemporary feminine single life, and, as in the early twentieth century, this has been facilitated by media (Sato, 2003, p. 17).

Popular usage of the term *ohitorisama* along these lines was boosted by the development of an eponymous television drama broadcast on TBS in 2009. *Ohitorisama* focuses on the life, loves and travails of Akiyama Satomi (played by Mizuki Arisa), a 33 year-old private high-school teacher who embodies the ideal *ohitorisama* as envisaged by Iwashita. Satomi is highly intelligent, driven and devoted to her work. Her commitment to work is counterbalanced by her inability to perform domestic tasks (cooking, cleaning), but she is depicted as content to eat and drink alone, and to pursue a range of (expensive) hobbies with her boss/mentor (who might be seen to embody Ueno's version of a never-married *ohitorisama*). The storyline of *Ohitorisama* follows Satomi's travails at work and in love, as she develops romantic feelings for a much younger, less-experienced and gentle-natured male colleague, Kamisaka Shin'ichi (played by Koike Teppei). The drama depicts the tensions of the *ohitorisama*'s life, when the couple becomes engaged and Satomi is required to choose between her job and her relationship with her colleague. This dilemma is ultimately resolved by a plot line that sees Shin'ichi transferred to Okinawa for work (Dales, forthcoming; Collins, 2011; Freedman and Iwata-Weickgenannt, 2011).

The versions of *ohitorisama* that appear in this program demonstrate the glossy appeal of models presented by Iwashita. The lead female character is an urban-dwelling, financially secure professional who consumes without concern and lives alone, without care responsibilities. It is likely that this depiction of *ohitorisama* is most current in the public imagination, at least in part because it is the model that most closely resembles earlier tropes of the single woman. In the case of the *ohitorisama*, as in earlier discourses of the single woman, the model remains tied (if implicitly) to the prospect of marriage. As in the television drama, a second key theme of popular *ohitorisama* discourse is its ultimate deference to marriage.

While Ueno's more recent discussion focused on ageing singles (also known as "single-again", through divorce or widowhood), the trope created by Iwashita and promoted through popular media focuses predominantly on the childless, never-married (or divorced) single woman. The tenacity of marriage as an underlying theme, even in a discourse that focuses on individuality, reflects the centrality of marriage as a normative marker of maturity in women's lives. Marriage marks the "passage into responsible adulthood", and implies the forthcoming birth of children (Maree, 2004, p. 541). In fact, as Hertog argues, marriage "is the necessary condition to ensure a suitable environment for children" (2009, p. 154). Since the level of extramarital fertility in Japan is so low, being *ohitorisama*, at least according to the popular discourse, implies forgoing childbearing (Hertog, 2009).

Thus while the focus remains on marriage as the ultimate goal, the *ohitorisama* model also reframes a period of uncertainty – the period in which a woman is unmarried – that is otherwise imbued with negative social value. The promotion of the term through television and other popular media underscores the possibilities for this period to be lively, fun, fulfilling and agentive.

The question of what it means to be unmarried elicits two further questions: how do others see unmarried women, and how do unmarried women see themselves? If *ohitorisama* is a social label, questions remain about how well this label fits the experiences of women, and whether it is perceived by women themselves to represent the unmarried experience. To answer these questions, I turn to recent research interviews.

Being Single, Being *Ohitorisama*

The women introduced below were interviewed as part of an on-going research project begun in 2009. In this project Beverley Yamamoto and I have to date interviewed 34 "unconventional" women. We use the term "unconventional" (*tenkeiteki janai*) to mean women whose life courses diverge from the stereotypical, including never-married and divorced women, single mothers, women who cohabit with a man, and women who marry late. The women range in age from 30–49 years, with nearly half of the sample aged 30–35 years. At the time of interview 21 women were never-married, eight were divorced, three were married and two were cohabiting. None of the women identified as lesbian or queer. Five of the women have children, and another was pregnant at the time of interview.[7]

This sample is patently non-representative, developed through contacts and the snowballing technique. One notable feature of the sample is that it is more educated than average – 14 interviewees have postgraduate qualifications. While extended education represents one factor in delayed marriage and declining fertility in Japan, it is tightly intertwined with factors such as class, family support, residence (urban or rural) and financial capacity (Shirahase, 2000, p. 48). In this research the interviewees' experiences of singlehood and perceptions of marriage appear to be less specifically influenced by their education levels than by these other related factors.

None of the women introduced here had read Iwashita or Haishi's books, although all had heard of the term, and some had read Ueno Chizuko's best-selling work. That is to say, all were aware of the variety of popular constructions of single womanhood, but few felt that the terms suitably encapsulated their own experiences. Their affiliation with or rejection of the term *ohitorisama* offers insights into their perception of what constitutes a good or ideal life course for women in general. It tells of what they believe *should* be possible, as well as what they perceive to be appropriate or attainable for themselves. For each woman, specific circumstances have enabled specific life choices, while disabling others, illustrating the diversity that exists within the category "unmarried woman".

Okubo-san is a 32 year-old, never-married academic who lives alone. She openly – and quite cheerfully – admits she has never had a romantic relationship, and decided as a teenager that she would never marry. Okubo has embraced research and an academic career and sees her work as her passion:

> The most important thing for me is to continue my work and continue my study the way I want. As far as I am in the situation (that) I can do the best with my study, (romance) doesn't matter (Okubo, 32 years).

Okubo's singlehood is assisted by her education, her skills and her physical and psychological capacities for an independent life. Her professional status, urban lifestyle and financial stability suggest that Okubo might experience singlehood in a similar way to the *ohitorisama* constructions in Iwashita's book and television dramas. Okubo herself defines *ohitorisama* thus:

> The image is particularly one of women, one who can do anything and go anywhere by herself. I don't particularly use the term myself, but I think I could be called one.

In stark contrast to Okubo, Suzuki-san is a subdued, 38 year-old never-married woman who lives with her ageing parents in a semi-rural area about one hour from Tokyo. Suzuki is a university graduate, but due to mental illness has never held a full-time job and has been unemployed for most of the last decade. Suzuki, her mother and father subsist on his pension, but he is rapidly becoming demented. Suzuki worries how she will survive, both financially and practically, when her parents die. She does not go shopping, lacking the financial and psychological capacity for this activity, and she is not interested in the kinds of entertainments that she perceives to be typical feminine hobbies:

> On TV you see only young women, pretty and fashionable and they go shopping in fashionable places, eating gourmet foods. And that sort of thing is totally foreign (to me), a different world (Suzuki, never-married, 38 years).

While she does not associate her own version of the *ohitorisama* model with the depiction of singlehood in the TBS drama, Suzuki regards media depictions of typical young women's lives as alien. Nonetheless she values the term, seeing the *ohitorisama* discourse as an alternative to the version of femininity she sees most frequently – the married housewives engaged in childrearing in her neighbourhood:

> I think (the idea of *ohitorisama*) is really good. Around me there are no *ohitorisama*. I <u>might not</u> end up having one of those families, getting married and having children... (Suzuki, never-married, 38 years) (emphasis added).

Suzuki remains alienated by the aspect of the *ohitorisama* lifestyle that makes it most marketable to mainstream women – its fundamental expectation of consumption as a means to fulfilment. Thus, the life of the *ohitorisama* is as distant as that of the full-time housewife – but for Suzuki, the former is valuable as an innovative challenge to dominant expectations of women's performance of relational care. In Suzuki's reading, the *ohitorisama* model operates as a discursive counterweight to the idealised housewife role, providing a legitimate alternate path to fulfilment for women who do not marry and have children.

Kuroda-san, a never-married woman in her late 30s, is a writer and activist on issues relating to women's poverty and unemployment. She currently lives alone in Tokyo, but lived with her mother until their relationship deteriorated and she was forced to leave. She has never seriously thought about marriage or living with a man, and sees the lack of affordable housing and unemployment as twin barriers to women's independence. Here she suggests that the term evokes a level of consumer power beyond the scope of most women, a power borne of consumption per se (Ortner, 2001). She also suggested that women's unemployment (and ergo their poverty) is obscured by an implicitly standard progression in feminine life course:

> People think you can just be supported by your husband. Japanese people tend to think if you've got family then you're ok – it's all right if you have a father or a husband. It's an obvious female stereotype (Kuroda, never-married, late 30s).

Kuroda notes that dependence on family or husband is normative, and that the single woman without familial support (financial or emotional) is an invisible, or perhaps obscured, social presence. This is a nod to both the centrality of marriage as an ideal for women, and the marginality of unmarried women, which in practical terms can mean economic insecurity, and to the agency of the unmarried woman, who contradicts the "obvious female stereotype", but at the cost of financial stability. For Kuroda, in contrast to the *ohitorisama* of Iwashita's model and the TBS drama, living in the capital city makes (luxury) consumption less feasible, and less likely to bring fulfilment or pleasure.

Also residing in Tokyo, Kinoshita-san is a 31 year-old single mother, a high-school graduate with a 13 year-old son. Divorced shortly after the birth of her son, she is opposed to marriage and objects to the "idea of systematising human relations". In the past she has lived with her mother and her son, alone with her son, and with friends in cooperative housing arrangements. She differs radically from the professional, affluent and single-living heroine of the TBS television series. In relation to the *ohitorisama* label, she laughs: "I've got no money, so I can't do that kind of thing. It's irrelevant to me" (Kinoshita, divorced, 31 years). Kinoshita appears to reference the version of *ohitorisama* espoused by Iwashita and promoted in the television drama, and one can see that both her politics and her financial situation as a single mother push her beyond the borders of this lifestyle. Kinoshita's resistance to dominant feminine norms, evident in her explicitly political position against marriage, suggests that she employs discursive agency to positively define her socially marginal, financially difficult position as a single mother.

Some women distance themselves from the category because they see it as politically loaded, or implying a lack of romantic relationships. This perception of *ohitorisama* implies resistance, whereby being single is a directed act "aiming to defy, subvert, undermine or oppose the power and repression of dominant forces" (Parker, 2005b, p. 87). Hatsumoto-san, a 30 year-old never-married woman who lives with her parents, sees the typical *ohitorisama* as more than just an individual who happens to be single:

> (*Ohitorisama* is) one who chose to be that way – not just a single person. Maybe it doesn't go as far as an ideology, but in effect... I haven't really thought deeply about it but I like men, so I want to share my life with someone. So to be completely alone ... though *ohitorisama* are not all single ... and they're not unwaged, are they?
>
> I've only ever thought about (marriage) in a vague way, but I suppose if you get pregnant it is more convenient to get married. If you have kids and you're not married you have to fight for so many things. And that takes a huge amount of time and energy... In any case I think if I can just do what I want to do and make a proper career from it, marriage and that sort of thing will come later (Hatsumoto, never-married, 30 years).

Hatsumoto is an artist who holds down a number of part-time jobs, and at the time of our discussion was worried about her financial situation. Ideally she would "earn enough that I could live by myself", but at this point it is impossible. Hatsumoto's personal aversion to the *ohitorisama* lifestyle is therefore two-pronged – it is not feasible for her emotionally to be "completely alone"; neither is it possible economically for her to manage alone. Thus, in her own eyes, according to her definition of the term, she lacks the motivation to be *ohitorisama* – the desire to subvert the hegemony of marriage or romantic coupling. Perhaps more significantly, she is also precluded from her own definition of *ohitorisama* by virtue of her economic vulnerability. A decision to live (permanently) as a single is rendered inoperable by the structural impossibility of such a lifestyle. Hatsumoto also recognises that marriage and children are the normative set, and that the decision to live as a single mother requires significant commitment – resistance beyond her personal capacity. Rather than being concerned about her unmarried status per se, Hatsumoto addresses the structural obstacles to her ideal life – namely, her lack of job security and economic independence. Hatsumoto is less concerned with resistance, and more with the operation of what Ortner terms the agency of intention: an agency of "projects, purposes and desires" (Ortner, 2001, p. 79).

Economic capacity clearly makes a difference to the kind of life, and the options for agency, that an unmarried woman can enjoy. Ogawa-san is a never-married woman in her mid-40s with postgraduate qualifications. She has studied and worked overseas for many years, and speaks fluent English. Ogawa lives alone, working in a senior policy and research position. She notes that while she has not read Iwashita's book, she has read Ueno's discussion of ageing and singlehood, and interprets the term *ohitorisama* positively:

> Some of my single friends say that they can't go to a restaurant alone, but I don't mind going alone... I take the term positively rather than negatively ... what (Ueno) is basically saying is that everyone is alone when we are born and when we die, so her message is for people to be more independent (Ogawa, never-married, 46 years).

The popularised *ohitorisama* lifestyle is fixed on particular assumptions of women's socioeconomic capacities that limit its inclusivity, and in this sense it is as prescriptive as the full-time housewife ideal. Nonetheless, the discourse of *ohitorisama* should be valued as an alternative ideal, insofar as it acknowledges that marriage is not a universal feature of contemporary Japanese womanhood. As Suzuki observes:

> It would be good if it were more recognised, wouldn't it – that women's lives aren't just about marrying and having kids, but that the *ohitorisama* way of living is a possibility too (Suzuki, never-married, 38 years).

Suzuki notes that the possibility that she might not marry is what makes alternative paths relevant to her. She may not be the typical *ohitorisama*, but it is nonetheless an aspirational ideal. This acknowledges her own position – as an unmarried woman who in fact is unlikely to "achieve" a mainstream ideal feminine life pattern – and also locates her within a community of sameness (other unmarried women) that adopts a critical perspective on the dominance of particular ideals.

Ohitorisama: Not "All the Single Ladies"[8]

Singlehood features in an increasingly significant way in the lives of Japanese women. Evidently it is not always a chosen state, and as the women in this study have observed, it may be an unanticipated status. The experience of singlehood is diverse and dependent on a range of factors, and must be set against the broader backdrop of economic uncertainty and an employment market that is increasingly comprised of contract and part-time work. In this sense, self-sufficiency, in economic terms at least, is not necessarily a realistic or attainable goal for some single women. In the discourse discussed here, the archetypal *ohitorisama* embodies agency as it might be envisioned in Western liberal thought. The *ohitorisama* is unencumbered by the obligations of care that shackle her typically married, childrearing sisters. The *ohitorisama* is not "a lonely woman" (Haishi, 2004, p. 12). She is sociable, self-contained, self-motivated and as strategic in deciding where to eat as she is in deciding where to take her career. The assumptions implicit in this model have already been carefully and comprehensively dismantled in the feminist literature on agency and resistance (Mohanty, 1991; Mahmood, 2001; Parker, 2005a; Dales, 2005). The capacity for individual women to become *ohitorisama* – whether Iwashita's archetype, Ueno's older, single-by-default version, or some other interpretation – rests upon a range of factors, including individual ability, physical and mental health, familial support, and opportunity, all of which are located in the broad socioeconomic landscape. The ability to act – and to embody the *ohitorisama* – develops in relation to the varied and accumulated experiences of the individual, as she navigates a life course. In this way agency is contingent upon the successful negotiation of broader changes, such as economic downturn, that potentially destabilise the individual. The degree to which the individual is destabilised is intrinsically tied to the factors just mentioned.

For Ogawa, postgraduate education has led to a stable, well-paying position and a degree of reflexivity about her status as a single woman. Like Okubo, the young academic, Ogawa does not necessarily describe herself as *ohitorisama*, but her status suggests that she could well be described thus by others. She is sensitive to the social implications of being a single woman, both in Japan and abroad, but does not appear to need the structural support offered by a defined social label. While Okubo and Ogawa's respective careers have no doubt contributed to their self-containment, Ogawa notes explicitly that her personality, as well as the tides of social change, has enabled her career choices:

> I seem to be quite independent. I didn't really realise, but one day I was told this by a British person, and until he said that to me I didn't really realise it…

> (It) was a lucky thing that Japanese society had been changing. Probably one generation before me, if (women) were over 30 and unmarried, neighbours would say something. But you know, fortunately (at that time) women's options were expanded, so even one of the neighbours said to me "Nowadays it's good that women can do anything they like" and we have more options than women from two generations prior. So in a sense I'm lucky (Ogawa, never-married, 46 years).

Family support represents an additional strut in the scaffolding. The relative absence of familial pressure to marry experienced by the women in this study might be reflective of a more accepting Japanese society, and of changing social mores. Certainly none of the women in this study indicated that being unmarried had brought any familial exclusion or sense of shame or disappointment from their family.[9]

The relative neutrality of this situation might also be seen as enabled by the relative wealth of the baby-boomer generation, which has largely enjoyed the seniority-based wage system that characterised postwar Japanese employment (Ogawa, 2009). Families with a senior worker may be able to subsidise an adult child co-residing, particularly when the child contributes to the household finances. However, in light of the imminent retirement of baby-boomers, the stress upon the pension system and medical systems, and the effects of nearly two decades of recession, it is likely that the number of families with the economic capacity to maintain this pattern will decline. The agency of the individual, situated within the family and subject to familial relationships of care and obligation, is thus tied to the capacities of her family. The exercise of agency as an unmarried daughter may also require the negotiation of constraints that married women avoid – "bargains with patriarchy" of a different kind – by moving outside the parental home (Kandiyoti, 1988). Certainly the capacity of a family to support an unmarried daughter is a salient factor in the lives of unmarried women, particularly women in insecure employment. The effects of economic support are most noticeable when threatened, as in the case of Suzuki and her elderly parents, and in cases where the single daughter may need to take on the care of her parents. The physical and/or financial support of elderly parents was not explicitly a concern for the other women introduced here, but nonetheless represents an area of possible tension in unmarried women's life courses, particularly for working-class women. Hatsumoto's decision to work in a relatively unstable arts industry allows her personal freedom, but undercuts her financial leverage and precludes living alone. Her optimism about future possibilities in work as well as romance reflects her good health and youthful vitality, and stands her in direct contrast to Suzuki, also unmarried and living with her parents. Suzuki's prospects for agency and her perspective on future possibilities are delimited by her long-term struggles with mental illness and her subsequent lack of employment experience. Paradoxically, it is her limited capacity (and potential) for financial independence that makes the *ohitorisama* ideal appealing to Suzuki. The promise of agency, and specifically the agency of power, may be attractive precisely because it is less attainable to Suzuki than to the other women (Ortner, 2001).

Agency and Singlehood

> The idea of agency is a key mediating category through which the inter-connections between cultural and economic forces, identity formations and social structures can be examined (McNay, 2005, p. 177).

As McNay observes, the question of agency requires contextualisation. Insofar as an act enables individuals, it also acknowledges the barriers that would otherwise prevent action. Being unmarried, particularly after the age of 30, draws attention to the predominance of marriage in Japan, to normative notions of femininity as entwined in wifehood and motherhood. The markers of difference vary according to the type of singleness: never-married women in childbearing years are marked by their childlessness, while divorced women are marked by their divorce as failure to maintain the ideal. Sakai's (2003) critique of this social separation of women sees "loser dogs" separated from "winners" along the lines of marriage, so that even successful, financially independent women in their 30s are "losers" if they have never married.

While typicality is a matter of discursive construction, women who are not married between the ages of 35 and 74 are both numerical and discursive minorities (Mackie, 2002, p. 203; NIPSSR, 2012). While single women constitute a majority of their age group until they reach 29 years, marriage is a socially-inscribed goal attained by the majority of women during their childbearing years (NIPSSR, 2008). The decision to live outside marriage does not necessarily reflect political intent; indeed, it may not always be a decision, but rather an unintended outcome. This may be agency, but it is certainly not resistance (Parker, 2005b, p. 87). For women who idealise or aspire to marriage, being unmarried may be a concession to circumstances beyond individual control. The limited take-up of the label *ohitorisama* could be understood as a nod to the resilience of this feminine ideal, even among women who do not (or cannot) put it into practice.

Although being unmarried is a state, rather than an act per se, we can see that the daily practices required by life outside marriage are constructed as less natural, or at least less desirable, than the practices involved in married life. Eating out alone, going on holidays alone and drinking alone at a bar are everyday acts that do not preclude married people from participation, but as *ohitorisama* acts, they exemplify the kind of unconventional behaviour for unmarried women that requires explanation, justification and/or advocacy. They are the kind of acts that invoke literary interventions such as those offered by Iwashita, Haishi and Ueno, suggesting both marginality (experiences beyond the norm that require interpretation) and significance (in a shifting society where heretofore normative life courses are destabilised). It is the perceived need for explanation, justification or celebration engendered by these everyday acts that renders the term *ohitorisama* salient in an examination of contemporary Japanese society.

While the *ohitorisama* model might represent one path for the validation of unmarried life, its scope is limited and unable to encompass the experiences of all unmarried women, particularly those with children, those who experience ill health, and those with limited financial capacity or security. The agency engendered by new discourses of femininity is not insignificant – as interviewee Suzuki notes above, the existence of a new trope of womanhood in itself brings hope – but there is an unequivocal gap between the ideal and the lived reality. The ideal of the agentic *ohitorisama* does not diminish the reality of the struggling, isolated or under-employed woman, and financially independent Ogawa lives in the same socio-cultural space and time as unemployed Suzuki. The *ohitorisama* model does, however, draw attention to hitherto under-recognised possibilities for women in the realms beyond marriage.

Roseneil (2007, p. 91) observes that being single can produce a self "experienced as in conflict, fractured and dislocated, sometimes in relation to its past, sometimes from a sense of futurity", but it can, through practices of self-care and the cultivation of supportive relationships and networks also "suture the [psychologically damaged] self". This self-care may be manifest in the practices of consumption outlined by Iwashita, but it may also occur through the cultivation of resilience and fortitude, in the making of decisions relating to work, domicile and family responsibilities. For some of the Japanese women interviewed in this research, life outside marriage presents opportunities, real and symbolic, that would not exist within marriage. For Okubo, being single means freedom from the expectations of care implicit in the role of wife:

> Well of course it depends on the person, but usually Japanese men are so lazy about keeping house. If they require me to do all these house matters, obviously I would say "no, I'm too busy"… The most important thing for me is to continue my work and continue my study the way I want. As far as I am in that situation (where) I can do the best with my study, (a romantic relationship) doesn't matter (Okubo, never-married, 32 years).

For Kinoshita, singlehood allows commitment to relationships that are otherwise subjugated to romance: "If you don't fit into a couple, you don't have a place" (*ibasho ga nai*). Living outside marriage enables flexibility, in contrast with couple-hood, which requires a narrowing of both physical activities and social participation. "Not having a place" means marginalisation, but it also opens up possibilities for new ways of living communally, beyond the reproductive family.

In describing agency, I would add to Ahearn's neat definition that it is both possible and meaningful only within the specific confines of the socio-cultural context. This is not to say that an act – for example, a Japanese woman's refusal to acquiesce to familial pressure to marry – cannot be understood as agency except within the context of Japanese society. (Surely feminist scholars worldwide would spot the agency in this act!) Rather, it is to say that the meaning, the scope, and the implications of this act cannot be fully gauged without reference to the socio-cultural context in which it occurs. The differences are significant because, as Parker (2005a, p. 16) observes,

> agency is mainly an issue of power; it necessarily addresses relations of social inequality; and it comes into play in the operation of power differentials between genders and between other social groups, as well as between individuals.

Thus we see power differentials within the single women group, as well as between single women and single men, unmarried women and married women.

Hertog (2009, p. 155) has observed, when writing of unwed mothers in Japan, that even though pressures on women may be similar in different societies, the outcomes of these pressures can vary greatly. Just as it is "the different meanings imbued" in a concept that shape women's actions, so the actions themselves have different meanings depending on the society. This is easily argued in the case of *ohitorisama*, where linguistic difference – a term that does not translate easily into English – might be taken as representative of a substantive difference in being single in Japan and Anglophone societies.[10] Yet because the model of *ohitorisama* does not fully encapsulate the realities of being an unmarried woman, we must be aware that the account of agency in singlehood is inevitably more complex than a linguistic innovation (McNay, 2005, p. 182).

Conclusion

For Japanese women who live outside marriage, the capacity to act (or not act) is more than the function of a missing wedding band. As illustrated in this discussion, the lives of unmarried women diverge on several planes. The differences between unmarried women are glossed over in popular discourses of singlehood, just as they are in normative constructions of femininity based on marriage and mothering. If we are to assess agency, it must be within the context of these broader differences. Without this context the category of "unmarried" woman empties of meaning and lends itself to caricaturing, in the manner of the "parasite single" or the "Christmas cake".

Ohitorisama, though variously nuanced in its interpretations, represents a particular vision of singlehood, although in its early iterations at least it was not limited to unmarried women. The *ohitorisama* lifestyle promoted by Iwashita and Haishi attempts to renovate and reform the female self that is excluded from popular ideals of the feminine life course, centred on marriage and childrearing. In this *ohitorisama* model, being single – or acting alone – does not preclude social legitimacy for women. On the contrary, Iwashita suggests that it is a polished performance of being single that makes a woman mature and competent as a social actor. Further, the discourse challenges acceptance of societal norms:

> If you don't know what happiness is for you, you may end up aiming for what the world around you calls happiness. There is no unhappiness greater than being

convinced that you are unhappy because you're different from others (Iwashita, 2001, p. 249).

Haishi's model of *ohitorisama*-as-married-woman also challenges assumptions about the ideal romantic relationship, perhaps demonstrating a shift from notions of *amae* (Doi, 1973; Borovoy, 2005) and care (Long, 1995; Borovoy, 2005) that have been seen to typify modern Japanese marriages and the role women play within them. This is not the model evoked in media discussions of *ohitorisama*, evidenced by the TBS drama; neither is it apparent in the conceptualisations of the women interviewed in this research project. Such popular understandings of *ohitorisama*, typified by the lead character in the television series, may challenge marriage as a universal or inevitable goal for women, but neither Iwashita's nor Ueno's model assumes an anti-marriage ideology. Nor do they address the effects of heteronormativity (Iwashita, 2001). Furthermore, the limitations of the *ohitorisama* category echo other exclusivities that have marked feminist discussions of women's lives – class and economic capacity, geography and (dis)ability.

The interviews conducted in this project thus far suggest that the label *ohitorisama* has been taken up less than one might have expected. Almost all of the women had heard the term, and had some sense of its meaning as consonant with Iwashita's original definition and the media construction, or reflective of Ueno's focus on seniors, but few identified with it. The disconnect between the model and the reality of unmarried life parallels the disconnect between the residual ideal of marriage, and the reality that increasing numbers of Japanese women will live more of their lives unmarried. That few women identify as *ohitorisama* reflects the multiple interpretations of the term and their uneven spread across different media. It also suggests that the term should not be seen as a catch-all, any more than the earlier pejoratives "Christmas cake" or *makeinu*. Rather, like these terms, *ohitorisama* presents an entry point for discussions of singlehood as it is perceived by broader Japanese society, its demerits and its potential. If it is not a solution to the marginalisation of unmarried women, it is perhaps a new way of viewing the peripheral space.

This space, between model and practice, ideal and reality, can also be understood as a generative space for agency. Where unmarried women speak one way and act differently, or where they behave in a way that challenges what is expected of them, we see the possibilities for broader change. Innovation at the discursive level, in the appearance and popularisation of the term *ohitorisama*, is an example of the ways in which women's experiences find a foothold in the public imaginary. This is a link between "small-scale, everyday, possibly less self-consciously reflective conduct and more explicit, public and macro moments in relation to social change" (Beasley, 2011, p. 27).

Unmarried women, whether or not they call themselves *ohitorisama*, embody the tension between ideals and reality. They demonstrate what can be understood as the agency of the everyday, in which individuals create spaces or opportunities for acts that allow self-expression, self-promotion or other expansion of personal capacity.

As Kuroda-san (above) observes, marriage is understood to shield women from the need to be independent, and indeed it may well enable agency among women who otherwise lack the earning capacity to live alone, to secure a legitimate social status and a degree of economic stability. In reality, however, the increasing divorce rate and economic recession mean that marriage does not necessarily secure anything, at least not permanently, for women. Because it remains the social ideal, women who sit outside its realm are required ipso facto to find alternative paths to a legitimate social space or identity and to economic stability. The discourse of *ohitorisama* may help with the former, but contributes little to the more significant problem of the latter.

The daily negotiation of work and family on the periphery requires some work. This may be the psychological work, invisible and/or unconscious, involved in bolstering the self and identity. It may be physical work, required to build the resources for running a household alone, in the present or in the future. Or it may be discursive work, the subtle resistance to suggestions and presumptions about being unmarried, and the hegemony of wifehood and motherhood as a feminine ideal. I argue that this work bolsters the individual as a legitimate social actor. It constitutes agency, extending the possibilities for women to make meaning of their lives, in relation to others and within the confines of multiple, intersecting structural constraints. Being single in a familialist society suggests the transgression of boundaries, even as or when they are recognised as ideal. While there may be no overarching project of empowerment or emancipation at play, there is nonetheless scope for the exercise of women's agency, if only in the moments of justification, explanation, or planning inevitably involved in living as a single woman in Japan.

Acknowledgments

This article is the product of a collaborative research project conducted with Beverley Yamamoto in the Graduate School of Human Sciences at Osaka University, funded by a Japan Society for the Promotion of Science Postdoctoral Fellowship. I am very grateful to Beverley for her work on this project, to Lyn Parker at The University of Western Australia for her insightful comments, and to the reviewers of the paper for their detailed and constructive advice.

Notes

1. In Japanese these categories may be separated out with different terms: *mikon* for never-married, *rikon* for divorcees and *mibōjin* for widows. *Shinguru mazā* (single mothers) are women who have children and are currently unmarried, but may be divorced or cohabiting with a partner.
2. Haishi notes "But *ohitorisama* is not just for singles – being married or single is irrelevant. *Ohitorisama* is for all women" (Haishi, 2004, p. 15).
3. While the term is not explicitly gendered, there is evidence – for example, Ueno's second publication, 'The path to old age for single men' (*Otoko no ohitorisma michi*) and work published by authors prior to Ueno's books – to suggest that the term most obviously connotes a single woman.
4. An emic perspective centres on the subject's experience and perception, while an etic perspective prioritises the researcher's interpretation of a behaviour, event or situation (Pelto and Pelto, 1978).
5. Iwashita notes that old-fashioned Japanese inns may reject single female guests, on the grounds that "they might commit suicide" (2001, p. 5).
6. Indeed, the hotel offers several women-targeted packages, including the "Reward yourself for working hard" Sanctuary Stay (28,785 yen/night). See http://www.fourseasons-tokyo.com/event/ladys.html, accessed 22 August 2011.
7. Okubo-san and Ogawa-san (introduced below) chose to speak in English during their interviews. While other quotes are translated from Japanese, their quotes are verbatim.

8. This quote references the 2008 hit song 'Single Ladies (Put a Ring on It)' by American artist Beyonce Knowles. The song ostensibly celebrates single women's freedom, while exhorting men to marry their girlfriends or risk losing them.
9. This might be contrasted with single women in other societies. See Rozario (2007).
10. It should be noted that scholars on singlehood in the West have identified similar pejorative tropes among depictions of singles and singlehood (Gordon, 1994; Trimberger, 2005; De Paulo, 2007).

References

Ahearn, Laura (2001) Language and agency. *Annual Review of Anthropology* 30, pp. 109–37.
Beasley, Chris (2011) Libidinous politics: Heterosex, "transgression" and social change. *Australian Feminist Studies* 26(67), pp. 25–40.
Borovoy, Amy (2005) *The too-good wife: Alcohol, codependency and the politics of nurturance in post-war Japan* (Berkeley: University of California Press).
Collins, Kristie (2011) '*Hatarakiman*', 'Around 40' and '*Ohitorisama*': Media narratives of single Japanese women, in *IGALA6 Book of Proceedings*, Selected Papers from the 6th International Gender and Language Association Biennial Conference, pp. 77–84 (Tokyo: Tsuda University).
Dales, Laura (2005) Lifestyles of the rich and single: Reading agency in the "parasite single" issue, in Lyn Parker (ed.), *The agency of women in Asia*, pp. 133–57 (Singapore: Marshall Cavendish).
Dales, Laura (forthcoming) Suitably single? Representations of singlehood in contemporary Japan, in Tomoko Aoyama, Laura Dales and Romit Dasgupta (eds), *Configurations of the family in contemporary Japan* (London: Routledge).
Davies, Bronwyn (1991) The concept of agency: A feminist poststructuralist analysis. *Social Analysis* 30, pp. 42–53.
De Paulo, Bella (2007) *Singled out: How singles are stereotyped, stigmatized, and ignored, and still live happily ever after* (New York: St Martin's Griffin).
Doi, Takeo (1973) *The anatomy of dependence* (New York: Kodansha International).
Freedman, Alisa and Kristina Iwata-Weickgenannt (2011) "Count what you have now. Don't count what you don't have": The Japanese television drama *Around 40* and the politics of women's happiness. *Asian Studies Review* 35(3), pp. 295–313.
Gordon, Tuula (1994) *Single women: On the margins?* (New York: New York University Press).
Haishi Kaori (2004) *Kakkoii onna wa "ohitorisama" jōzu* (Tokyo: PHP Press).
Hertog, Ekaterina (2009) *Tough choices: Bearing an illegitimate child in contemporary Japan* (Stanford: Stanford University Press).
Hilsdon, Anne-Marie (2007) Introduction: Reconsidering agency – feminist anthropologies in Asia. *The Australian Journal of Anthropology* 18(2), pp. 127–37.
Iwashita Kumiko (2001) *Ohitorisama* (Tokyo: Chuokoron-shinsha).
Jeffery, Patricia (1998) Agency, activism and agendas, in Patricia Jeffery (ed.), *Appropriating gender: Women's activism and politicized religion in South Asia*, pp. 156–76 (New York: Routledge).
Kandiyoti, Deniz (1988) Bargaining with patriarchy. *Gender and Society* 2(3), pp. 274–90.
Long, Susan Orpett (1995) Nurturing and femininity: The ideal of care-giving in post-war Japan, in E. Anne Imamura (ed.), *Re-imaging Japanese women*, pp. 156–76 (Berkeley: University of California Press).
Mackie, Vera (2002) Embodiment, citizenship and social policy in contemporary Japan, in Roger Goodman (ed.), *Family and social policy in Japan*, pp. 200–29 (Cambridge: Cambridge University Press).
Mahmood, Saba (2001) Feminist theory, embodiment, and the docile agent: Some reflections on the Egyptian Islamic revival. *Cultural Anthropology* 16(2), pp. 202–36.
Maree, Claire (2004) Same-sex partnerships in Japan: Bypasses and other alternatives. *Women's Studies* 33(4), pp. 541–49.
Mohanty, Chandra Talpade (1991) Introduction, in Anna Russo, Chandra Talpade Mohanty and Lourdes Torres (eds), *Third World women and the politics of feminism*, pp. 1–50 (Bloomington: Indiana University Press).
McNay, Lois (2005) Agency and experience: Gender as a lived relation. *Sociological Review* 52(2), pp. 173–90.
National Institute of Population and Social Security Research (NIPSSR) (2008) Population statistics of Japan: Households and living arrangements. Available at http://www.ipss.go.jp/p-info/e/psj2008/PSJ2008-07.pdf, pp. 78–85, accessed 17 December 2012.

NIPSSR (2010) Data packet of demographic statistics (Table 6-23). Available at http://www.ipss.go.jp/syoushi-ka/tohkei/Popular/P_Detail2010.asp?fname=T06-23.htm&title1= per cent87Y per cent81D per cent8C per cent8B per cent8D per centA5 per cent81E per cent97 per centA3 per cent8D per centA5 per cent81E per cent94z per cent8B per centF4 per cent8A per centD6 per cent8CW per cent95 per centCA per cent90l per cent8C per centFB&title2= per cent95 per cent5C per cent82U per cent81 per cent7C23+ per cent90 per centAB per cent95 per centCA per cent90 per centB6 per cent8AU per cent96 per centA2 per cent8D per centA5 per cent97 per centA6 per cent82 per centA8 per cent82 per centE6 per cent82 per centD1 per cent8F per cent89 per cent8D per centA5 per cent94N per cent97 per centEE per cent81i per cent82r per cent82l per cent82 per cent60 per cent82l per cent81j per cent81F1920 per cent81 per cent602005 per cent94N, accessed 21 July 2010.

NIPSSR (2011) Data packet of demographic statistics (Table 6-12). Available at http://www.ipss.go.jp/syoushi-ka/tohkei/Popular/P_Detail2011.asp?fname=T06-12.htm&title1= per cent87Y per cent81D per cent8C per cent8B per cent8D per centA5 per cent81E per cent97 per centA3 per cent8D per centA5 per cent81E per cent94z per cent8B per centF4 per cent8A per centD6 per cent8CW per cent95 per centCA per cent90l per cent8C per centFB&title2= per cent95 per cent5C per cent82U per cent81 per cent7C12+ per cent91S per cent8D per centA5 per cent88 per centF7 per cent82 per centA8 per cent82 per centE6 per cent82 per centD1 per cent8F per cent89 per cent8D per centA5 per cent82 per centCC per cent95 per centBD per cent8B per centCF per cent8D per centA5 per cent88 per centF7 per cent94N per cent97 per centEE per cent81F1899 per cent81 per cent602009 per cent94N, accessed 3 September 2011.

NIPSSR (2012) Population statistics of Japan 2012 (Table 6.22). Available at http://www.ipss.go.jp/p-info/e/psj2012/PSJ2012.asp, accessed 4 March 2014.

Ogawa, Naohiro (2009) Changing intergenerational transfers and rapid population ageing in Japan. *Report for United Nations Expert Group Meeting on family policy in a changing world: Promoting social protection and intergenerational solidarity.* Available at http://social.un.org/index/LinkClick.aspx?fileticket=wtiORn-fiX6Ypercent3D&tabid=215, accessed 31 October 2011.

Ortner, Sherry (2001) Specifying agency: The Comaroffs and their critics. *interventions* 3(1), pp. 76–84.

Parker, Lyn, ed. (2005a) *The agency of women in Asia* (Singapore: Marshall Cavendish).

Parker, Lyn (2005b) Resisting resistance and finding agency: Women and medicalised birth in Bali, in Lyn Parker (ed.), *The agency of women in Asia*, pp. 62–97 (Singapore: Marshall Cavendish).

Pelto, Pertti J. and Gretel H. Pelto (1978) *Anthropological research. The structure of inquiry* (Cambridge: Cambridge University Press).

Roseneil, Sasha (2007) Queer individualization: The transformation of personal life in the early 21st century. *NORA—Nordic Journal of Women's Studies* 15(2–3), pp. 84–99.

Rozario, Santi (2007) Outside the moral economy? Single female migrants and the changing Bangladeshi family. *The Australian Journal of Anthropology* 19, pp. 154–71.

Sakai Junko (2003) *Makeinu no toboe* (Tokyo: Kodansha).

Sato, Barbara Hamill (2003) *The new Japanese woman: Modernity, media, and women in interwar Japan* (Durham: Duke University Press).

Scott, James (1985) *Weapons of the weak: Everyday forms of peasant resistance* (New Haven: Yale University Press).

Shirahase, Sawako (2000) Women's increased higher education and the declining fertility rate in Japan. *Review of Population and Social Policy* 9, pp. 47–63.

Shoji, Kaori (2005) Better left on the shelf than a downtrodden wife? Japan Times. Available at http://www.japantimes.co.jp/text/ek20050602ks.html#.T-gWue3gwRk, accessed 4 March 2014.

Trimberger, E. Kay (2005) *The new single woman* (Boston: Beacon Press).

Ueno Chizuko (2007) *Ohitorisama no rōgo* (Tokyo: Hōken).

Yamada Masahiro (1999) *Parasaito shinguru no jidai* (Tokyo: Chikuma Shobou).

Masculinities in Asia: A Review Essay

CHIE IKEYA

Rutgers University

Chandrima Chakraborty. *Masculinity, Asceticism, Hinduism: Past and Present Imaginings of India.* Delhi: Permanent Black, 2011.

Kale Bantigue Fajardo. *Filipino Crosscurrents: Oceanographies of Seafaring, Masculinities and Globalization.* Minneapolis: University of Minnesota Press, 2011.

Michele Ford and Lenore Lyons, eds. *Men and Masculinities in Southeast Asia.* London and New York: Routledge, 2012.

Abstract: *Masculinity as an analytical concept has received limited attention in historical and cultural studies of Asia, and particularly of South and Southeast Asia. Only a small number of works produced in South and Southeast Asian studies address the historical construction and evolution of masculinities in the regions and even fewer offer in-depth inquiries into the extent to which historical forms of masculinity governed social relations. The specific dynamics of the relationship between ideologies and the ways that manhood is interpreted, experienced and performed in daily life in the past and in present times remain underexplored. This essay reviews three recent publications that demonstrate that masculinity has been crucial to ideologies and techniques of rule in colonial, national and globalised contexts and, as such, needs to be placed at the centre of analyses of empire, nation and globalisation. It directs attention to promising areas for future comparative research on masculinities in Asia.*

Since R.W. Connell, Jeff Hearn and Michael S. Kimmel (2005, p. 9) pointed out that research on men and masculinities remained, despite the growth in the field, a "First World enterprise", significantly more scholarship on the subject has been produced in the context of Asia. Though still nascent, the study of men and masculinities in Asia has already emerged as an important component of gender studies as a whole, one indication of which is the proliferation of edited volumes that serve as "readers" for masculinities in Asia and its various sub-regions (Brownell and Wasserstrom, 2002; Louie and Low, 2003; Chopra et al., 2004; Srivastava, 2004; Frühstück and Walthall, 2011). In East Asia, pioneering studies such as Kam Louie's work on Chinese masculinity (Louie, 2002), which argued that "the cerebral male model tends to dominate that of the macho, brawny male" (p. 8), and the influential volume by Roberson and Suzuki (2003), which challenged the "salaryman" model of middle-class masculinity in Japan, have been followed by a variety of research on masculinities too numerous to recapitulate here – ranging from investigations into the construction of masculinity in late imperial Chinese literature (Song, 2004; Huang, 2006; Vitiello, 2011) to analyses of the emergence of a transnational corporate masculinity (Hird, 2009; Dasgupta, 2010) and the "softer", sensitive and feminised "New Man" (Louie and Low, 2003; Iida, 2005; Jung, 2011).

Scholarship on South and Southeast Asia has been slower to catch on to "masculinity studies". Yet, South Asian studies has produced seminal work on colonial masculinities and their legacies, and has led the scholarly effort to push back the terrain of inquiry beyond the nineteenth century to attend to pre-colonial codes and hierarchies of masculine identities (Sinha, 1995; O'Hanlon, 1999). Broadening the scope of existing research on gender and Buddhism, which has focused almost exclusively on representations of the feminine (Cabezon, 1992; Gross, 1993; Wilson, 1996),[1] the ground-breaking work of John Powers (2009) has examined early Buddhist discourses relating to masculinity and male sociality.

Although the field of gender studies in Southeast Asia has tended to focus primarily on women,[2] similarly important steps have been taken there as well. There is now considerable research on transgenderism and homoeroticism that shows that understanding masculinity requires delinking it from "male bodies" as well as from heteronormatively gendered, "woman-desiring" men (Blackwood, 1998; Boellstorff, 2005; Garcia, 1996; Jackson and Sullivan, 1999; Johnson, 1997; Sinnott, 2004; Bhaiya et al., 2007; Peletz, 2009). Recent scholarship on heteronormative masculinity (Clark, 2004) that draws on R.W. Connell's theory that there are culturally exalted, "hegemonic" forms of manhood that predominate has added to classic works on "men of prowess" and other idealised masculinities of self-restraint, discipline, control and charisma that have influenced paradigmatic understandings of gender relations in Southeast Asia (Anderson, 1965; Anderson, 1972; Geertz, 1973; Brenner, 1998; Spiro, 1997; Wolters, 1999).

Nevertheless, masculinity as an analytical concept has received limited attention in historical and cultural studies of Asia, particularly of South and Southeast Asia. Only a small number of works produced in South and Southeast Asian studies address the historical construction and evolution of masculinities in the regions, and even fewer present in-depth inquiries into the extent to which historical forms of masculinity govern social relations. The specific dynamics of the relationship between ideologies and the interpretation, experience and performance of manhood in daily life, both in the past and in present times, remain underexplored.

The three books reviewed here – a monograph on India and one on Philippines, plus an edited volume on Southeast Asia – thus mark important contributions to the study of men and masculinities in Asia. They not only illuminate the historical plurality and variability of masculinity and the dynamic and intersectional nature of gender identities and relations, but also provide deep insight into the complexities of doing and redoing masculinity. Importantly, they demonstrate that masculinity has been crucial to ideologies and techniques of rule in colonial, national and globalised contexts and, as such, needs to be placed at the centre of our analyses of empire, nation and (economic and cultural) globalisation.

Chandrima Chakraborty's *Masculinity, Asceticism, Hinduism: Past and Present Imaginings of India* offers a nuanced historical and literary study of Hindu ascetic masculinity in colonial and postcolonial India. Scholars of South Asia have made significant progress in analysing the ineluctably intertwined process of "imagining" women and the nation in anti-colonial and nationalist politics in the nineteenth and twentieth centuries, but much less attention has been paid to reimagining men and the nation. Chakraborty seeks to fill this lacuna. Through a close reading of the writings and speeches of Indian literati and nationalists as well as newspaper reports, films and Hindu Right websites and blogs, she documents the deployment of what she calls "ascetic nationalist masculinity" in the struggle to reclaim indigenous masculinities, produce national(ist) subjects, and create a modern nation-state. In so doing, she casts new light on the well-worn topic of (Hindu) nationalism in India.

The first chapter investigates formulations of ascetic martial masculinity and revolutionary violence by Bankim Chattopadhyay. In response to the colonial discourse of the manly Englishman and the effeminate Bengali *babu*, Bankim creatively merged the traditional Hindu masculine archetypes of Kshatriya (warrior) and Brahmin (priest) and established martial heroes and warrior ascetics of the past as models for normative Hindu masculinity. As Chapter 2 shows, Bankim's ideal of ascetic martiality was both embraced and critiqued. In analysing select works of Rabindranath Tagore, Chakraborty reveals that the former swadeshi activist came to reject ascetic martiality and condemned swadeshis for employing violence to assert masculine power in the name of the nation. His vision of ideal masculinity emphasised, instead, a notion of ethical manliness founded on respect for difference and civic friendship. In Chapter 3, Chakraborty looks at how Mahatma Gandhi rewrote swadeshi ideology to reconfigure the nationalist ascetic as a self-controlled subject and disciplined, saintly body. His radical articulation of nonviolent resistance elevated the ascetic values of nonviolence, voluntary suffering, patience and endurance as ideal masculine attributes.

These three chapters offer an insightful discursive and genealogical investigation into the Hindu male ascetic. British scholar-administrators blamed Indian asceticism for the "inadequacies" in the Indian constitution: indolence, corporeal and moral weakness, lack of martial spirit, and so on. The colonial government saw Hindu ascetics as personification of the absolute renunciation of worldly duties or, at worst, religiously inspired criminality. It is in response to such assertions about the deleterious effects of Hindu asceticism that nationalist ideologues such as Bankim, Tagore and Gandhi directed their attention to the figure of the male Hindu ascetic, turning him into a powerful symbol of anti-colonialism. The masculine ascetic, attributed with indigenous models of masculinity and a superior morality that called for nationalist emulation, enabled the indigenous elite to decolonise and remasculinise the colonised individual, social and national Indian body. Bankim, Tagore and Gandhi thus reworked the terms of the colonial discourse of Hindu/Indian emasculation and challenged colonial ideologies of masculinity.

These chapters serve as background for the last chapter on Hindutva. Chakraborty persuasively argues that the Hindu Right, in its bid to legitimise its agenda of turning

India into a Hindu state, draws heavily and selectively on texts from the nation's past, glossing over the historical heterogeneity of earlier nationalist articulations of asceticism to authorise more radical formulations of ascetic nationalist masculinity. No longer an embodiment of protest, the figure of the ascetic nationalist male is transformed into an "angry Hindu" who defends the nation against its enemies, notably Muslims and the West. These aggressive, muscular Hindu nationalists assert their dominance over internal "others" – such as dissident Hindus and religious minorities – and demand overt and continual reassurances by Indian women of their chastity and obedience to heteronormative family values.

Chakraborty's examination of ascetic nationalist masculinity suggests promising areas for comparative research on masculinities in South and Southeast Asia. As mentioned above, spiritual potency or "prowess", harnessed through self-control, discipline and ascetic practices that restrain carnal desires, has long been an idealised – if also contested – masculine attribute in Southeast Asia. And in the colonial period, male asceticism was perceived, by both sides of the colonial struggle, as a source of subversive potential and revolutionary power, as evinced by the widespread involvement of monks and ascetics in popular millenarian and anti-colonial protests throughout Southeast Asia, from the Spanish Philippines to British Burma.[3] In more recent times, the ascendancy of the Hindu Right in India has found a striking parallel in the masculinist, nationalist "969" movement in Myanmar led by Buddhist monks. The cultural and political efficacy of "ascetic nationalist masculinity" and the violent entanglement of religion, masculinity and the nation in both South and Southeast Asia deserve comparative scrutiny.

Another line of possible comparative inquiry concerns the question of indigenous response to (neo)colonial and Orientalist discourses of manliness. As Michael Pante reveals in his article in this issue, the Filipino elite, like their Indian counterpart in British India, frequently faced charges of political immaturity and effeteness (Pante, 2014). Across South and Southeast Asia colonised subjects actively appropriated and reconfigured the masculine norms and practices that were most valued by the colonials in their attempts at remasculinisation. Yet, as Pante reminds us, asymmetries in socioeconomic status produced significant discrepancies in responses to dominant ideologies and institutions of masculinity. Jessica Hinchy's piece in this issue on the "failed" masculinity of the transgender *hijra* in British India serves likewise as an instructive counterpoint to Chakraborty's study which focuses on canonical nationalist writings by elite men, and highlights the need to consider expressions of male respectability by not only the colonial and native elite but also those beyond the dominant class (Hinchy, 2014).

The two remaining works under review represent critical interventions in this regard. Kale Bantigue Fajardo's *Filipino Crosscurrents: Oceanographies of Seafaring, Masculinities and Globalization* is a rich and provocative ethnography of working-class Filipino seamen who emerged as key figures of state- and corporate-generated Filipino masculinity at the turn of the twenty-first century. Parallelling the recent historiographical return to thalassology (Horden and Purcell, 2006), Fajardo's oceanography – what the author describes as "situated traveling fieldwork" – accentuates seaborne interactions and connectivity, and the dynamic nature of oceanically connected lives shaped by "crosscurrents". This is a fitting approach to the cultural politics of seafaring, Filipino masculinities, and globalisation, one that brings focus to the large-scale processes under examination and offers a fascinating look at Filipino masculinities in their complex totality.

Fajardo argues that as a result of neoliberal capitalist globalisation and the Philippine state's institution of Filipino/a overseas migration as a key long-term economic development strategy, Philippine state officials, multinational corporations, and the seamen themselves, often deploy hetero-patriarchal narratives that portray Filipino seamen as geographically and sexually mobile, heroically nationalistic, simultaneously family-oriented or heteronormative, and macho. Essential to this story is the feminisation of the Filipino/a and, more generally, Southeast Asian global labour; Orientalist, misogynistic and racist representations of the Philippines and other Southeast Asian countries and people as hyperfeminine, weak, subservient and pliant remain persistent today. At the same time, the Philippine state has played an active role in promoting and regulating Filipino labour migration and crafting narratives of heroism and masculinity to reinforce it. For example, Fajardo analyses in Chapter 1 the ways in which Philippine state officials and corporate elites co-opt the history of Manila-Acapulco galleons and "heroic" Filipino sailors as compelling narratives and figures in order to attract capital investment and naturalise the "global city-ness" of the new port development and free trade zone in Manila. Imaginaries of Filipino seafarers – and other overseas Filipino workers – as *bagong bayani* (new heroes) should be read as a product of multiple interlocking conditions that materially and discursively subordinate and discipline Filipino/a subjects and labour.

Fajardo's vivid ethnographic accounts of the lives of Filipino seamen at sea and in ports, and at home and in diaspora, acknowledge that the seafaring *bagong bayani* has served as a powerful formulation of Filipino masculinity. In recalling with pride the galleons and indio/native sailors who travelled the vast expanse of the Pacific during the Spanish colonial period, Filipino seamen linked their own hardships and courageous masculinities to those of past "Filipino" seafarers, and emphasised the parallels between the high-quality Filipino seamanship found today and what they believe existed in the past. Yet, this gendered script of the nation describes only some aspects of some Filipino seamen's experiences and identities. As Fajardo demonstrates, rather than enacting and consolidating state-driven hegemonic masculinities, Filipino seamen have been able to carve out non-normative and non-conventional ways to be Filipino men. For instance, Filipino seamen who "jumped ship" in ports outside the Philippines removed themselves from the oppressive and inequitable state-sanctioned program of Filipino/a labour migration and, furthermore, articulated a counterdiscourse of *bagong bayani* that resisted state constructions of seamen who jump ship as "deserters".

Another telling counternarrative of masculinity came from Filipino seamen who expressed camaraderie with Filipino transgender "tomboys" as working-class Filipino male/masculine subjects who, in Fajardo's words, "coexperience" and "conavigate" oppressive socioeconomic conditions. Eschewing dominant understandings of the Filipino man as emotionally repressed, detached or macho, many of the seamen Fajardo encountered stressed the masculine quality of *pakikiisa* – the ability to emotionally connect with and depend on each other. In these and other ways, Fajardo deftly uncovers fissures in recurring narratives about Filipino seamen's heroic nationalism, heteronormative family values and macho-ness.

The themes of transnational labour migration, globalisation, and competing masculinities reappear in *Men and Masculinities in Southeast Asia*, which brings together ethnographic studies of hegemonic and non-hegemonic masculinities in present-day Philippines, Thailand, Vietnam, Singapore, Cambodia, Timor-Leste and Indonesia. Edited by

Michele Ford and Lenore Lyons, the volume focuses on heteronormative masculinities in an effort to offset the predominance of non-heteronormative genders and sexualities in the literature on masculinity in Southeast Asia. As the editors explain in the introductory chapter, a central concern of the volume is the impact of cultural and economic globalisation on gender relations. Critical of the idea of globalised/globalising forms of masculinities, the volume argues for scholarship that foregrounds the study of localised masculinities while also taking into consideration translocal and crosscultural flows of ideas, people and capital that shape relations of power in Southeast Asia.

The first three essays in the collection explore the masculinities of Filipino seafarers (McKay and Lucero-Prisno), Thai migrant construction workers in Singapore (Kitiarsa), and low-wage Vietnamese immigrant men to the United States (Thai), focusing, much like Fajardo, on the varied strategies that these men develop to mitigate their marginalised socioeconomic status and anxieties about masculine inadequacy and disempowerment. In the workplace, these men may emphasise a "dutiful" professional masculinity of self-discipline, competence and endurance of hardship whereas their off-duty and pleasure-oriented activities in port bars, red-light districts and living quarters tend towards a hypermasculinity that accentuates physical dominance, gallantry and risk-taking heterosexuality. Still, back home in their local or national communities, the toiling migrant workers can transform themselves – if only temporarily – into successful marriageable partners, family breadwinners and overseas adventurers, and by so doing recover their sense of masculine self-worth.

The increasing scholarly attention to migrant men and masculinities is timely and welcome, given that millions of men and women from Southeast Asia leave their homes each year as transnational migrant labourers. In fact, this is a phenomenon common to both South and Southeast Asia – Philippines, India and Bangladesh are the world's leading international labour exporters – and, as such, represents another research area ripe for comparative and collaborative work among South and Southeast Asia specialists. Yet, what about male/masculine subjects in these regions whose labour and everyday practices are marked less by the kinds of far-reaching movements and mobilities that characterise the lives of transnational and transoceanic labour migrants? How do they understand and embody their masculinities? What difference does it make that their masculinities are (re)produced primarily "at home" rather than overseas, in borderlands, or in diaspora?

These questions are addressed in the remaining essays of *Men and Masculinities in Southeast Asia*. Taking an innovative approach to the study of hegemonic masculinities in Singapore, Sophie Williams, Lyons and Ford analyse members-only online discussions by and about Chinese Singaporean male sex tourists to the nearby Indonesian island of Batam. Trudy Jacobsen examines how Cambodian men understand and negotiate seemingly contradictory tropes of idealised manhood: whereas traditional paradigms of Cambodian masculinity posit that the "good" man is family-focused and limits his entertainment to wholesome pursuits, notions of modern manhood cast the "successful" man as unbound by such constraints. In both cases, performance and discourse of virility emerge as a key vehicle for masculinity and fraternity, rather than sexual pleasure or eroticism. It is not only among migrant labourers that overt expressions of sexual experience and capability serve as vital means of enhancing one's sense of manliness.

The next two essays interrogate the relationship between masculinity and violence and the struggle among men with limited resources to acquire masculine respectability. In an ethnographic study of violence-prone, male-dominated groups in Timor-Leste – gangs, martial arts groups and ritual arts groups – Henri Myrttinen uncovers how members of these disaffected groups attempt to come to terms with a double alienation from "traditional" Timorese masculinity and an urban, "modern" and post-conflict masculinity. Ian Wilson similarly contends that the resurgence of *jago* (local strongmen) masculinity among disenfranchised young men in Jakarta's slums and poor neighbourhoods represents resentment towards the post-New Order state and its failure to adequately redress the institutionalised inequalities of the New Order. The "underworld" masculinities of gangs and the *jago* illuminate the fraught combination of a sense of entitlement, victimhood and agency that has become constitutive of the self-image of Timorese and Indonesian young men as virtuous protectors of the people whose acts of violence are motivated by a sense of honour and justice that exceeds that of the law and the state.

The final essay explores the relationship between military service, masculinity and citizenship as experienced by Malay Muslim men in Singapore (Lyons and Ford). The military and its relationship to masculinity have not been given due consideration in the extensive body of scholarship on gender and the nation.[4] The connection between the military and manhood remains naturalised and intact in much of Asia, where many countries mandate military service for men. Countries with no compulsory "national service" such as Pakistan, India, Indonesia and Thailand have some of the world's largest active and reserve militaries, while others such as Myanmar and Philippines have long histories of military governments and armed insurgencies. It is only fitting then that the concluding chapter considers how the military functions as a forum for institutionalising values associated with manliness, valorising masculinism and recognising masculine standing.

In Chinese-dominated Singapore, Malay men have long been stereotyped as intellectually and otherwise indolent (in sharp contrast to the stereotype of the hardworking and high-achieving Chinese race). As national subjects whose loyalty to the nation-state is invariably questioned because of their race and religion, Malay Muslim men are denied high-ranking positions or prestigious combat roles in the military. Yet, precisely because of the systemic discriminations that Malay men face, the military serves as a venue through which they can partake of the traditional association of military men with physical and mental fortitude and patriotism. Many Malay men expressed a sense of pride and achievement in their military service and characterised themselves as "more loyal citizens" than Chinese servicemen who supposedly viewed military service as a waste of time. Lyons and Ford provide new and much needed insight into the way that gender ideologies lead subaltern men to participate in and comply with a state institution that helps to uphold hegemonic codes that contribute to their own social, economic and political marginalisation.

Some readers will undoubtedly take Ford and Lyons to task for their failure to address why, despite the variety of localised masculinities to which *Men and Masculinities in Southeast Asia* attends, status, sex and violence emerge as prominent themes. That these themes recur throughout the volume may be a logical outcome of its preoccupation with the links between the performance of heterosexuality and dominant constructions of masculinity. On the one hand, this emphasis facilitates, as intended by the editors, an analysis of how women and their bodies function as sites for the production and recognition of masculinity. On the other hand, it limits the volume's analysis of the relationship between women and masculinity and risks reducing women to the stereotypical role of objects of desire and victims of violence. The conceptual privileging of Connell's notion of hegemonic masculinity, defined by exclusive heterosexuality and sexual conquest, also has the effect of at times essentialising the Southeast Asian masculine subject. One is left to wonder what the volume may have gained from a more critical assessment of the merits and demerits of studies that give primacy to heterosexuality in constructions, performances and narratives of masculinity.

Collectively, the various histories and ethnographies of masculinities in South and Southeast Asia discussed here serve as evidence of the centrality and continued relevance of masculinity to analyses of colonialism, nationalism and globalisation. They demonstrate that all of these processes have relied upon the elaboration and management of a shifting hierarchy of masculinities, and underscore the highly gendered nature of political, military and economic institutions. Another important insight that emerges from these books collectively is, as Michael Roper and John Tosh (1991, p. 1) have stressed, that masculinity has been and continues to be defined to a large extent in relation to "the other". Throughout South and Southeast Asia, colonials achieved their manliness by insisting on their difference from the "emasculated" colonised men and the "civilising" effect of imperial masculinity. Visions of remasculinised man and nation have depended no less on the denigration of variously gendered, racialised, classed and sexualised others: just as there is no masculine Hindu defender of the nation without the Muslim enemy in India, the figure of the "lazy", "inept" and "weak" Malay Muslim animates the hegemonic masculinity of the industrious and daring Chinese man in Singapore. It is therefore critical that any understanding of masculinity be situated within broader analyses of the unequal relations of power and discourses of difference and otherness that make possible and sustain normative constructions of masculine identity and behaviour.

Finally, the three reviewed works highlight the need for comparative and interdisciplinary dialogues on masculinities that engage scholars of gender in Asia from a variety of geographical locations, theoretical perspectives and disciplinary approaches in a conversation. The point is not to identify a "regional hegemonic masculinity" (Connell and Messerschmidt, 2005, p. 850) or a unique "Asian" view on manhood. The heterogeneous and conflicting norms and practices of manliness explored in the reviewed works illustrate the difficulties of discerning a singular national – let alone regional – masculinity. Cross-border dialogue and thinking will allow us to explore a wide range of competing articulations and experiences of masculinity within Asia itself and denaturalise taken-for-granted ideas about masculinities *in/and* Asia. Such conversations, in turn, will enable us to deconstruct essentialised understandings of Asia and its knowledge field.

Acknowledgments

I wish to thank the editors and anonymous referees of *Asian Studies Review* for their helpful suggestions on earlier drafts of this article. Special thanks go to Michael Barr, the chief editor of this journal, for his encouragement and support for my article. All errors and omissions are my own.

Notes

1. Gender analyses of Buddhism in the Southeast Asian context have tended, similarly, to focus on discourses about the feminine.
2. The notable exception, for a long time, was Ong and Peletz (1995).
3. See Adas (1979), Ileto (1979) and Tai (1983).
4. Historical scholarship on Philippines, notably the work of Alfred McCoy and Norman Owen, stands out in this regard (McCoy, 1999; Owen, 1999).

References

Adas, Michael (1979) *Prophets of rebellion: Millenarian protest movements against the European colonial order* (Chapel Hill: University of North Carolina Press).

Anderson, Benedict (1988 [1965]) *Mythology and the tolerance of the Javanese* (Ithaca, NY: Modern Indonesia Project Monograph Series, Southeast Asia Program, Cornell University).

Anderson, Benedict (1972) The idea of power in Javanese culture, in Claire Holt (ed.), *Culture and politics in Indonesia*, pp. 1–69 (Ithaca, NY: Cornell University Press).

Bhaiya, Abha, Evelyn Blackwood and Saskia E. Wieringa, eds. (2007) *Women's sexualities and masculinities in a globalizing Asia* (New York: Palgrave Macmillan).

Blackwood, Evelyn (1998) Tombois in West Sumatra: Constructing masculinity and erotic desire. *Cultural Anthropology* 13(4), pp. 491–521.

Boellstorff, Tom (2005) *The gay archipelago: Sexuality and nation in Indonesia* (Princeton, NJ: Princeton University Press).

Brenner, Suzanne A. (1998) *The domestication of desire: Women, wealth, and modernity in Java* (Princeton, NJ: Princeton University Press).

Brownell, Susan and Jeffrey N. Wasserstrom, eds. (2002) *Chinese femininities and Chinese masculinities* (Berkeley, CA: University of California Press).

Cabezon, Jose (1992) *Buddhism, sexuality, and gender* (Albany: State University of New York Press).

Chopra, Radhika, Caroline Osella and Filippo Osella, eds. (2004) *South Asian masculinities: Context of change, sites of continuity* (New Delhi: Women Unlimited).

Clark, Marshall (2004) *Maskulinitas: Culture, gender and politics in Indonesia* (Melbourne: Monash Asia Institute).

Connell, R.W., Jeff Hearn and Michael S. Kimmel, eds. (2005) *Handbook of studies on men & masculinities* (Thousand Oaks, London and New Delhi: Sage).

Connell, Raewyn and James Messerschmidt (2005) Hegemonic masculinity: Rethinking the concept. *Gender and Society* 19(6), pp. 829–59.

Dasgupta, Romit (2010) Globalisation and the bodily performance of "cool" and "uncool" masculinities in corporate Japan. *Intersections: Gender and Sexuality in Asia and the Pacific* 23, January.

Frühstück, Sabine and Anne Walthall (2011) *Recreating Japanese men* (Berkeley, Los Angeles and London: University of California Press).

Garcia, J. Neil C. (1996) *Philippine gay culture: The last thirty years* (Quezon City: University of the Philippines Press).

Geertz, Clifford (1973) *Interpretation of cultures* (New York: Basic Books).

Gross, Rita M. (1993) *Buddhism after patriarchy: A feminist history, analysis, and reconstruction of Buddhism* (Albany: State University of New York Press).

Hinchy, Jessica (2014) Obscenity, moral contagion and masculinity: *Hijras* in public space in colonial North India. *Asian Studies Review* 38(2), pp. 274–94.

Hird, Derek (2009) White-collar men and masculinities in contemporary urban China. Unpublished PhD thesis. University of Westminster, United Kingdom.

Horden, Peregrine and Nicholas Purcell (2006) The Mediterranean and "the New Thalassology". *American Historical Review* 111(3), pp. 722–40.

Huang, Martin W. (2006) *Negotiating masculinities in late Imperial China* (Honolulu: University of Hawaii Press).

Iida, Yumiko (2005) Beyond the "feminization of masculinity": Transforming patriarchy with the "feminine" in contemporary Japanese youth culture. *Inter-Asia Cultural Studies* 6(1), pp. 56–74.

Ileto, Reynaldo (1979) *Pasyon and revolution: Popular movements in the Philippines, 1840–1910* (Manila: Ateneo de Manila University Press).
Jackson, Peter and Gerard Sullivan, eds. (1999) *Lady boys, tom boys and rent boys* (Binghamton, NY: The Haworth Press).
Johnson, Mark (1997) *Beauty and power: Transgendering and cultural transformation in the Southern Philippines* (Oxford: Berg).
Jung, Sun (2011) *Korean masculinities and transcultural consumption: Yonsama, Rain, Oldboy, K-Pop idols* (Hong Kong: Hong Kong University Press).
Louie, Kam (2002) *Theorising Chinese masculinity: Society and gender in China* (Cambridge: Cambridge University Press).
Louie, Kam and Morris Low, eds. (2003) *Asian masculinities: The meaning and practice of manhood in China and Japan* (London and New York: Routledge).
McCoy, Alfred (1999) *Closer than brothers: Manhood at the Philippine Military Academy* (Manila: Anvil Publishing).
O'Hanlon, Rosalind (1999) Manliness and imperial service in Mughal North India. *Journal of the Economic and Social History of the Orient* 42(1), pp. 47–93.
Ong, Aihwa and Michael G. Peletz, eds. (1995) *Bewitching women, pious men: Gender and body politics in Southeast Asia* (Berkeley, CA: University of California Press).
Owen, Norman (1999) Masculinity and national identity in the 19th-century Philippines. *Illes i imperis* 2, pp. 23–47.
Pante, Michael D. (2014) A collision of masculinities: Men, modernity and urban transportation in American-Colonial Manila. *Asian Studies Review* 38(2), pp. 253–73.
Peletz, Michael G. (2009) *Gender pluralism: Southeast Asia since early modern times* (London and New York: Routledge).
Powers, John (2009) *A bull of a man: Images of masculinity, sex, and the body in Indian Buddhism* (Cambridge and London: Harvard University Press).
Roberson, James E. and Nobue Suzuki, eds. (2003) *Men and masculinities in contemporary Japan: Dislocating the Salaryman doxa* (London and New York: RoutledgeCurzon).
Roper, Michael and John Tosh (1991) Introduction: Historians and the politics of masculinity, in Michael Roper and John Tosh (eds), *Manful assertions: Masculinities in Britain since 1800*, pp. 1–24 (London and New York: Routledge).
Sinha, Mrinalini (1995) *Colonial masculinity: The "manly Englishman" and the "effeminate Bengali" in the late nineteenth century* (Manchester, UK and New York: Manchester University Press).
Sinnott, Megan (2004) *Toms and dees: Female same sex sexuality and transgender identity in Thailand* (Honolulu: University of Hawaii Press).
Song, Geng (2004) *The fragile scholar: Power and masculinity in Chinese culture* (Hong Kong: Hong Kong University Press).
Spiro, Melford E. (1997) *Gender ideology and psychological reality: An essay on cultural reproduction* (New Haven and London: Yale University Press).
Srivastava, Sanjay, ed. (2004) *Sexual sites, seminal attitudes: Sexualities, masculinities, and culture in South Asia* (New Delhi and Thousand Oaks: Sage).
Tai, Hue-Tam Ho (1983) *Millenarianism and peasant politics in Vietnam* (Cambridge, MA: Harvard University Press).
Vitiello, Giovanni (2011) *The libertine's friend: Homosexuality and masculinity in late Imperial China* (Chicago: University of Chicago Press).
Wilson, Liz (1996) *Charming cadavers: Horrific figurations of the feminine in Indian Buddhist hagiographic literature* (Chicago: University of Chicago Press).
Wolters, O.W. (1999) *History, culture, and region in Southeast Asian perspectives* (Ithaca, NY: Southeast Asian Program Publications, Cornell University).

A Collision of Masculinities: Men, Modernity and Urban Transportation in American-Colonial Manila

MICHAEL D. PANTE

Ateneo de Manila University

Abstract: *Early twentieth-century Manila saw the motorisation of its urban transport system. This was a significant transformation not only because of the technological changes it brought about but more importantly because of its role in shaping the highly gendered discourse of colonial modernity. Motorised vehicles, like the streetcar and the automobile, were trumpeted as masculine and modern machines by America's civilising mission. This colonial discourse was continuously shaped and subverted by a collision of masculinities coming from different directions. This essay will focus on four different male groups in an effort to understand how transport motorisation influenced their sense of masculinity. White American colonisers imagined themselves as modern men destined to bring civilisation to the colony through technology. The native elites used the coloniser as their model by appropriating the symbols of masculine modernity. While the male workers of the modern transport sector gained knowledge of and access to the domains of those in power, those in the traditional sector became targets of vilification by the native and colonial elites. Instead of a duel between two sets of masculinity (coloniser vs. colonised) what emerged was a complex set of relationships influenced by the socioeconomic differences that separated these four groups.*

In the early twentieth century, American-occupied Manila saw the transformation of its urban transportation system.[1] Change came in the form of motorisation: vehicles that did not rely on human or animal power were introduced and integrated into the urban fabric. The electric streetcar and the automobile served as the best examples and symbols of this technological transformation. As the motorised transport modes became more popular, non-motorised modes suffered a decline. Yet, the transformation was not simply technological; motorisation changed the discursive landscape of colonialism. The colonisers viewed the streetcar and automobile not only as enhancers of mobility but also as vehicles of modernity. Motorisation was viewed as progress brought by the civilised American to the uncivilised colony and, thus, a justification for imperial rule. Transportation became a site and an instrument by which the colonisers evaluated the readiness of the colonised natives to become citizens, a status defined according to White masculine norms. As such, this notion of modernity was framed in highly gendered terms. This discourse became dominant given the colonial set-up, but not without contestation from various sections of Manila society, whose responses were informed by their different socioeconomic positions. Subverting colonialism, the colonised subjects appropriated transportation as a way to assert their position in society.

This article will use masculinity as a key construct in revisiting Manila's urban history. This theoretical approach to Philippine historiography is not yet popular, and arguably, theorising gender in Philippine scholarship is still largely understood to be limited to women and LGBT concerns – as if the concept of gender is not applicable to heterosexual men. Nonetheless, a number of pioneering historians have been successful in deploying the construct of masculinity to uncover hitherto uncharted territory, especially in the historiography of the colonial period. The tussles between the coloniser and the colonised, and the projects of imperialism and nationalism, cannot simply be understood as manifestations of universal political ideas. The preeminent position of men and masculine ideas was significant in the propaganda campaign of late nineteenth-century *ilustrado* nationalism (Owen, 1999; Reyes, 2008), in the extension of the American imperial project in the Philippines (Kramer, 2006; de Chavez, 2008; Halili, 2006), and even in the martial imaginings of a soon-to-be independent nation state (McCoy, 2000).

The works mentioned above are concerned with masculinity in relation to overtly political agenda. Though foregrounding masculinity, this essay veers away from tying this notion to formalised relations of power in order to seek the embeddedness of masculinity in more "mundane" facets of colonial society – in this case, urban transportation. More importantly, it contributes to historiographical literature by showing how socioeconomic divisions accentuate the gendered discourse of colonial modernity. Raquel Reyes (2008) and Paul Kramer (2006) have been successful in showing the clashes (as well as the continuities) between the native elite and the Western colonial powers in terms of their ideas regarding masculinity. But what about the men who were outside elite circles? Indeed, there are a variety of masculinities, and even within the colonised population, varied notions do exist, especially between the elites and the working classes. The title of this essay calls to mind Cristina Blanc-Szanton's (1990) concept of "collisions of culture" and the consequent collision of gender systems. This essay tries to factor in gender and how it "complicates" the already complex web of colonial society stratified according to race and class.

Motorised Machines and Modern Man

Late nineteenth-century Manila was a rapidly urbanising Southeast Asian port city and the capital of one of Spain's few remaining colonies. Its economic growth was based on its status as an international port opened by Spain to foreign merchants in the name of liberalised trade. As such, its role was to serve as the main link between the Philippines and the industrialised West: for exporting to the West cash crops harvested from its hinterlands and importing from the West manufactured goods (Legarda, 1999). This socioeconomic status of Manila continued and was even reinforced when the United States assumed colonial rule in the early twentieth century. Supporting Manila in the late nineteenth century was an urban transport network that featured only two types of vehicles: small watercraft and horse-drawn vehicles. Motive force was solely dependent on human and animal power.

This transport system was highly stratified. The masses relied on cheap means of mobility; many took the *banca*, a canoe-like watercraft that plied inland creeks, or walked to their destination.[2] Middle-class residents had more options: *carromatas*, or the so-called commoners' carriages; *calesas*, which were more elegant carriages; and the horse-drawn streetcar, the only transit system at that time. Stylish *victorias*, carriages pulled by two or more horses, were reserved for the elite. Due to such stratification, the private carriage was a symbol of affluence and power (Roxas, 1970, p. 31) since buying and maintaining one was expensive.[3]

When the Americans replaced the Spaniards as the new colonial rulers at the turn of the twentieth century they found Manila's urban transport system inadequate (Wilson, 1903, p. 259). They were clearly frustrated, and the most vivid articulation of this frustration came from the Philippine Commission (1901, p. 29), the highest executive and legislative body of the newly established colonial state:

> There is no city in the world which is so much in need of electric railways as the city of Manila. The cab system is most defective, and it is necessary for the government to maintain a large number of government cabs for the use of the public offices during business hours... Of far greater importance, however, is the inconvenience to the public arising from a lack of proper street transportation.

The colonial community, including both state and non-state sectors, called for improvements in transportation. The solution came in the form of motorisation, which was viewed as Western technology. It was a relief for Americans to see the electric streetcar and the automobile plying the city streets in the first decade of the century. Americans particularly lauded the arrival of the electric streetcar, which had its inaugural run on 10 April 1905, replacing the horse-drawn tram.[4] Through the next three decades, the Americans ensured the continued integration of motorised vehicles into Manila's transport system, a phenomenon seen as a process of "modernisation". The electric streetcar, operated by the Manila Electric Railroad and Light Company (Meralco), became the centrepiece of a transit system. Automobiles were also used as public transport. Public autobuses were introduced in the 1920s, while metered taxis became popular in the 1930s. On the eve of the Pacific War, Manila already had 20,634 registered motor vehicles: 14,916 automobiles, 5,422 trucks and 296 motorcycles (Bureau of the Census and Statistics, 1939, p. 160).

Transport "modernisation" not only changed the patterns of conveyance in Manila; it also altered the city's occupational structure. It created new jobs that provided opportunities for socioeconomic mobility (Doeppers, 1984, pp. 33–34, pp. 59–60). According to the 1903 Census (US Bureau of the Census, 1905, Vol. II, p. 883, p. 1004), Manila had a population of 219,928 but only a handful of urban transport workers: 5,649 *cochero*s (carriage drivers), around 20 to 40 employees for the horse-drawn streetcars, and 1,418 boatmen. By 1939 there were new lines of work with a sizeable labour force (see Table 1).

What motorisation failed to change, however, was the male bias in the occupational structure that had been entrenched since the nineteenth century (LeRoy, 1968, p. 54; Gealogo, 2010, p. 48). Although Meralco employed a number of female streetcar conductors in 1919, this "experiment" failed to make a dent in the company's male-dominated labour force.[5] Manila's transport system was still a man's world, from owners and managers to its rank and file. In fact, it was only in 1939 that Manila had its first female *cochero*.[6]

Before going further, we should take note that the aforementioned notion of transportation "modernisation" emerged from a colonial discourse that was Western, if not Anglo-Saxon, in perspective and highly dichotomising. In this discourse, the oppositional categories of "modern" and "traditional" were often congruent to "Western" (i.e. "American") and "native", respectively. To begin with, the American character of the "modern" modes was unambiguous. Meralco was an American company and the majority of the automobiles that roamed Manila's streets were American-made. Moreover, the modern transport modes were defined by their reliance on non-traditional sources of

Table 1. Persons 10 Years Old and Over in Manila Classified by Usual Occupation and Sex, in the Urban Transport Sector, 1939

Occupational Group	Total Labor Force	Males	Females
Street railroad transportation	440	440	0
Officials	16	16	0
Agents, conductors, drivers, inspectors	320	320	0
Labourers and other workers	104	104	0
Bus and truck transportation	1,121	1,119	2
Owners and officials	110	108	2
Agents, conductors, and drivers	810	810	0
Labourers and other workers	201	201	0
Taxi transportation	1,061	1,061	0
Owners	26	26	0
Drivers	1,035	1,035	0
Calesa, carretela, and carreton transportation	4,690	4,601	89
Owners	1,333	1,245	88
*Cochero*s and other workers	3,357	3,356	1
Chauffeurs	5,751	5,751	0
Working for private owners	3,395	3,395	0
Working for other employers	2,356	2,356	0

Note: Occupational groups presented were taken from the census category, "Transportation and Communication". Occupational groups in the said category that represented lines of work outside the urban transport sector were not included.
Source: Philippine Commission of the Census, 1940–43, Vol. I, Part 3: Manila, p. 32.

motive power: the electric motor and the internal combustion engine, innovations that symbolised the West's scientific triumphalism at the height of imperial expansion (Adas, 1989). Americans, who grew up in US cities transformed by innovations in transportation, communication, sanitation and energy (Adas, 2006, p. 139), linked modernity to the use of science in all aspects of life, a modernity that served to separate themselves from Filipinos as un-modern others (Adas, 1989, p. 194). Transport modernisation represented civilisation, and the reverse also held true: an inadequate transport system indicated a level of savagery in its people (Philippine Commission, 1900, p. 71; Elliott, 1968, pp. 279–80; Forbes, 1945, p. 202).

At the same time, however, Americans saw that civilisation and modernity could be "given" to the Filipinos. Moreover, technological advancement became the barometer with which Americans measured the Filipinos' progress in material prosperity and modernity (Kramer, 2006, pp. 312–13). Transportation was one key rubric (Robb, 1932, p. 16, p. 52; Pante, 2011), an aspect that one American described as "dearest to [their] hearts" (Daniels, 1905, p. 5). Modernising Manila was envisioned as part of the colonisers' "duty to [themselves], to civilisation, to a downtrodden people" (Daniels, 1905, p. 5). Techno-modernism, a discourse of modernity largely defined in terms of scientific and technological progress, also served to justify American colonial rule. The new colonisers persistently presented themselves as benevolent administrators who stood in contrast to the "lethargic and decadent Spanish overlords" (Adas, 2006, p. 154) of the previous regime. Using technological progress as a gauge, the Americans blamed the Spaniards for "the underdeveloped state of the Philippines" (Adas, 2006, p. 154). Simultaneously, the Americans depicted their own rule as progressive and modern.

In this civilising mission, the idea of masculinity played a crucial role. On the one hand, the discourse of colonial modernity entailed "unmanning the [colonised] other" (de Chavez, 2008, p. 137; cf. Halili, 2006, pp. 43–80; Hoganson, 1998, p. 135) and tied masculinity to the notion of "capacity". According to Kramer (2006, p. 312), when the Americans arrived in the Philippines, they "represented Filipinos as misbehaving male children to be disciplined through violence, recognised as 'little brown brothers', and through the workings of education and collaboration, assimilated to semi-manhood. The discourse of capacity was that of a watchful elder brother or father overseeing an increasingly potent, but potentially troublesome, male adolescent". Filipinos had the potential to be "reformed" but were still unfit to be independent. Thus, they needed American tutelage in order to be worthy of civilisation (Rafael, 2000, p. 54; Anderson, 2007, p. 56; Adas, 2006, pp. 146–47). On the other hand, the civilising mission itself was a product of a crisis of White masculinity happening in American society at the turn of the century (Filene, 1998, p. 74). The colonial civilising mission was thought to be a remedy for this, although at the same time it was also part of the predicament. Technology, which had been the foundation of the modernist ideology that brought about imperialist expansion, was remaking American masculinity in the process. Ironically, advances in transportation weakened traditional notions of American masculinity. The new relations of production that gave birth to railways and automobiles emasculated working-class men as they lost autonomy in the sphere of production. The rise of middle-class streetcar and automobile suburbs blurred men's identity in the domestic realm (Filene, 1998, p. 84). The surge of new immigrants, blacks moving into cities, and the first wave of women industrial workers and activists compounded the crisis (Filene, 1998, pp. 114–15; Kimmel, 1996, pp. 81–85; Mosse, 1996, pp. 78–79).

"Over-civilisation" also worried the White man. It was a fear that there was a lack of "rough" activities to reinforce his manliness. Late nineteenth-century bourgeois men became "worried that modern males – particularly themselves and their sons – had become so civilised that their relationship with their own primal needs was now dangerously disrupted" (Rotundo, 1993, p. 232). Reflecting these concerns was the emergence of neurasthenia as a "disease" resulting from overwork, especially among middle-class men who could not keep up with over-civilisation (Kimmel, 1996, p. 134). The end result was that men became "over-sophisticated and effete" (Kimmel, 1996, p. 122), at a time when America's continental frontier, which had been a place for the "perennial rebirth" of masculinity, was drawing to a close (Kimmel, 1996, p. 87; Hoganson, 1998, p. 12).

Many Americans saw the solution to this crisis in the extension of the American frontier to the new colonies, such as in the Philippines where the majority of the expatriate colonists were white, middle-class American males. In the "frontier-tropics" the White American male sought not only to fulfil his duty of spreading civilisation but also to retrieve his masculinity, which was being eroded at that time (Hoganson, 1998, p. 112, p. 183; Filene, 1998, p. 76; see also Rafael, 2000, p. 55). The colony was thus a locus for displaying a "virile and robust American masculinity" (de Chavez, 2008, p. 135). Clearly, the "male, white engineering identity" that emerged from the 1890s to the 1930s and was increasingly "cast into a middle-class identity" was also "firmly linked to overseas expansion" (Oldenziel, 1999, pp. 16–17).

Colonial Transmission, Elite Response

To some extent, transportation provided the Americans with a precarious tool in their civilising mission. It was a symbol of the myriad threats to masculinity back at home, but in the colony it was the hallmark of the modern American male. Somehow, the fast-paced and energetic nature of the electric streetcar and the automobile fits Theodore Roosevelt's ideal masculinity: "Man is made for action, and the bustling scenes of moving life" (Rotundo, 1993, p. 168). Technology in general provided the backbone for a renewed type of American masculinity as the nation embarked on overseas expansion.

The American entrepreneurs who dominated Manila's urban transport system greatly contributed to the "masculinisation" of this sector. Given their troubles in terms of physical mobility at the turn of the century, it was not surprising that a handful of Americans ventured into the transportation business. The livery stable, a transport service that competed with public carriages, became a prominent business venture among Manila Americans (Gleeck, 1977, p. 7). Motorisation compelled these entrepreneurs to incorporate automobiles into their fleets, until it came to the point that cars completely replaced carriages. Thus, the livery garage was born (Gleeck, 1977, p. 79, p. 131).[7] Examples of such entrepreneurs were Emil Bachrach, who was also a pioneer in bus and air transportation in Manila (Gleeck, 1977, pp. 120–21, p. 132), and Harry Rosenberg.[8] As successful businessmen, they became part of a select group of "representative men" in early twentieth-century Manila (Nellist, 1931, p. 25). Partly due to the success of the electric streetcar, Meralco officials were also recognised as members of Manila's cream of the crop. The best example was James Rockwell, who became company president in 1938 (Gleeck, 1977, pp. 161–62).

Motorisation saw the automobile replace the *victoria*, a special type of four-wheeled carriage reserved for the elite (Pante, 2012, p. 431), as the symbol of male respectability. The first car enthusiasts were prominent American men, led by Philippine Commission member Dean Worcester, who was even described as an "enthusiastic automobilist" (Bellairs, 1902, p. 205), Governor-General W. Cameron Forbes, Bachrach, and BPW Director Warwick Greene. Through proper traffic decorum, American colonial officials demonstrated their urbanity and modernity as a counterpoint to the supposed autocracy of the previous Spanish colonial regime, earning the respect of elite Filipino politicians. Manila Mayor Felix Roxas (1970, p. 31) recalled the blatant display of power of carriage-riding Spanish governors and archbishops, and juxtaposed this with the new colonisers' demeanour: "When we meet the Governor-General on the Escolta, his car awaits its turn". It was as if the arrival of the Americans transformed the carriage – a symbol of aristocratic rule – into an automobile, which became a testament to American rationality, self-control and democracy. Roxas's statement echoed Walter Robb's (1939, p. 351) praise for Governor-General William Taft, who, during the pre-motorised years, never allowed his personal carriage to drive against the traffic flow, unlike the state officials of the previous colonial regime.

Motorised transport, which became a vehicle for a virile lifestyle in America (Heitmann, 2009, p. 92), served a similar purpose in Manila. It redefined American men's access to their "preferred" places of entertainment. Santa Ana Cabaret, an American-owned dance hall that was popular among expatriates, advertised itself as: "10 minutes by motor car from downtown districts" (American Express, [1937?], p. 38); "about 15 minutes in a taxi from Luneta" (Anon., 1934, pp. 35–36); "just one minute away from the car line" (Philippine Carnival Association, 1921, n.p.). American soldiers and sailors who wanted "a little diversion of an evening" (Lyons, 1921, p. 11) became regular patrons since the cabaret was just one streetcar ride away from their barracks. Yet, the frontier-tropics were not simply for the Americans' recovery of masculinity. They also involved spreading modernity to the colonised, and in their civilising mission, the most willing recipients were the native elites. This was not surprising, because the Western-oriented, rich and educated Filipino, desiring to prove his readiness for political self-rule, regarded the White male as his model for masculinity and the motorised transport modes as "classrooms" for learning civilisation (Pante, 2011).

Native elites immediately acquired the dominant, macho culture of motorised transportation, and saw it as a way of asserting their capacity for civilisation, a response that paralleled the Indonesian nationalists' use of Western clothing as a retort to accusations of effeminacy and immaturity and as a statement of their modernity and right to become citizens of an independent nation (Gouda, 2007). Many imbibed the car culture since the automobile was a widely regarded status symbol. As early as 1912, many of the registered car owners in Manila were Filipino men. By 1931 Filipino car enthusiasts had formed the Philippine Motor Association (PMA). The PMA comprised prominent male citizens in the country, and its officers came from elite families (Automobile Association of the Philippines, n.d.). By the 1930s the majority of the owners and managers of transport-related businesses in Manila were Filipinos such as well-known businessman and auto dealer Teodoro Yangco (Philippine Commission of the Census, 1940–43, Vol. I, Part 3: Manila, pp. 32–33).

One important effect of transport motorisation was the demise of the *paseo*, a late nineteenth-century urban ritual in Manila that displayed elitist masculinity. Members of the upper classes paraded their carriages along the main boulevards of the city such as the streets of Luneta Park, which provided a suitable location for viewing the scenic sunsets of Manila Bay. As one American described it: "hundreds of carriages drive along the shore facing the bay, or stop for a few moments as near the [band] stand as possible, while gentlemen alight to talk to friends in other carriages" (Devins, 1905, p. 54). This evening promenade was an "opportunity for ostentatious display and gossip … the scene of flirtation and gossip. Who was who, who was there, who was with whom were the burning questions whispered discreetly by men and women as they ambled or sat in a slowly rolling carriage" (Reyes, 2008, p. 27). In the *paseo* a man flaunted both his *cochero*-driven carriage (the more horses, the better) and his lady, who sat behind him inside the carriage. He displayed both his sexual prowess if seen with a woman and his manly authority based on his power over his male *cochero*. Middle-class men who aped this elite culture paraded their *carromata*s (LeRoy, 1968, p. 63), an act that probably satisfied their desire to display their masculinity.

The *paseo* continued into the early American colonial period and Manila Americans even joined the ritual (Kramer, 2006, p. 189). The rise of the automobile did, however, lead to its eventual decline. American John Robb (1932, p. 52) explained the demise of the *paseo* as one of the "accompanying penalties" of Manila's "modernisation" that the masculine automobile embodied. His use of dichotomous gendered images was apparent:

> The old victorias today rest under a blanket of spider webs. The Luneta custom is no more. The automobile is too fast, too powerful, too impatient a vehicle to content itself with driving at snail's pace around the park; and besides, the roar of a gasoline motor drowns out the sound of the band, and the fumes from the exhaust utterly destroy the sweetness of milady's perfume. No, with the coming of the automobile the picturesque Luneta custom had to disappear…

One can argue that the *paseo* as a locus of elite masculinity gave way to the cabaret. By the 1920s the display of masculinity among elite Filipinos and Americans involved driving flashy automobiles to their favourite dance halls.

In the 1930s, the display of power through motorised transportation was seen in another new form. Since powerful government officials were issued car licence plates according to their rank, licence plate numbers became a symbol of manly authority. Plate number 1 was issued to the highest official, down to the "lowest" official who was issued with number 250. This spawned a so-called "licence plate aristocracy" as Filipinos became fascinated with low-numbered cars.[9] With the onset of the Commonwealth period (1935–41), during which Filipinos gained considerable autonomy, plate number PI-1 was designated to President Manuel Quezon (Horn, 1941, p. 23). Quezon further displayed his authority as he rode his official car with motorcycle outriders (Robb, 1939, p. 3). American Florence Horn (1941, p. 24) called this "mad scramble to get low numbers" Manila's "social register", a practice that was true for both Filipino and American officials.

As seen in the examples above, one key feature of elite masculine culture was the centrality of "visual impact" (Reyes, 2008, p. 95). Elites had to display their masculinity, and motorised transportation provided the means for conspicuous consumption. This propensity for display was also a function of the native elites' desire to show their modernity and "knowledge of the foreign". It spoke of their urbanity that "symbolized a turning away from rusticity towards sophistication" (Reyes, 2008, p. 11; see also Carpo-Manawis, 1932, p. 49). It was a case of the native elite's conscious imitation of colonial models (see Sinha, 1987, p. 230). This act of imitation was a conscious response similar to the way in which Filipino students in Europe, known as *ilustrado*s (literally, the "enlightened ones"), displayed their masculinity as a response to their encounter with metropolitan culture (Reyes, 2008, pp. xxvi–xxix). For the elites of early twentieth-century Manila, imbibing the car culture was a matter of defence against accusations of being unmanly, uncivilised, and unprepared for self-government (Reyes, 2008, pp. 96–98; Kramer, 2006, pp. 369–77). This was especially crucial at a time when they were already in political positions to represent Filipinos as lawmakers and executive officials, yet their struggle for independence was thwarted by allegations of being politically immature, charges that could very well be translated to "infantilism, effeminacy and effeteness" (Reyes, 2008, p. 95). The Filipino elites' use of motorised transportation served as a visible marker to support their claims that they were civilised. They used the language of urban transportation to craft "rebuttals of colonial assertions" (Owen, 1999, p. 23) hurled against their modernity and masculinity. That many of them were heavily influenced by or were themselves *ilustrado*s only underscores their relatively easy acceptance of colonial modernity: they had been previously immersed in the same Western intellectual currents that informed American techno-modernism.

The seemingly easy transmission of metropolitan masculinity therefore could not be hastily explained as a manifestation of the way in which the native elite blindly accepted American culture. In fact, they already possessed their own notions of modernity and masculinity with which they approached a new-but-familiar discourse introduced by American imperial expansion. This act of mimicry should not be construed as indicating the Americans' absolute success in cultural imposition, but as a way with which the Filipino elites asserted their place in the colonial order. This was "fiesta politics", to borrow Paul Kramer's (2006, p. 190) words, which involved a "Filipino construction of U.S. culture" and the "employment of identifiably 'American' imagery". This was not simply assimilation for "such adoption gave Filipinos possession of this imagery, enabling them to rework it along unforeseen lines" (Kramer, 2006, p. 190).

Potential Modernity, Potential Threat

Changes in the notions of modernity and masculinity also took place among the middle-class/lower middle-class workers who operated the new transport modes and became an important segment of the city's growing proletariat. Since they occupied a socioeconomic position entirely different from that of the native elites, these changes were different from those described above. To begin with, while motorisation affected the elites as consumers, it affected workers mainly in their capacity as "producers" of conveyance services.

Transport motorisation provided Manila's booming population with new avenues for socioeconomic mobility. The electric streetcar and the automobile from the "upper circuit" provided more remunerative job opportunities than the "traditional" transport modes of the economy's "lower circuit". Streetcar conductors, motormen, taxi drivers and chauffeurs earned higher incomes than their counterparts in the traditional sector (Doeppers, 1984, pp. 88–91). Meralco was even swamped with job applications during its initial years of operation because it offered salaries that were considerably higher than those most Manila-based companies could offer (Figure 1).[10]

Transport workers in the upper circuit were also generally more literate, had longer work experience and residency in the city, and of course, were male. For Americans, streetcar employees compared favourably with other Manila workers. They supposedly exhibited an "unusually high degree of intelligence". Meralco even boasted that 80 per cent of its conductors had "considerable fluency" in the English language, while 20 per cent of its motormen were "acquainted" with the language.[11] Livery garage chauffeurs were also appraised in the same way. Garage companies took pride in their

Figure 1. Meralco employees (from left to right): Engineer, Conductor, Motorman and Lineman, 1910. Source: MMA.

"English-speaking Drivers" (American Express, 1939, back cover). The socioeconomic status that the employees of modern transport services attained served to separate them somehow from those in the lower circuit. The latter were typified by the *cochero*. They earned less and were considerably younger and less literate. Differences in income and literacy created significant differences between them in terms of lifestyle (Doeppers, 1984, pp. 90–91).

In Manila's altered urban environment, motorised transportation served as a way to measure the workers' capacity for modernity, and to some extent, their very masculinity. At the start of colonial rule, Americans doubted the feasibility of employing native workers, who were regarded as lazy and unreliable (Daniels, 1905, p. 5; Clark, 1905). Initially, American businessmen even favoured Chinese coolies.[12] This presented a thorny situation: "attributions of Filipino laziness frightened away foreign capital, but claims of energetic Filipino labour – so closely tied to notions of thrift, property, and self-restraint – could easily be mistaken for recognition of Filipino capacities, perhaps including those for nationality and self-rule" (Kramer, 2006, p. 313). The apprehensions toward native labour held true for the transport sector. Although Filipinos showed their capacity to learn fast, there was still a hint of ambivalence from foreign capitalists. A manager of the Manila Railways Company praised Filipino shop mechanics, but also pointed out that they only worked half as fast as American or English mechanics. Moreover, he noted that: "They can not use figures or calculate and must have white foremen over them. In 14 years we have not been able to train up a traffic inspector from their numbers" (Clark, 1905, p. 856).

The Americans' initial apprehension in Meralco's case was remarkably similar to the employers' hesitation to rely on Filipino workers described in the previous paragraph. Manila Americans at first doubted Meralco's decision to hire Filipino workers for the railway construction. Doubts turned to praise, however, after the successful construction phase. When Meralco began its transport services, all 35 motormen were Americans. Although there were Americans who thought that the "undersized Filipinos" were incapable of operating the cars (Gleeck, 1975, p. 22), company policy mandated the original motormen to guide and train native male employees, who would eventually take over.[13] The reins were given to the Filipinos only after they had shown efficiency and care in operating the cars.[14] Praise was again showered on the workers. Yet, this did not put an end to attacks against Filipino workers, attacks that were often racially tinged and questioned the labourer's masculinity. According to Katherine Mayo (1925, p. 226):

> One direct consequence of the Filipino's small bodily strength is seen in high costs of production. The experience of the Manila Electric Company [Meralco] illustrates this point. It shows that while Filipino and American may be exchanged, man for man, in the light jobs, as street-car operators, three to four Filipino track labourers are required to do the work that in America one white man does.

Such apprehensions about the capacity of Filipino transport workers persisted until the 1930s. The mainstream press was pessimistic that Manila would be rid of the reckless use of horns, which it attributed to a seemingly inherent trait among native workers: "the carromata and the irresponsible cochero, the almost equally irresponsible driver of the auto-calesa and even of the taxi, and the general don't-give-a-damness of the average chauffeur and, sad to say, of not a few owner-drivers".[15] These statements revealed a colonial anxiety regarding the perceived dual character of modern technology: while it provided the colonised with tools for civilisation, it also posed a danger if it fell into the hands of unfit natives. Such an anxiety can be read in the insights of American schoolteacher Mary Fee. For Fee (1912, p. 141), Filipinos had skills to manipulate but owned no factories that would create, and this led them to make the mistake:

> of assuming that their aptitude in learning to press the button is equivalent to the power of creating the system. They are like some daring young chauffeur who finds that he can run an automobile, and can turn it and twist it and guide it and control it with the same ease that its inventor does, and who feels that he is as fully its master – as indeed he is, till something goes wrong.

From Fee's standpoint the Filipino worker's attitude toward technology was more of a delusion of having unlimited access and control over modernity, which in this case came in the form of mechanised technology. She feared having Filipino workers exercise control over mechanised technology given their supposed inadequate knowledge. This situation presented opposite potentialities for the colonisers and the colonised: for the former, it could sow chaos and disturb the colonial urban order; for the latter, it presented possibilities for improving their skills and knowhow, their chances for employment, and ultimately their socioeconomic position within a competitive urban labour market. Illustrating this threat/potential dichotomy stemming from the natives' access to mechanised transport technology was a story of Filipino boys pretending to be chauffeurs. A *Manila Times* editorial alleged that they were city lads who, after gaining a modicum of knowledge about automobiles by simply observing mechanics in garages, presented themselves as chauffeurs to unwitting customers. Accordingly, the editorial demanded mandatory licensing of professional chauffeurs.[16] On the one hand, this incident seemed to confirm the colonisers' fears surrounding the Filipinos' control over mechanised technology. On the other hand, from the boys' point of view, what they did was to simply take advantage of what modernity "offered" them. Rather than being mere passive operators of the "machines of their masters", Filipino workers harnessed modern, mechanised technology and the knowledge that came with it on their own terms despite their subordinate position as colonised and labourer.

Such an appropriation of knowledge and the discourse of techno-modernism occurred not only within the colony but also in the metropole. In a study of Filipino immigrants' perceptions of the US and their "familiarity" with the metropole, the Social Science Institute of Fisk University discovered that "the urban environments of the West Coast felt familiar" especially to those immigrants who had lived in Manila: "When he had difficulty catching a streetcar, Native at first attributed it to racism of a white conductor, but after pulling himself on board, he learned that he was merely hailing it incorrectly" (Kramer, 2006, p. 403). At times, the threat of the transport worker was an affront not only to the urban order but to bourgeois masculinity. The very nature of his work accounted for this. Exemplifying this was the chauffeurs' ability to "intrude" into the personal lives of their upper-class employers and customers. Their position granted them access to the life of vice and lust in which a number of elite American and Filipino males engaged.

The chauffeur's critical position was best articulated in a *Philippines Free Press* article entitled 'Confessions of a Chauffeur'.[17] Although it is highly unlikely that a real chauffeur wrote this piece or that this was a true "confession" at all, the narrative gave the impression that it might have been based on a true story/ies of a chauffeur/s. The persona in the article claimed to be a migrant worker from Pampanga province who had spent five years in Manila and had held four jobs – all as a private driver. He started working for "a rich Filipino merchant and real estate owner" in Pasay, then worked for a "*politico*" for two years. After he was fired, he was employed by a "young unmarried American", and then finally, worked for a "Spanish mestizo who [was] very high in society".[18] At the very start of the article, he reflected on the precarious nature of his job because of his rather "intimate" relations with his boss. He was also aware of the chauffeurs' subordinate position and the "appropriate" behaviour their male masters expected of them. He learned early on that: "chauffeurs, like little children, should be seen and not heard. I was paid to drive a limousine and keep my mouth shut. Nobody wanted my opinion on any subject except driving the car".[19]

Despite, or perhaps because of, his "muted" presence, he was able to enter his employer's personal space. Speaking of his personal and his fellow chauffeurs' collective experience, he stated that though rendered mute, he could not be made deaf and blind:

> But I heard plenty. After all, our employers cannot expect us to stuff our ears with cotton when they are discussing a big business deal with a friend or making love to a pretty young lady in the back seat at night.
>
> It seems to me that the inside of a limousine lends itself to informality and indiscretion. I know of men who are ordinarily tight-lipped, but no sooner do they settle themselves comfortably in the back seat than they start revealing many of their secrets to their guests.[20]

Here the persona understood the automobile both as a symbol and an arena to showcase the owner's masculinity, especially in terms of sexual adventure (see Heitmann, 2009, pp. 91–92). However, although the male employer seemed the undisputed master in his automobile where he displayed his masculinity, in business or romance, he was also rendered vulnerable due to his chauffeur's "permitted incursion" into his private realm. While the chauffeur's presence did show the owner's masculinity through a display of vertical power relations, this very presence also empowered the ostensibly subordinate worker.

Acquiring "knowledge" was one key component of the persona's job. When he served under a politician, presumably a Filipino, he became aware of shady deals unknown to the general public. After he was fired, he worked for a young American, "a wild young man about 25 years old". His new employer "introduced [him] to a new set of faces and places". As the American's chauffeur, he somehow crossed racial boundaries and was exposed to a new world of masculinity: "I became familiar with the Manila hotel, Santa Ana cabaret and a number of brothels and bar-rooms scattered about the city".[21] His knowledge of his employers' secrets and scandals gave him leverage in a number of situations, even when he was fired from his job. He was fully aware that in his "automobile universe" a hierarchy of masculinities existed: "Some men are born to own automobiles and others are born to drive them".[22] Nonetheless he enjoyed his work and its pay, and believed that he could earn the respect of his employer. To a large extent this "automobile universe" was a contact zone, a frontier within a frontier. It was a locus for the coloniser's display of power over the colonised, yet it also represented the threat of the coloniser's proximity to the colonised. Although the chauffeur could not alter his position vis-à-vis his employer, the very nature of his job created in the terrain of subordination possibilities for negotiation.

While the abovementioned chauffeur asserted his masculinity by using his access to his employers' private realm, there were also cases in which modern transportation aided its workers in their attempt to display their masculinity in the public domain. As was true for the Filipino elite, the visual impact of the car became an indelible part of a chauffeur's masculinity: "A chauffeur without a car is like a turtle without its shell".[23] Many took advantage of this chance to display their masculinity – sometimes to the detriment of other road users. Contemporary editorial cartoons evoked such realities. Meralco motormen were criticised because while they did not stop the streetcar for the elderly to board, they immediately halted it for pretty passengers. Due to the recklessness of many chauffeurs, they were caricatured as "*Ang Tsuper ng Kamatayan*" ("The Chauffeur of Death"), a bane of society (Anastasyo Salagubang, 1923, p. 16). Another cartoon branded the taxi driver as the new "emperor of the streets" (McCoy and Roces, 1985, p. 85). Due to the number of deaths it caused, the recklessness of many chauffeurs was perceived as a threat to the modern, urban order, and it became the topic of many contemporary editorials (McCoy and Roces, 1985, p. 37).

Most threatening to the bourgeois order, however, was the capacity of the workers to organise themselves and challenge the system itself. As knowledge of unionism, economic nationalism and imperialism began to enter workers' consciousness, opposition became more systematic. Throughout the early twentieth century, Meralco workers and garage chauffeurs engaged in a number of strikes, often with the help of fellow organised labourers from other sectors (Kerkvliet, 1992, pp. 122–31).

The *Cochero:* Unmanly and Hypermasculine

If transport workers in the modern sector were a potential threat to the urban order, the elite saw clear threats coming mainly from the traditional sector. The constant allegation of the Filipinos' infantile disorder was usually hurled against those who were perceived to be the antithesis of modernity, those who operated traditional transport modes. The *cochero,* in particular, earned the ire of the White man and the native elite.[24]

Almost from the outset, many Americans had a low regard for the *cochero*. Although not all foreigners felt this way toward them (Foreman, 1985, pp. 558–59), the foreigners' overall perception of *cochero*s was that they were reckless and generally incompetent (Wilson, 1903, p. 259; Devins, 1905, p. 50). The Americans harped on the supposed laziness of *cochero*s, as opposed to the bustling, manly activities of modern transport modes. The American colonial state, for its part, tried to "modernise" the "savage" *cochero*. In the early years of colonial rule, local ordinances in Manila mandated that drivers of all vehicles should be at least 16 years old, "of intelligence and good character, and free from infections or contagious disease" (Malcolm, 1901–09, p. 20). With motorisation, the Americans envisaged the inevitable disappearance of *cochero*s (Elliott, 1968, p. 279).[25] The American-controlled mainstream media proclaimed the end of the *cochero*s' "prosperous days" as the "autocratic reign" of the electric streetcar began.[26] On the day the streetcar was introduced, the *Manila Times* ran an editorial predicting:

> that the day of the antiquated, dilapidated, ill-regulated and altogether execrated quilez and carromata is a thing of the past. It means that the seats of the mighty where his exalted highness THE COCHERO has so long held sway, spurning the worms who crossed his path, will soon be vacant.[27]

The same newspaper unleashed another attack on the *cochero*s the following day. An article mockingly lamented the "passing of the autocratic King Cochero" as he "gazes with wondering eyes at the big swift running cars and as he remembers that the demand for their dilapidated vehicles is nearing its end, mutters strange and savage Tagalog oaths beneath his breath".[28]

*Carromata*s and *cochero*s persisted throughout the next three decades despite these predictions. Consequently, the elites' optimism gave way to frustration. Newspapers, until the 1930s, were still predicting the *cochero*s' demise with Meralco's incorporation of autobuses, the *cochero*s' supposed "mortal dread", in its transport system.[29] Such a prediction only underscored the *cochero*s' unexpected persistence. Meralco officials themselves admitted in a 1944 company report that the company had been "badly harassed with competition" from small horse-drawn vehicles (Meralco, 1944, appendix). Around 7,000 carriages still plied Manila's streets prior to the outbreak of the Pacific War in 1941 (Simpich, 1940, p. 409; Horn, 1941, p. 26).

More important than mere persistence was that *carromata* owners and *cochero*s claimed their own space, both literal and figurative, within the urban landscape even as it was being dominated by modern modes. Despite driving the slowest of vehicles, many *cochero*s refused to yield to cars and blocked roads instead of pulling over to give way to other vehicles.[30] There was also a prevalent perception that *carromata* owners and *cochero*s secured their interests through the Municipal Board (Simpich, 1940, p. 411; McCoy and Roces, 1985, p. 72). Many speculated that the local government failed to regulate *carromata*s and *cochero*s because Municipal Board members needed the support of this sector due its capacity to turn in a good number of votes during elections. This was the so-called "calesa vote" (McCoy and Roces, 1985, p. 84; Horn, 1941, pp. 26–27). The elites' frustration at this stage transformed the perception towards *cochero*s: from condescension to vilification. From being remnants of savagery they were now seen as barriers to modernity. The upper classes often depicted *cochero*s as Manila's villains who, along with petty criminals, ruled over the city especially during the last two decades of the colonial period (McCoy and Roces, 1985, p. 84).[31] Mainstream media regarded them as "scheming", "irresponsible", "unreliable" and "rude".[32] Good *cochero*s were seen as an exception to the rule. In a *Philippines Free Press* article that narrated how a traffic altercation led a chauffeur to shoot a *cochero* dead, *cochero*s received blame instead of sympathy from the newspaper, which also demanded the regulation of *cochero*s.[33]

Contemporary editorial cartoons reflected and reinforced the *cocheros*' negative reputation (McCoy and Roces, 1985, p. 67, pp. 72–73, p. 84). One remarkable feature in these cartoons was how *cocheros* were usually drawn as visually ugly characters. It was as if the illustrator erased all marks of respectable manly attributes from the *cochero*'s character, unlike the way in which American men or native politicians were usually drawn in similar cartoons. The unmanly depiction of the *cochero* was not surprising. His deformities served as a representation in mainstream media of his supposed lack of modernity, a "trope" used in other contexts. His "ugliness referred not only to bodily but also to mental characteristics ... [his] disordered outward appearance signalled a mind that lacked control over passions, where male honour had become cowardice, honesty was unknown, and lustfulness had taken the place of purity" (Mosse, 1996, p. 59). In the case of British-colonial India, Mrinalini Sinha revealed a similar case in how the Bengali's puny and diminutive physique became a "source of mirth and derision" in the British colonisers' imagination (Sinha, 1987, pp. 226–27). These "deformed depictions" also bore a striking resemblance to the visual representation of the Filipino's "savagery" in American cartoons during the initial years of occupation (Halili, 2006). Filipinos were caricatured as "half-child, half-devil" (Kramer, 2006, p. 198), "both too little and too much of a real man" (Kimmel, 1996, pp. 194–95). The *cochero* was both unmanly and hypermasculine, and not a real man. The mainstream media was also the source of this hypermasculine characterisation of *cocheros*. Editorials that called for the regulation of *cocheros* usually included stories of harassed women passengers, as documented in articles[34] and illustrated in cartoons (McCoy and Roces, 1985, p. 72). Notwithstanding the increasing acceptability of "passion" and "animal instincts" as proper masculine values in turn-of-the-century America (Rotundo, 1993, p. 227; Kimmel, 1996, p. 182), such "primitive sexual behaviors" associated with *cocheros* were interpreted differently.

At the same time, it is reasonable to attribute such a strong feeling of contempt for the *cocheros* to the reality that they were also asserting their masculinity within colonial society. They were active in defining and defending their manly dignity in the face of a transport regime biased against them (Doeppers, 1984, p. 134). This was seen in the persistence of *carromatas*, their everyday fight over road space, and even in organised political action. Despite differences between the modern and traditional sectors, there were instances when workers from the two circuits collaborated against common enemies. Solidarity among the *cocheros*, Meralco workers and organised labour was strategically forged in the face of what they saw as American oppression, which Meralco aptly represented. In a March 1909 strike of Meralco employees, strikers "called upon all Filipinos ... to boycott the street cars and patronise the street rigs, the drivers of which ... would make special rates to enemies of the street railway company".[35] Acts of solidarity were also seen in workers' propaganda.[36] An article in a pro-workers' publication denounced Meralco owners as "imperialists" and enemies of Philippine independence. It also asserted that Meralco's streetcars and autobuses threatened the livelihood of transport workers in the traditional sector. To counteract Meralco's "imperialist ways", transport workers floated the idea of having various *carromata* owners forge a viable business entity to compete with Meralco autobuses.[37]

Tenuous Modernity and Masculinity

American imperialism brought transport motorisation to Manila, and consequently motorisation provided new tropes for the imperial discourse of colonial modernity. As shown in this essay, the White middle-class American notion of masculinity was embedded in this discourse as it was deployed in the city. From this standpoint, the Filipinos – from car-owning elites to their chauffeurs and even *cochero*s – were all substandard copies of the ideal masculine modernity. As Sinha (1987, p. 230) argues in her analysis of British India:

> The dichotomy of manliness and effeminacy did not refer simply to the discrimination between mother culture and alien culture, but rather to the mother culture and its bastards, the self and its doubles. Effeminacy was not the complete opposite but the bastardized or incomplete form of manliness.

Whereas bastardised manliness here can be read as failed assimilation from the coloniser's point of view, for the colonised it was a deliberate process of appropriation of symbols and knowledge to gain leverage or to push for their objectives. While the elite's choice to embrace car culture was an assertion of their status as modern male citizens, the transport workers' acquisition and appropriation of "knowledge" allowed them to survive in a rapidly urbanising city. Clearly, Eurocentric notions of modernity led "to diverse ways for expressing ideals of a domestic domain, for demonstrating status, and indeed for showing that a man or a woman could be 'modern' in a variety of ways" (Stoler and Cooper, 1997, p. 32). Yet, the diverse ways of being modern and masculine also underscore the demarcations among the socioeconomic groups. Class differences had a profound impact on how the various sections of Manila society responded to the dominance of techno-modernism and how they redefined their own masculinities accordingly. When the Filipino elite asserted their masculinity and modernity through motorised transportation, it was assertion through conspicuous consumption. It involved buying flashy vehicles to display their licence plates or to frequent Manila's cabarets. In contrast, workers tried to establish their own masculinity and modernity mainly by harnessing the knowledge they acquired as part of the transport sector's labour force. One could even argue that their position as labourers put them in an inherently antagonistic position vis-à-vis their employers, be they Filipino or American. Moreover, their socioeconomic status precluded them from mimicking the modern and masculine culture in the same way that the native elites did. And even among the workers, there was a significant difference. Although there were cases of cooperation between labourers from the two circuits, their socioeconomic differences still created a significant gap. As perceived by both American and Filipino elites, streetcar employees and chauffeurs had the capacity for progress; *cochero*s on the other hand were relics of a backward past. More importantly, socioeconomic indicators such as wage levels, literacy rates and employment rates gave streetcar employees and chauffeurs a clear upper hand compared to *cochero*s.

Evidently there was no unified Filipino masculinity pitted against the colonial ideal. Although colonial modernity painted a highly dichotomous picture of Manila society, a more fitting description would be a collision of masculinities coming from different directions.

Acknowledgments

This essay was originally presented as a conference paper at the workshop 'Masculinities in Asia' organised by the Asia Research Institute, National University of Singapore, in August 2011. I would like to thank the workshop's organisers and participants, especially Kaira Alburo, Megan Sinnott and Dinah Sianturi, for their questions and suggestions, which greatly improved this work. Likewise, this article benefited from the insights of two anonymous reviewers. I am also grateful to Roberto Paterno for giving me permission to use materials from the Meralco Museum and Archives. Lastly, Chie Ikeya has been there, from the workshop proper to the production process, to support the publication of my paper, and as such deserves special mention.

Notes

1. The use of the term "urban transportation" in this paper will be limited to intra-city passenger conveyance. Thus the word "urban" must be understood in contrast to "regional" ways of travelling (e.g. trains, inter-island shipping) and not as the opposite of "rural".
2. The first great American investment in the Philippines, *Manila Times Anniversary Issue*, 1910, p. 24.
3. Memories of Manila in 1895, *American Chamber of Commerce Journal*, March 1930, p. 4.
4. This is a red letter day in the history of the Philippines, *Manila Times*, 10 April 1905, pp. 1–2.
5. Meralco has girls on cars, *Manila Times*, 12 April 1919, p. 1.
6. Manila's first woman cochero, *Philippines Free Press*, 23 September 1939, p. 17. The novelty of having a woman *cochero* was apparent in this statement: "Grammarians are now trying to coin the feminine equivalent of 'cochero'".
7. See also: Rosenberg's carriage works and livery stables, *Manila Times Anniversary Issue*, 1910, p. 98.
8. Ibid., p. 98.
9. Our license plate aristocracy, *Philippines Free Press*, 16 May 1931, p. 8, pp. 42–43. On p. 27 of the 26 August 1939 issue of the same newspaper, a cartoon strip criticised the owners of cars with "low numbered" plates. Apparently, a common pet peeve of Manila residents was the arrogance of these car owners who parked their vehicles almost anywhere.
10. Lookout for the trolleys by April 1, *Manila Times*, 22 March 1905, p. 1.
11. Ibid., p. 1.
12. Another witness for the native laborers, *Manila Times*, 17 April 1905, p. 2.
13. This is a red letter day in the history of the Philippines, *Manila Times*, 10 April 1905, p. 2.
14. The first great American investment in the Philippines, *Manila Times Anniversary Issue*, 1910, p. 25.
15. Mussolini did it, *Philippines Free Press*, 2 September 1939, p. 17.
16. License the chauffeurs, *Manila Times*, 18 June 1910, p. 4.
17. Confessions of a chauffeur, *Philippines Free Press*, 6 August 1932, pp. 20–21, p. 52.
18. Ibid., p. 20. Pasay is a town that borders Manila to the south.
19. Ibid., p. 20.
20. Ibid., p. 20.
21. Ibid., p. 52.
22. Ibid., p. 20.
23. Ibid., p. 52.
24. For an extensive discussion of the *cocheros*' notoriety during the American colonial period, see Pante (2012).
25. See also: This is a red letter day in the history of the Philippines, *Manila Times*, 10 April 1905, p. 1.
26. Lookout for the trolleys by April 1, *Manila Times*, 22 March 1905, p. 1.
27. Inauguration of the trolley, *Manila Times*, 10 April 1905, p. 4. Emphasis in original.

28. Many street cars running, *Manila Times*, 11 April 1905, p. 1.
29. Transportation business in Manila has received an impetus through the Meralco, *Philippines Herald*, 30 September 1930, p. 3.
30. The rule of the cochero, *Philippines Free Press*, 21 February 1931, p. 1.
31. See also ibid., p. 1.
32. The carnival of life, *Philippines Free Press*, 30 January 1932, p. 1; The cochero again, *Philippines Free Press*, 23 April 1932, p. 32.
33. The rule of the cochero, *Philippines Free Press*, 21 February 1931, p. 1.
34. Chivalry among cocheros, *Philippines Free Press*, 16 May 1931, p. 44.
35. 'Act' and 'Boycott', *Manila Times*, 8 March 1909, p. 1.
36. Tinututulan ang pisong lisensiya sa mga kutsero, *Ang Manggagawa*, 30 August 1929, p. 18.
37. Hindi dapat mamalagi ang pagsasamantala ng Meralko, *Ang Manggagawa*, 30 December 1928, p. 18, p. 20.

References

Adas, Michael (1989) *Machines as the measure of men: Science, technology, and ideologies of Western dominance* (Ithaca: Cornell University Press).
Adas, Michael (2006) *Dominance by design: Technological imperatives and America's civilizing mission* (Cambridge: Harvard University Press).
American Express (1937?) *Manila and the Philippines* (Manila: American Express).
American Express (1939) *Manila and the Philippines* (Manila: American Express).
Anastasyo Salagubang [pseud] (1923) [Untitled editorial cartoon]. *Ang Manggagawa*, 6 June, p. 16.
Anderson, Warwick (2007) *Colonial pathologies: American tropical medicine, race, and hygiene in the Philippines* (Quezon City: Ateneo de Manila University Press).
Anon. (1934) *Gateway to Manila (Shopping in old Manila): A complete practical guidebook to the Orient's most charming city* ([Manila]: n.p.)
Automobile Association of the Philippines ([n.d.]) Company profile. Available at http://www.aaphilippines.org/about.aspx?pages=aap-company-profile, accessed 30 June 2011.
Bellairs, Edgar (1902) *As it is in the Philippines* (New York: Lewis, Scribner).
Blanc-Szanton, Cristina (1990) Collision of cultures: Historical reformulations of gender in the lowland Visayas, Philippines, in Jane Monnig Atkinson and Shelly Errington (eds), *Power and difference: Gender in island Southeast Asia*, pp. 345–84 (Stanford: Stanford University Press).
Bureau of the Census and Statistics (1939) *Yearbook of Philippine statistics* (Manila: Bureau of Printing).
Clark, Victor (1905) Labor conditions in the Philippines. *Bulletin of the Bureau of Labor* 58, pp. 721–905.
Carpo-Manawis [pseud] (1932) When a provinciano comes to Manila. *Philippines Free Press*, 19 November, p. 49.
Daniels, Bradford (1905) The re-making of Manila. *Manila Times*, 12 October, pp. 3–5.
de Chavez, Jeremy (2008) The brown man's burden: American colonial masculinity and the problem of resistance in Maximo Kalaw's *The Filipino rebel*, in Priscelina Patajo-Legasto (ed.), *Philippine studies: Have we gone beyond St. Louis?*, pp. 134–43 (Quezon City: University of the Philippines Press).
Devins, John Bancroft (1905) *An observer in the Philippines* (Boston: American Tract Society).
Doeppers, Daniel (1984) *Manila, 1900–1941: Social change in a late colonial metropolis* (Quezon City: Ateneo de Manila University).
Elliott, Charles (1968) *The Philippines to the end of the Commission Government: A study in tropical democracy* (New York: Greenwood).
Fee, Mary (1912) *A woman's impressions of the Philippines* (Chicago: A.C. McClurg).
Filene, Peter (1998) *Him/her/self: Gender identities in modern America*, 3rd edition (Baltimore: Johns Hopkins University Press).
Forbes, W. Cameron (1945) *The Philippine Islands*, revised edition (Cambridge: Harvard University Press).
Foreman, John (1985) *The Philippine Islands* (Mandaluyong City: Cacho Hermanos).
Gealogo, Francis (2010) Gender and work in four late nineteenth century Tagalog *Padrones Generales*. *Philippine Population Review* 9(1), pp. 27–56.
Gleeck, Lewis (1975) *American business and Philippine economic development* (Manila: Carmelo & Bauermann).

Gleeck, Lewis (1977) *The Manila Americans (1901–1964)* (Manila: Carmelo & Bauermann).

Gouda, Frances (2007) From emasculated subjects to virile citizens: Nationalism and modern dress in Indonesia, 1900–1949, in Stefan Dudink, Karen Hagemann and Anna Clark (eds), *Representing masculinity: Male citizenship in modern Western culture*, pp. 235–57 (New York: Palgrave Macmillan).

Halili, Servando, Jr. (2006) *Iconography of the new empire: Race and gender images and the American colonization of the Philippines* (Quezon City: University of the Philippines Press).

Hoganson, Kristin (1998) *Fighting for American manhood: How gender politics provoked the Spanish-American and Philippine-American wars* (New Haven, CT: Yale University Press).

Horn, Florence (1941) *Orphans of the Pacific: The Philippines* (New York: Reynal and Hitchcock).

Heitmann, John (2009) *The automobile and American life* (Jefferson, NC: McFarland).

Kerkvliet, Melinda Tria (1992) *Manila labour unions, 1900–1950* (Quezon City: New Day).

Kimmel, Michael (1996) *Manhood in America: A cultural history* (New York: The Free Press).

Kramer, Paul (2006) *The blood of government: Race, empire, the United States, and the Philippines* (Quezon City: Ateneo de Manila University Press).

Legarda, Benito, Jr. (1999) *After the galleons: Foreign trade, economic change, and entrepreneurship in the nineteenth-century Philippines* (Quezon City: Ateneo de Manila University Press).

LeRoy, James (1968) *The Philippines circa 1900, Book One: Philippine life in town and country* (Manila: Filipiniana Book Guild).

Lyons, Norbert (1921) The scenic route to Montalban. *American Chamber of Commerce Journal* 2(6), pp. 9–12.

Malcolm, George, ed. (1901–09) *Ordinances, City of Manila* (Manila: n.p.)

Manila Electric Company (Meralco) (1944) Estimate for reconstruction. Unpublished company report, Item No. D17020003. Meralco Museum and Archives (MMA).

Mayo, Katherine (1925) *The isles of fear: The truth about the Philippines* (New York: Harcourt, Brace).

McCoy, Alfred (2000) Philippine Commonwealth and the cult of masculinity. *Philippine Studies* 48(3), pp. 315–46.

McCoy, Alfred and Alfredo Roces (1985) *Philippine cartoons: Political caricature of the American era, 1900–1941* (Quezon City: Vera-Reyes).

Mosse, George (1996) *The image of man: The creation of modern masculinity* (New York and Oxford: Oxford University Press).

Nellist, George (1931) *Men of the Philippines: A biographical record of men of substantial achievement in the Philippine Islands* (Manila: Sugar News Co).

Oldenziel, Ruth (1999) *Making technology masculine: Men, women and modern machines in America, 1870–1945* (Amsterdam: Amsterdam University Press).

Owen, Norman (1999) Masculinity and national identity in the 19th-century Philippines. *Illes i imperis* 2, pp. 23–47.

Pante, Michael (2011) Ang sasakyan at lansangan bilang paaralan: Modernisasyon ng transportasyong panlungsod at lipunan sa Manila, 1900–1941. *Malay* 23(2), pp. 111–26.

Pante, Michael (2012) The *cocheros* of American-occupied Manila: Representations and persistence. *Philippine Studies: Historical and Ethnographic Viewpoints* 60(4), pp. 429–62.

Philippine Carnival Association (1921) *Official program: Magallanes Carnival and Exposition: January 29th to February 6th, 1921* (Manila: Philippine Carnival Association).

Philippine Commission (1900) *Report of the Philippine Commission to the President* (Washington: Government Printing Office).

Philippine Commission (1901) *Report of the Philippine Commission to the President, 1901* (Washington: Government Printing Office).

Philippine Commission of the Census (1940–43) *Census of the Philippines, 1939*, Vol. 1, Part 3 (Manila: Bureau of Printing).

Rafael, Vicente (2000) Colonial domesticity: Engendering race at the edge of empire, 1899–1912, in *White love and other events in Filipino history*, pp. 52–75 (Quezon City: Ateneo de Manila University Press).

Reyes, Raquel (2008) *Love, passion and patriotism: Sexuality and the Philippine propaganda movement, 1882–1892* (Singapore: National University of Singapore Press).

Robb, John (1932) Manila after thirteen years. *Philippines Free Press*, 6 February, p. 16, p. 52.

Robb, Walter (1939) *Filipinos* (Manila: Carmelo and Bauermann).

Rotundo, E. Anthony (1993) *American manhood: Transformations in masculinity from the Revolution to the modern era* (New York: Basic Books).

Roxas, Felix (1970) *The world of Felix Roxas: Anecdotes and reminiscences of a Manila newspaper columnist, 1926–36*, trans. Angel Estrada and Vicente del Carmen (Manila: Filipiniana Book Guild).

Simpich, Frederick (1940) Return to Manila. *The National Geographic Magazine*, October Issue 78, pp. 409–51.

Sinha, Mrinalini (1987) Gender and imperialism: Colonial policy and the ideology of moral imperialism in late nineteenth-century Bengal, in Michael Kimmel (ed.), *Changing men: New directions in research on men and masculinity*, pp. 217–31 (Newbury Park, CA: Sage).

Stoler, Ann Laura and Frederick Cooper (1997) Between metropole and colony: Rethinking a research agenda, in Ann Laura Stoler and Frederick Cooper (eds), *Tensions of empire: Colonial cultures in a bourgeois world*, pp. 1–57 (Berkeley: University of California Press).

US Bureau of the Census (1905) *Census of the Philippine Islands, taken under the direction of the Philippine Commission in the year 1903* (Washington, DC: US Bureau of the Census).

Wilson, William (1903) *Description of the Philippines: Official handbook* (Manila: Bureau of Printing).

Obscenity, Moral Contagion and Masculinity: *Hijras* in Public Space in Colonial North India

JESSICA HINCHY

Nanyang Technological University

Abstract: *In the 1850s, the British "discovered" a community of transgender eunuch performers, the* hijras, *and legislated for their surveillance and control under the Criminal Tribes Act (CTA) in 1871. This article examines how the British dealt with transgender colonial subjects and the implications for our understanding of colonial masculinities. In particular, I analyse colonial attempts to erase* hijras *as a visible socio-cultural category and gender identity in public space through the prohibition of their performances and feminine dress. This case study demonstrates, first, how masculinity intersected with a broad range of colonial projects, agendas and anxieties. Focusing on the problematic presence of cross-dressing and performing* hijras *in public space, I examine how colonial attempts to order public space and reinforce political borders dovetailed with discourses of masculinity, obscenity and contagion. Second, I argue that attempts to discipline masculinity and obscenity were uneven in practice, meaning the CTA had varying localised impacts upon* hijras. *The lack of interest of some British officials in regulating* hijras, *inadequate policing resources, and pragmatic compromises opened up gaps in surveillance that* hijras *grasped and expanded, frustrating colonial attempts to transform their bodies and behaviours.*

Hijras are generally male-born persons who describe themselves as emasculates or "eunuchs from birth", wear feminine clothing, usually adopt feminine names and have a socio-cultural role as performers at the time of births. Yet to the British in nineteenth-century India, *hijras* were "habitual sodomites" and gender deviants. Their performances were an obscenity, according to colonial officials, while their clamorous public presence was a moral outrage. This article examines the disciplining of *hijra* gender and sexuality for what this reveals about the relationship between masculinity and colonialism. In particular, I focus upon British attempts, beginning in the 1870s, to erase *hijras* as a visible social category and gender identity in public space through the prohibition of performance and transvestism.

Badhai, or performance, was central to the social role of *hijras* in the nineteenth century, and is still significant to *hijra* identities in contemporary India (Reddy, 2005b, pp. 78–84). When a child was born or a wedding occurred, *hijras* routinely visited the house, performed songs and dances, and received (or demanded) payment from the family. *Hijras* claimed a right to alms because their role had religious significance: as infertile persons, they had the power to either bless or curse the fertility of others. *Hijras* also performed their songs and dances in public spaces, such as markets and religious fairs, and for the entertainment of Indian rulers. Yet *hijras* were often considered outcastes due to their castration. Despite the importance of Hindu mythology to the social role of *hijras* and their worship of particular Hindu deities, many described themselves as Muslims and *hijra* identity and customs were religiously syncretic. In northern India, *hijras* wore female clothing, which was an important mark of *hijra* identity, and adopted feminine names upon their initiation.[1] The *hijras* of a particular town or neighbourhood usually lived together in households that were structured by relationships described through kinship terms and by *guru-chela*, or teacher-disciple, hierarchies (Amson, 1872; Castle, 1878; Crooke, 1896, p. 495; Dalmahoy, 1865a; Dalmahoy, 1865b; Enthoven, 1997 [1922], pp. 226–28; Low, 1836; Preston, 1987, p. 376; Robertson, 1866; Rose, 1907, p. 243; Rose, 1911, pp. 331–32; Russell, 1916, pp. 207–08; Simson, 1860; Simson, 1866; Shortt, 1873, p. 209, p. 403; Tiernan, 1871; Williams, 1865).

Hijras challenged the binary division of gender, and despite their self-description as "neither males nor females" (Enthoven, 1997 [1922], p. 228) colonial officials referred to *hijras* as "men". The use of the masculine pronoun was, in fact, a linguistic strategy to erase *hijras* as a distinct gender category and restore the binary division of gender that *hijras* challenged. Masculinity was central to the British construction of the category of "eunuch". From the 1860s, the British in north India discovered several groups that were not castrated but seemingly resembled *hijras* (Elliot, 1871b; Hobart, 1876a). These transgender groups were loosely categorised as "eunuchs" under law, even though they were not emasculated, highlighting that the transgression of normative masculinity was fundamental to the definition of eunuch-hood in British India.[2]

Masculinity was also fundamental to British ideologies of rule in India, in which British men were represented as the masculine ideal. According to colonial discourses, British men had a manly physical appearance, treated their women in a protective and yet liberal manner, occupied their time with manly pursuits such as hunting and sports, and above all, ruled the subcontinent in a just and enlightened manner (thereby glossing over the violence of colonialism). Colonised men were characterised as inherently inferior, but were differentiated through a hierarchy of manliness that distinguished "martial tribes", such as Sikhs, Pathans and Muslims, from "effeminate races", such as Bengalis. Mrinalini Sinha has used the term "colonial masculinity" to describe the relational construction of British and Indian masculinity, along multiple "axes" of power and difference "among or within the colonisers and the colonised as well as between the colonisers and colonised" (Sinha, 1995, p. 1). Interestingly, homosexuality[3] was usually associated in colonial discourse with the "martial races", not with "effeminate"

Bengalis. Yet the colonisers perceived the figure of the *hijra* as effeminate, sexually "deviant" *and* "impotent" – as a figure of failed masculinity.

In 1871, the Government of India enacted the Criminal Tribes Act (CTA). The first part of the CTA applied to the criminal tribes (whose caste professions were labelled criminal), and the second part provided for the registration and control of "eunuchs". The CTA applied to the North Western Provinces (NWP), Oudh and the Punjab. (In 1877, the NWP and Oudh merged. I refer to these provinces collectively as NWP&O throughout this paper.) While the CTA was not fully enforced in the Punjab (Barron, 1910; Griffin, 1872), the NWP&O government considered this "peculiarly nasty" matter (Tyrwhitt, 1874) an "important branch" of judicial and police administration (Webster, 1880). Under the CTA, eunuchs were defined as "all persons of the male sex who admit themselves or on medical inspection clearly appear, to be impotent" (Government of India, 1871). Yet only eunuchs who were "reasonably suspected" of kidnapping, castration or sodomy would be registered; thus, the Act required the classification of eunuchs into "respectable" and "suspicious" categories. The NWP&O government established that either performing in public or wearing female clothing would render a eunuch "suspicious" and liable to registration (Elliot, 1873). In the long term, the aim of the CTA was the extermination of eunuchs through the prevention of emasculation, which would cause eunuchs to "die out" (Elliot, 1871a; Simson, 1865). The immediate aim, however, was to erase *hijras* as a visible socio-cultural category and gender identity. Thus, the Act provided for the imprisonment for up to two years with fine of "[a]ny eunuch ... who appears, dressed or ornamented like a woman, in a public street or place, or in any other place, with the intention of being seen from a public street or place, or who dances or plays music, or takes part in any public exhibition", thereby criminalising *hijras*' primary means of income (Government of India, 1871). The CTA also "virtually deprive[d]" eunuchs "of civil rights" (Elliot, 1871a), including the right to write a will and be the guardian of a child, while police removed children residing with eunuchs in order to prevent emasculation (Government of India, 1871). The CTA was enforced until 1911 in the NWP&O (Government of India, 1911; Jenkins, 1910).

The central questions this article asks are, how did the British in north India govern transgender colonial subjects and what are the implications for our understanding of colonial masculinities?[4] First, colonial attempts to discipline *hijras* demonstrate that discourses and projects of colonial masculinity were over-determined by a range of broader colonial agendas, anxieties and priorities. Colonial moral panics about *hijras* can only be understood through an analysis of how gender and sexuality intersected with numerous broader concerns. The author's broader research project demonstrates how various colonial preoccupations following 1857 were manifest in moral panics about *hijras*, from concerns with peripatetic groups to anxieties about child sexuality. This paper focuses specifically on the intersections of masculinity with broader attempts to order and "clean" public space and to prevent the spread of moral and physical "disease" after 1857. Discourses of masculinity were bound up with concepts of hygiene, contagion and obscenity. In the British view, the performances and transvestism of *hijras* posed a threat of moral and sexual contagion to both Indian men and colonial public space.

Second, this article examines the impacts of the colonial regulation of obscenity and masculinity. Mrinalini Sinha, Sikata Banerjee and Charu Gupta have shown that masculinity was intimately bound up with colonial policies, debates about social reform, and Indian nationalism (Sinha, 1995; Banerjee, 2005; Gupta, 2010). This article extends these studies by examining what happened when the colonisers used codes of masculinity as a means of policing indigenous society. To what extent could the colonisers transform the minutiae of *hijras*' gendered practices and public acts? I argue that the disciplining of *hijra* gender and sexuality was uneven and fissured at the local level. Whereas some *hijras* felt the full brunt of the law – or were subject to excessive applications of the CTA – lax enforcement elsewhere facilitated *hijras*' breaking of the law. The varied impacts of the regulation of performance and feminine dress were due to several factors. Inadequate policing resources and resulting gaps in surveillance made *hijra* evasion possible, while British district administrators prioritised other areas of local administration. British conceptualisations of obscenity varied and officials held differing opinions on the necessity of regulating *hijras*' public acts, producing a diversity of policies at the district level. Moreover, *hijras* took advantage of, widened and generated gaps in colonial power through various strategies of everyday resistance, evasion and negotiation. This study illuminates the fissured nature of colonial attempts to regulate obscenity, gender and sexuality. More broadly, this article resonates with historical studies of "colonial governmentality", which have shown how colonial attempts to manage populations and discipline bodies were often limited in practice, due to the imperative to maintain colonial dominance and the prioritisation of extractive economic policies (Heath, 2010, Chapter 1; Legg, 2007, pp. 5–24; Prakash, 2002, pp. 87–89; Nair, 2009, p. 330).[5]

The registration of eunuchs under the CTA has not received in-depth scholarly analysis, meaning an important episode in the history of the *hijra* community is yet to be told.[6] This article extends the anthropological literature on *hijras* through a historical focus (Dutta, 2012; Hall, 1997; Hossain, 2012; Lal, 1999; Nanda, 1989; Reddy, 2005b). While anthropologists have generally neglected the issue of masculinity and privileged the lens of "third gender" in their accounts of the *hijra* community (Osella et al., 2004, p. 2), I argue that masculinity was central to the historical marginalisation of *hijras*. This article also contributes to the aforementioned studies of "colonial masculinities", which have primarily presented a dialogue between British masculinities and upper-caste Hindu masculinities (Banerjee, 2005; Sinha, 1995), with the recent notable exception of Charu Gupta's work on Dalits (Gupta, 2010). This article analyses colonial masculinities from the margins, examining the deployment of masculinity against gender, sexual and caste subalterns, as well as the agency of *hijras* in response. Finally, this article contributes to studies of the regulation of sexuality in the British Empire. Studies of the regulation of female prostitution have considered the ordering of space (Levine, 2003, pp. 297–322; Tambe, 2010, pp. 58–63), yet there has been little research on the intersections between space, sexuality and masculinity.[7]

The Ethnographic and Historical Context

Hijras were not the only group the British classed as "eunuchs" in north Indian society. *Khwajasarais*, eunuch slaves who were employed in the feminine quarters of elite homes and were courtiers and administrators, could rise to positions of prominence in the Mughal Empire and regional Indian states (Lal, 2005, pp. 195–96; Chatterjee, 2000, pp. 64–65). The author's broader research project examines *khwajasarais* in

Awadh, a regional power in north India. *Khwajasarais* had diverse duties that traversed the domestic and political, but they were particularly prominent in intelligence, diplomatic and military roles. *Hijras* and *khwajasarais* were distinct social roles in the eighteenth and nineteenth centuries (Faiz Bakhsh, 1889 [c.1818]; Khan, 1870). *Khwajasarais* were male-identified and, despite their slave status, were of considerably higher social standing than *hijras*. Nevertheless, the communities had some similarities: both were internally structured by *guru-chela* (teacher-disciple) hierarchies and by non-biological kinship relationships (Faiz Bakhsh, 1889 [c.1818]). The power of *khwajasarais* gradually declined over the nineteenth century. From the beginning of the century, *khwajasarais* were less important as transmitters of intelligence (Bayly, 1999, pp. 94–96). By the mid-nineteenth century, in the lead-up to the British annexation of Awadh, the British deemed *khwajasarais* politically "corrupt" and inappropriate administrators and in 1848 pressured the Awadh ruler to prohibit them from "official" positions (Richmond, 1848; Padshah of Awadh, 1848). *Khwajasarais* resisted colonial interference with some success (Outram, 1855) until British annexation of Awadh in 1856, which resulted in a dramatic decline in their power (Nazir ud-Daula, 1874). The power of *khwajasarais* also gradually diminished in the state of Murshidabad in Bengal (Chatterjee, 1999, pp. 44–57, pp. 73–77, pp. 150-51, p. 215). Efforts to regulate *khwajasarai* labour in Awadh highlight the fact that the CTA was not the only colonial intervention aimed at eunuchs. Yet *hijras* provoked deeper colonial anxieties and more wide-reaching interventions than did *khwajasarais*, who were not, in the colonial view, "habitual criminals" and sexual "deviants".

Hijras' bawdy performances and feminine embodiment were situated in a broader context of gender-crossing and cross-dressing in mythology, religious worship and popular culture. Mythology and folklore in the Hindu tradition contains numerous examples of mythological figures that change sex, usually from male to female (Goldman, 1993; O'Flaherty, 1980, pp. 303–06, p. 334; Nanda, 1989, pp. 21–23; Lal, 1999, pp. 122–26). Several Hindu religious orders cross gender boundaries in their worship. For instance, the *rasiks* or *sakhis* ("female companions") of the Ramanandi monastic order – male devotees who perform feminine behaviours, dress as women and even observe the taboos of the menstruation period in the course of their devotion to Sita and Ram – were present in nineteenth-century north India and still exist today (van der Veer, 1988, pp. 162–69; Low, 1882; Smith, 1881; 1882). Moreover, in the nineteenth century there were diverse forms of female impersonation in theatre and popular culture, from performances of Hindu legends to urban, middle-class theatre (Hobart, 1876a; Hansen, 2004). The gendered and sexual meanings of these forms of gender-crossing were often ambiguous and scholars have interpreted them as variously reinforcing or destabilising dichotomous conceptions of gender (for opposing views, see Nanda, 1989, pp. 21–23; Goldman, 1993, p. 392). Nevertheless, *hijras* were one of several groups who transgressed dichotomous gender in north Indian society.

How, then, did north Indian society view *hijras*? The official records suggest that the songs and dances of *hijras* were inoffensive to a significant proportion of rural and urban society, even if *hijras* were socially marginal (Elliot, 1871b; Willock, 1873b). Indians the British labelled "respectable" reported that local *hijras* were merely "well behaved" singers and dancers (Willock, 1873a). Local intelligence reports from the 1870s show that *hijras* interacted with their neighbours on an everyday basis in the context of local ritual economies of alms-collection (Short, 1873). *Hijras*' performances had a wider range of religious and cultural associations to local communities than gender difference alone. Through performances and alms-collection, *hijras* evoked their identity as spiritual ascetics by giving the alms-giver a blessing on behalf of a deity and alluding to the creative power of infertile persons to bless or curse fertility (Russell, 1916, p. 209; Kirparam, 1988, pp. 506–08). Elite Indian opinion was nevertheless increasingly embarrassed by *hijras*' "abhorrent" and "unspeakable" practices (Khan, 1870) and their "extremely obscene ... effeminate speech, deportment, and movements" (Rai, 1889).

When we consider the broader context of colonial obscenity policy, the prosecution of *hijras*' cross-dressing and performance appears somewhat inconsistent. While *hijras*' public presence was characterised as "obscene", colonial administrators explicitly characterised the forms of theatrical and ritual transvestism mentioned above as "innocent" (Simson, 1866). In general, the colonial administration did not use the obscenity provisions of the Indian Penal Code of 1860 to prosecute transvestism. Moreover, British censorship laws were specifically framed to deal with "sedition" and sexually explicit theatre was not a key concern (Solomon, 1994, pp. 324–25).

Why then was the public presence of *hijras* so troubling to British officials in north India? First, according to colonial officials, the feminine embodiment of *hijras* was evidence of innate sexual and gendered deviance. While nineteenth-century definitions of obscenity usually turned upon the character of the audience (Heath, 2010, pp. 41–42), the definition of *hijra* obscenity turned upon the character of the performer. According to colonial officials, there was an inherent link between *hijras*' outward violation of gender norms and innate sexual "perversity", which rendered the generally "innocent" act of theatrical transvestism "obscene".

Second, the public performances of *hijras* evoked a wider set of anxieties that preoccupied British officials following the revolt of 1857, when the British lost control of much of north India. Colonial accounts of *hijras* in public space often mentioned *hijras*' overtly sexual dances; their "rude" and defaming talk; their alms-collection, characterised as "begging" and "vagrancy"; the exposure of their emasculated bodies when people refused to give alms; their "wandering habits"; and their "defilement" of public space. *Hijras* thus offended colonial sensibilities and concepts of proper public conduct in multiple ways. The colonial conceptualisation of *hijras*' public presence as "obscene" was not only related to their gendered embodiment and the sexually explicit content of their performances, but also to concepts of public space; sanitation projects and concepts of hygiene; anxieties over unproductive labour; discourses of criminality; and concerns with the uncontrolled movement of populations across political borders.

The British in north India were preoccupied with the order, purity and cleanliness of public space following the rebellion of 1857. For instance, Veena Oldenburg has shown how 1857 transformed the British view of Lucknow, henceforth seen as "sinister and dangerous". This resulted in the physical and social transformation of Lucknow as the British attempted to rid the city of labyrinth streets that facilitated rebellion and "clean" the city of "social disease" (Oldenburg, 1984, p. 27, pp. 124–25, pp. 143–44). The concern with *hijras* in public space thus intersected with broader projects of "imperial hygiene" (Bashford, 2004) that sought to order urban space, implement sanitary measures and prevent the spread of moral and physical "disease" (on Delhi: Legg, 2007; on Bombay: Kidambi, 2007). It is worth noting the disjunction between post-Enlightenment constructs of "public space" and early modern Indian concepts of common space.

The dominant conceptualisation of space in northern India and Bengal was a distinction between "inside" and "outside", in which the "outside" was "abandoned to an intrinsic disorderliness" (Kaviraj, 1997, p. 98, p. 101; see also Glover, 2008, pp. 185–202; Freitag, 1991b, pp. 7–8; Chakrabarty, 1991, pp. 19–26). In contrast, for the British, particularly following 1857, public space needed to be ordered since "[u]nordered space was potentially dangerous, suggesting contagion and dissent" (Levine, 2003, p. 299).

Colonial anxieties over *hijras* in public space also intersected with projects to control and suppress groups deemed "habitual criminals" in the 1860s and 1870s. *Hijras* were apparently "addicted" to sodomy, kidnapping and forcibly castrating children, while their alms-collecting practices were associated with "begging" and "vagrancy". Sandria Freitag writes that "the British perceived collectively criminal actions to be either directed against, or weakening, the authority of the state" (1991a, p. 230). Since the late eighteenth century, the British had been particularly concerned with the uncontrolled movement of populations and the porous quality of political borders (Sinha, 2008), and these anxieties were heightened following the revolt of 1857 (Freitag, 1991a). *Hijras'* mobility in public space and regular tours of the countryside for alms-collection connected the community to non-sedentary or "wandering" populations perceived as criminal, such as the "criminal tribes", groups labelled "hereditary criminals" because their caste occupations were believed to be criminal. The concern with the perceived criminality of itinerant groups following 1857, and the association between the *hijra* community and the criminal tribes, is evidenced by the regulation of both groups under the CTA in 1871. More broadly, the "deviant fringe" of Indian society was targeted for experiments in "population management" from the 1860s (Singha, 2003, pp. 92–94). The British enacted legislation to manage various marginal populations perceived as "deviant" and "criminal", including not only eunuchs and the "criminal tribes" but also the "infanticidal" castes, female prostitutes and lepers.

Ideologies of colonial masculinity thus intersected with a broad range of colonial projects following 1857 (Sinha, 1995, p. 2). In a context in which the British were preoccupied with the capacity of unordered public space, collectivities of "habitual criminals", and easily penetrated political boundaries to undermine British dominance of the subcontinent, *hijras'* "obscene" presence in public space was viewed as a direct challenge to British rule (Couper, 1861). Though the characterisation of *hijras* as a danger to British power in India was evidently overstated considering the social marginality and relatively small numbers of *hijras* – approximately 2,500 in the NWP&O (Simson, 1866) – this discourse is explained by the broader colonial anxieties with which the figure of the *hijra* intersected.

Obscene and Contagious Bodies: *Hijras* in Public Space

According to British officials in north India, *hijras* represented a threat of moral, sexual and physical contagion to both Indian men and public space itself. From the 1850s, British officials saw the registration of eunuchs as an exercise in containing the spread of certain "infections" or "contaminations", as well as cleansing the public space of Empire of "dirt" and "pollution" (North-Western Provinces Nizamut Adawlut, 1852; Drummond, 1865b). Following Deana Heath's recent work, I argue that obscenity should be viewed not merely as an issue of law or discourse, but as spatial and embodied in important ways (Heath, 2010, pp. 2–3). Through the reorganisation of spatial relations, the colonial government sought to stem transgender colonial subjects' perceived pollution of both bodies and public space. On the one hand, eunuchs were seen as agents of sexual contagion, as persons who physically infected others with the "disease" of "unnatural" sexual behaviour.[8] On the other hand, *hijras* apparently infected public space and undermined political borders between Indian-ruled and colonial territories.

According to colonial administrators, the public presence of eunuchs posed a threat of moral and sexual contagion to apparently deviant Indian males due to the perceived link between performance and prostitution (Smith, 1882; Sapte, 1865; Robertson, 1866; Roberts and Spankie, 1866). The logic behind the prohibition of performance and cross-dressing was described thus: "Because the dancing in public of eunuchs in female clothing afterwards leads to sodomy, therefore it should be prohibited" (Simson, 1866). Colonial officials opined that the "obscene songs and lascivious movements" (Wise, 1883, p. 39) of eunuchs existed in a direct causal relationship to the "spread" of sodomy (Hobart, 1882; Drummond, 1865b). The singing and dancing of eunuchs was often interpreted as an explicit form of advertising for sexual services, rather than as a performance with social and religious significance (Griffin, 1870). The NWP&O Inspector-General of Police wrote that preventing *hijra* performance would therefore suppress sodomy. Conversely, "so long as these creatures are allowed to go about singing and dancing in women's clothes [sodomy] will not be put a stop to" (Tyrwhitt, 1874). The colonisers claimed the public presence of *hijras* directly engendered sexual activity between *hijras* and Indian males due to the immorality, sexual deviance and unmanly character of Indian male audiences. Consequently, the deviant potential of Indian men was identified as a crucial racial difference between rulers and ruled, reinforcing hierarchies of colonial masculinity.

In the colonial view, the performances and transvestism of eunuchs also held the potential for the contamination of the public space of the British Empire. From the early nineteenth century, Europeans represented *hijras* as a multi-faceted infection of the public sphere. Early in the century, Flemish artist Baltazar Solvyns characterised the "ostentatious display" of deviant bodies and *hijras*' loud and clamorous public presence as an "infection" of "the streets and bazaars" and an "outrage" to public morality (Solvyns, 1808–12, plate IV). In 1852, in 'Government versus Ali Buksh', the first case to provoke concern with *hijras* in the NWP&O, the Mainpuri Sessions Judge wrote that legislation was required,

> ...to effectually rid the Company's dominions ... of such *pollutions*. There can be no difficulty in ferreting out and *clearing* the land of [these] wretches... [A]ny Magistrate [should have authority] to *sweep* his district of such a reproach to any country under Christian rulers (North-Western Provinces Nizamut Adawlut, 1852; italics added).

According to Unwin, the proper British intervention was one of "clearing" or "sweeping" colonial space and, in the process, erasing *hijras* as a visible social category and public presence. Colonial public space was specifically conceptualised as a masculine space, clearly demarcated in its public nature from the feminised private domain (Levine, 2003, p. 308). The visibility of femininely-dressed "habitual sodomites" in public undermined the masculine status of that space, as well as the social and spatial boundaries between the masculine and the feminine.

British administrators also characterised *hijras*' "obscene" performances and display of "deviant" bodies as the corruption of "colonial space", a supposedly purified domain, by the debauched culture of the "native state". The British conceptualised the symbolic geography of northern India as divided between colonial space and the few remaining native states, where debauchery, tyranny and immorality still apparently reigned. The visible public presence of *hijras* represented the infection of British India by the native state and therefore the undermining of the "rational" and "liberal" imperial project (Metcalf, 1994, pp. 24–25).[9] Masculinity was central to the ideologies of the colonial government and its symbolic geographies. The Indian principality was considered an unfortunately appropriate location for *hijras*, since the culture of the native state was at best effete and debaucherous, and at worst downright deviant (Low, 1836; Elliot, 1871b; Robertson, 1866). Colonial officials perceived the political, geographic, cultural and sexual boundaries of British India as dangerously porous. The threat of moral contagion from *hijras* thus required strategies of containment and quarantine. According to one judicial official, the aim of government was to contain *hijras* within the "more congenial limits" of the native state (North-Western Provinces Nizamut Adawlut, 1852). Prior to the CTA, some British officials made ad hoc efforts to "forcibly expel" *hijras* from British territories or institutions, such as army cantonments, "in consequence of the immoral and unnatural practices which public rumour assigned to them" (Ebden, 1856, p. 522). Through the CTA, the NWP&O government sought, at the very least, to ensure *hijras* were not *visible* in the public space of British India.

As we have seen, there were two perceived forms of contagion at stake in the performances and cross-dressing of *hijras*: first, the relationship between individual bodies, wherein deviant bodies posed a threat of contagion to other individuals through the "spread" of sexual vice; and second, the relationship between bodies and public space, wherein the spectacle of *hijras* threatened to infect colonial space. The public presence of *hijras* both reinforced and destabilised colonial masculinity: on the one hand, the perceived susceptibility of Indian male audiences to arousal and corruption by *hijras* confirmed their apparently deviant masculinity and sexuality, and therefore the notions of racial difference on which colonial rule was based; on the other hand, the presence of *hijras* in public undermined the symbolic geography of British India, representing an intolerable infiltration of Indian "immorality" and "effeminacy" into colonial space. While my analysis thus far has focused on the fears of contagion that underwrote the prohibition of *hijras*' transvestite performances, the following sections focus on the uneven implementation of the CTA and the contested boundaries of the obscene.

Prohibiting Performance and Transvestism

The NWP&O government considered the prohibition of the performance and cross-dressing of *hijras* a key priority of local policing (Colvin, 1875; Hobart, 1876b) and implored district officials not to let prudery hinder implementation: "It is not a pleasant [subject], but it is *work* and it must be done" (Tyrwhitt, 1879). Yet many British officials at the district level did not regard the "unpleasant" matter of eunuchs to be important administrative work. The colonial archive suggests an uneven pattern of enforcement, with relatively strict implementation in some districts, excessive applications of the CTA that widened its scope in other districts, and lacunas in prosecution elsewhere. This somewhat erratic implementation was a result of the limited reach of colonial surveillance and bureaucratic capacities on the ground and British officials' allocation of resources to other areas of administration considered more important, as well as the lack of interest or opposition of British district officials to the registration of eunuchs and *hijra* evasion of the police. Therefore, colonial projects to discipline *hijras'* gender and sexuality were internally fissured. My argument resonates with the findings of several historians that colonial attempts to manage populations and regulate bodies – for instance, in the context of urban planning and sanitation – were often limited in practice, due to pragmatic compromises and the imperative to maintain colonial control (Legg, 2007, Chapter 1, Chapter 4; Kidambi, 2007, Chapter 3; Nair, 2009, p. 330).

The prohibition of performance and cross-dressing got off to a slow start and in the first year of enforcement, 1872, there was only one successful prosecution (Tyrwhitt, 1874). Although the provincial government noticed "decided improvement" in the prosecution of performance and cross-dressing from the late 1870s (Hobart, 1877), enforcement continued to be uneven between districts. Police headquarters and the provincial government complained throughout the 1880s that there was "much laxity" in enforcement since the number of prosecutions was relatively small, generally fewer than a dozen per year (Tyrwhitt, 1878; Smith, 1884). The NWP&O government repeatedly sent circular orders to district authorities, reminding them that the punishment of public performance and cross-dressing was a government priority (Sparks, 1877; Robertson, 1878). Several years after the CTA was first implemented, dozens of eunuchs were still listed in the statistical returns as performing for a living (Robertson, 1879). In 1881, "in Muzaffarnagar and Kheri the occupation of some registered eunuchs [was] given as dancing and singing in male attire, though such conduct [was] expressly made penal in the Act". In Unao, too, registered eunuchs "still dress[ed] as women", while in Hardoi "registered eunuchs play[ed] in public in male attire". The NWP&O government concluded that the "police … appear[ed] inclined to wink at offences against the Act" (Robertson, 1881). The uneven disciplining of *hijras'* gender and public behaviour is also evident in the judiciary's enforcement of the prohibition on performance and cross-dressing, as sentences varied from a fine of a few rupees to rigorous punishment for several months, or even up to two years (Robertson, 1881; Smith, 1883).

Yet, in many districts, surveillance and the threat of prosecution made performance and cross-dressing impossible, with devastating impacts upon *hijras* who were denied their primary means of cultural expression, a key aspect of their social role and their primary source of income. In 1874, the Magistrate of Hamipur reported that the immediate impact of prohibition on local eunuchs was such that "the creatures hardly know what to do" (Tyrwhitt, 1874). In 1876, eunuchs in 15 of 22 districts had "been forced to abandon their former calling and to pursue honest and legitimate menial pursuits" (Hobart, 1876b). By 1896, less than 10 per cent of registered eunuchs earned a living "by some definite occupation without resort to begging" (Holderness, 1896). Although *hijras* were able to continue to collect alms from local communities, most were unable to perform and cross-dress under the CTA, or to find other work. In some districts, unregistered eunuchs were also forced to abstain from public performance and transvestism in order to prove their "respectability" and avoid registration. Consequently, the penal provisions of the CTA had a more wide-ranging impact in some areas than the number of prosecutions would suggest. Moreover, the devastating impact of prohibition was exacerbated by the excessive application of the Act, beyond the bounds of the law, in some districts. The prohibition of performance and cross-dressing to registered eunuchs gave the impression that *any* person who appeared to be a eunuch – regardless of whether they were legally registered under the Act – could be prosecuted for public performance and transvestism (Robertson, 1880). The CTA thus facilitated police harassment and the use of technically illegal measures against a range of persons who behaved in public space in a manner deemed "obscene" or "deviant". This represents a continuation of police abuse earlier in the nineteenth century. Prior to the CTA, colonial police harassed *hijras* and other transgender groups by "cut[ing] off their long hair, strip[ping] off their female attire and ornaments, and selling them[,] fit[ting] these people out with a set of men's clothes" (Hobart, 1876a).

The disciplining of *hijras*' gender and "obscene" public acts varied in different local contexts for a number of reasons. First, in many cases, the limited capacities of local police to keep *hijra* communities under surveillance meant that the police found it difficult to catch *hijras* "in the act", although they were "said" to perform and cross-dress in public. In Banda district authorities had intelligence that local eunuchs continued to perform in public, but the police had been unable to catch them doing so (Robertson, 1878). Gaps in surveillance were also a result of British district officials' prioritisation of other areas of local administration that appeared more pertinent to maintaining colonial control.

Second, there was disagreement between British officials – in the judicial as well as the police branches, and at every level of the provincial government – over the definition of obscenity and the necessity of regulation, highlighting that colonial understandings of obscenity and masculinity were by no means homogenous. What was it *precisely* about the performances of eunuchs that made them obscene? In particular, did the content of eunuchs' performances warrant the exercise of state power if the dress of the performer was "appropriately" gendered (Hobart, 1875; Colvin, 1875)? Oftentimes, local authorities punished femininely-dressed eunuchs but allowed those who agreed to wear male clothes to continue to perform in public (Hobart, 1876b; Webster, 1880). Several district Magistrates gave explicit, written permission to registered eunuchs to perform in male clothes, although this was illegal under the Act (Robertson, 1880; Smith, 1884). Aware that performing was the primary occupation of eunuchs, some British officials bent the rules (Tyrwhitt, 1874), while other administrators argued that eunuchs' performances were "harmless" – neither obscene, nor a threat of contagion (Tyrwhitt, 1879; Robertson, 1880). In sum, there were limits to the extent that British administrators were willing to police moral standards among the colonised due to both pragmatic considerations and varying official attitudes towards the necessity and legitimacy of regulating *hijra* morality.

According to many colonial officials, it was not the bawdy content of *hijras*' performances that required regulation, but the spectacle of *hijras* – figures of failed masculinity – dressed as women. While prosecuting transvestism, many local officials allowed registered eunuchs to perform in male clothing. In contrast, most British officials held that femininity needed to be entirely erased from the bodies of *hijras*, who should "uniformly wear men's clothes" (Robertson, 1879; see also Robertson, 1880). Some British district administrators even complained that *greater* policing powers were necessary to suppress cross-dressing and proposed that "it would be much easier" to suppress the public spectacle of *hijras* and other sexual "deviants" "if the law made it criminal for any man to appear in public in women's clothes" (Tyrwhitt, 1874). Since public transvestism was perceived as a visible manifestation of deviant gender and sexuality, British officials at the district level were on the whole in agreement that cross-dressing needed to be suppressed. Nonetheless, the significant variation in the disciplining of *hijras* suggests some plurality in colonial conceptions of obscenity and morality. The uneven regulation of *hijras* also highlights the fissured and incomplete nature of colonial projects to enforce codes of masculinity.

Modes of Resistance and Evasion

The prohibition of public performance and transvestism under the CTA had an uneven impact due to fractures in the colonial administration, but the enforcement of the CTA was also undermined by *hijras* themselves. In their everyday lives, *hijras* subverted colonial ideologies of masculinity and obscenity and legitimised their existence in the face of criminalisation. *Hijras* used various survival strategies to alleviate the impacts of the CTA and undermine colonial efforts to discipline their bodies and behaviours. Thus, *hijras* grasped, expanded and generated gaps in colonial power at the local level and frustrated colonial agendas. *Hijras* exploited "the tiny cracks within the overarching structures of patriarchy and colonialism", highlighting that "systems of dominance contain within them, as an integral part of them, spaces that allow for resistance" (Prasad, 2007, pp. 161–90; see also Haynes and Prakash, 1991, pp. 1–22; O'Hanlon, 1988, p. 222; Ghosh, 2007, pp. 13–15; Doron, 2009, pp. 16–17).

Subversive everyday practices

A range of *hijras'* everyday practices that were not criminalised under colonial law – such as alms-collection, ritual and the re-telling of oral traditions – helped *hijras* mitigate colonial interventions by providing them with a restricted means of income, subverting colonial discourses, legitimising their existence, and undermining colonial agendas. First, alms-collection was subversive in several respects. After 1871, the *hijras* of most districts in the NWP&O were still permitted to collect alms, as long as they did not perform (Oldham, 1875). Requesting alms provided *hijras* with a means of income – albeit a reduced income – following the prohibition of performance, and was an everyday strategy of survival. Alms-collection challenged the criminalising discourses of the colonial government by associating *hijras* with spiritual power, in particular a power to bless and curse fertility (Russell, 1916, p. 209; Kirparam, 1988, pp. 506–08). Alms-collection also directly challenged colonial projects through the implicit flip-side of giving. If money was refused, there was an understood threat of bawdy talk, skilful use of insult and "obscene" gestures and actions (Solvyns, 1808–12, plate IV; Hall, 1997), all of which undermined the NWP&O government's project to control *hijra* "obscenity" and erase *hijras* as a distinct socio-cultural category in public space. One colonial ethnologist reported, "If anyone fails to give them [*hijras*] alms they abuse him, and if abuse fails they strip themselves naked ... which is ... believed to bring dire calamity" (Enthoven, 1997 [1922], p. 228). In light of the prohibition of *hijras'* feminine dress, such actions challenged colonial control over *hijra* bodies by spectacularly drawing attention to bodily difference.

Second, *hijras* subverted colonial agendas and articulated an alternative socio-cultural and gender identity through the everyday re-telling of their communal mythology, derived from Hindu myths of androgynes and emasculates. One common *hijra* legend, which was included in a colonial ethnology, told the story of a prince named Jeto who was born impotent. The goddess Bahucharaji "appeared to Jeto in a dream and told him to cut off his private parts and dress as a woman", practices that all *hijras*, according to the legend, subsequently followed (Enthoven, 1997 [1922], pp. 227–28; see also Russell, 1916, pp. 207–09). Under the CTA, *hijras* evoked these mythological sources of authenticity on a daily basis by worshipping images of deities associated with the *hijra* community and visiting their shrines. Such myths legitimised *hijra* gender identity in the face of British attempts to enforce gender dualism.

"Obscene" performances and transgressive gender embodiment

Hijras deployed various strategies to continue to perform and wear feminine dress. Although *hijras* sent dozens of petitions to government appealing for permission to continue performing in public due to the negative impact of prohibition on their livelihood, the provincial government rejected eunuchs' petitions outright (North-Western Provinces Government, 1873; 1880a; 1880b; 1881). In light of the failure of petitioning, which was the only government-sanctioned form of redress, *hijras* evaded and resisted the laws against performance and feminine dress through multiple means. Therefore, the CTA limited, but did not entirely suppress, the illegal performances of *hijras* and their gender embodiment, despite the risk of prosecution.

First, some *hijras* illegally performed and cross-dressed in public while avoiding prosecution, highlighting the way in which gaps in surveillance created opportunities for resistance and evasion, which *hijras* grasped and widened (Robertson, 1878; Robertson, 1881). Second, the *hijra* community used mobility as a strategy to perform and cross-dress without prosecution. Many *hijras* migrated for short periods to Indian-ruled states, British provinces in which the CTA was not enforced, and other districts of the NWP&O where they were not registered. *Hijras* also constantly moved across political borders to evade police (Hobart, 1876b; Tyrwhitt, 1878; Smith, 1882). The lack of a pass system to prevent and control *hijra* mobility under the CTA allowed many *hijras* to perform and wear feminine clothing in public outside their district and thus gain a temporary reprieve from colonial interventions.

Third, *hijras* outwardly cooperated with normative masculinity to reduce the likelihood of prosecution for performance and thus collaborated with hegemonic ideologies in order to improve their livelihoods. Some *hijras* – for instance, those in Hardoi district – took a creative approach to their gendered embodiment, mixing elements of male and female clothing in order to superficially conform to masculinity, while simultaneously expressing their gender identity (Smith, 1881). Finally, most *hijras* performed and wore feminine clothing in domestic contexts, away from the gaze of the colonial police. The authorities in Mainpuri reported that performances were rarely "done in public" and most eunuchs secretly performed in "private" locations (Tyrwhitt, 1878). The authorities in Mordabad "proved that some registered eunuchs do dress in women's clothes in their own houses" (Webster, 1884). The "private" sphere provided a space in which *hijras* could perform their gender identity, maintain their livelihoods and subvert the colonial disciplining masculinity and obscenity. Despite calls from British district officials for intervention in *hijra* domestic space – through random night-time searches, for instance – the provincial government rejected such legislative changes and the "private" sphere remained a crucial space for *hijra* resistance to colonial projects (Webster, 1884; Smith, 1881; Connell, 1884).

Gaps in surveillance, inadequate resources, varying colonial attitudes, and the limits to which the provincial government was willing to intervene in *hijra* communities created small opportunities for *hijra* resistance to the colonial disciplining of their bodies and behaviours. *Hijras* grasped and expanded these fissures in colonial power, in the process frustrating colonial agendas.

Conclusion

In the second half of the nineteenth century, the colonial government in north India attempted to discipline the gender embodiment and "obscene" acts of *hijras* in order to erase the group as a distinct social category in public space. This was part of a wider project to cause *hijras* to "die out" as a physical and social entity through the enforcement of Part II of the Criminal Tribes Act of 1871. This article has examined what this project to police *hijras* tells us about colonial masculinity. First, I have argued that colonial moral panics about *hijras* were over-determined by several broader colonial agendas and anxieties. *Hijras* evoked wider concerns with the inability to know and control peripatetic groups; the colonial conceptualisation of Indian criminality in terms of collectives, perceived as a threat to British political authority; the purity of public space and projects of sanitation; the porous nature of political boundaries (both symbolic and physical) between Indian-ruled and British territories; and lacunas in intelligence and surveillance that demonstrated the tenuous nature of colonial power. This article has particularly examined the ways in which efforts to enforce masculinity and police *hijra* "obscenity" intersected with broader projects to clean and regulate public space following the 1857 revolt, when the British sought to re-draw the urban landscape to prevent dissent in urban space perceived as dangerously disordered. The presence in public space of *hijras* – conceptualised as "habitual criminals", gender and sexual "deviants" and carriers of moral contagion – was viewed as a direct challenge to British rule. *Hijras* were characterised as contaminating agents that infected both Indian men and colonial public space with moral and sexual "disease" associated with the "native states". According to British colonial officials, boundaries between bodies and between Indian- and British-ruled territories were both undermined by *hijra* "obscenity", requiring various strategies of containment to stem these flows of contagion. Thus, colonial discourses of gender and sexuality intersected with broader colonial projects – from sanitation policies, to urban planning, to efforts to control "wandering" groups – that were concerned with the order of public space and the stability of political borders in the post-1857 period.

Second, colonial efforts to regulate *hijra* bodies and their spatial location were inconsistent between local contexts, revealing the limits of the colonial government's attempts to discipline masculinity and suppress public "obscenity". The enforcement of the prohibition on transvestism and performance, and its impacts upon *hijras*, varied between districts, and even different local police jurisdictions. Some local authorities exercised an excess of coercive power, beyond the boundaries of the law, while elsewhere, local enforcement was lax. I suggest three reasons for the uneven disciplining of *hijras*. First, the capacity of the colonial government to minutely discipline the bodies and behaviours of *hijras* was limited at the district level due to inadequate policing resources, pragmatic compromises, and the prioritisation of other areas of local administration. Second, British colonial officials differed somewhat in their conceptualisation of obscenity and the extent to which the colonisers should control *hijras*. Some British district officials were simply uninterested in policing morality, which they did not view as crucial to British colonial rule. Third, *hijras* exploited and expanded fissures in colonial power at the local level to alleviate the impacts of the CTA on their everyday lives and directly undermined colonial efforts to suppress the visible public presence of *hijras*. *Hijras* maintained an aspect of their social role and their loud and raucous public presence through alms-collection; broke the law against performance and feminine dress while evading the police; partly collaborated with normative masculinity to reduce the risk of prosecution; and sang, danced and wore feminine clothing in domestic spaces, away from the gaze of the police.

The impact of colonial projects against *hijras* is still felt in post-Independence India. Anthropologist Gayatri Reddy shows that *hijras* are characterised by many in Indian society as a public nuisance, a threat to public order and a source of contagion. *Hijras* are "constructed in the popular imaginary as 'dirty', socially marginal outcasts" (Reddy, 2005a, p. 257), a perception that stems, on the one hand, from Indian notions of *sharam* (shame), and on the other hand, from concepts of public order and contagion with a colonial history. The CTA also established a pattern of police-*hijra* interactions premised on the criminality of the *hijra* community and the legitimacy of policing measures different from and more excessive than those applied to broader society, forming an important backdrop to the widely documented contemporary police abuse of *hijras* (People's Union for Civil Liberties, Karnataka, 2004). Yet the colonial government did not succeed in its ultimate aim: to cause *hijras* to "die out". Both the fissures of colonial power and the agency and resistance of *hijras* account for the long-term failure of colonial attempts to erase *hijras* as a socio-cultural and physical entity, notwithstanding the CTA's devastating (if uneven) impacts upon nineteenth-century *hijras*. The category and identity of the *hijras* fortunately survived colonial criminalisation.

Notes

1. *Hijras* adopted feminine names, with the exception of Punjabi *hijras*, who retained male names. These different naming practices have endured (Hall and Donovan, 1996, p. 252).
2. Police later de-registered dozens of "eunuchs" who had fathered children (Low, 1882).
3. In 1860, the Indian Penal Code criminalised "unnatural intercourse", usually interpreted as sodomy, under section 377 (Narrain, 2008).
4. The framework of "colonial masculinity" is not the only lens through which the history of the *hijra* community can be analysed. In my broader research project, I particularly analyse the ways in which power, agency and resistance were manifest in *hijras*' everyday lives and the intimate domain.
5. These studies have built upon Michel Foucault's concept of "governmentality" – a form of power that has as its object the management of populations through the production of knowledge (such as statistics) and deployment of various "tactics" to transform the population's conditions of life in an

"improving" manner – but have analysed how population management occurred in the colonial context. See Foucault (1991).
6. Shane Gannon's recent PhD dissertation on colonial representations of *hijras* examines the CTA in one chapter, but uses an exclusively discursive framework of analysis (Gannon, 2009, pp. 329–61).
7. On the neglect of symbolic geography in sexuality studies, see Mort (2000, p. xxiii); Phillips (2006, Introduction).
8. For a useful discussion of contagion, see Bashford and Hooker (2001, pp. 4–5).
9. The streets, markets and religious fairs in which *hijras* performed were usually defined as "native" spaces in contradistinction to the Civil Lines (Mills, 2005, pp. 105–13), but in this case were defined as "colonial" in contrast to the "native state".

References

Abbreviations for Archival Sources:

India Office Records, British Library, London
Government of India, Public and Judicial Department (BL/IOR/L/PJ)
North-Western Provinces Judicial Proceedings (BL/IOR/P)
North-Western Provinces Police Proceedings (BL/IOR/P)
North-Western Provinces and Oudh Judicial Proceedings (BL/IOR/P)
North-Western Provinces and Oudh Police Proceedings (BL/IOR/P)
Official Publications (BL/IOR/V)

National Archives of India, New Delhi
Foreign Department Political Consultations (NAI/FD/PC)
Home Department Judicial Branch Records (NAI/HD/JB)

Uttar Pradesh State Archives, Allahabad
Commissioner of Allahabad Records (UPSA/A/COA)
Commissioner of Meerut Records (UPSA/A/COM)
Commissioner of Varanasi Records (UPSA/A/COV)

Uttar Pradesh State Archives, Lucknow
Board of Revenue, Lucknow District (UPSA/L/BR/LD)

Sources:

Amson, J. (1872) Letter from Magistrate of Azamgarh, to Commissioner of Benares, 16 November, in UPSA/A/COV/119/12.
Banerjee, Sikata (2005) *Make me a man! Masculinity, Hinduism, and nationalism in India* (Albany: State University of New York).
Barron, C.A. (1910) Letter from Deputy Commissioner, Delhi, to Commissioner, Delhi, 22 August, in BL/IOR/L/PJ/5/82.
Bashford, Alison (2004) *Imperial hygiene: A critical history of colonialism, nationalism and public health* (New York: Palgrave Macmillan).
Bashford, Alison and Claire Hooker (2001) Introduction: Contagion, modernity and postmodernity, in Alison Bashford and Claire Hooker (eds), *Contagion: Historical and cultural studies*, pp. 1–14 (London: Routledge).
Bayly, C.A. (1999) *Empire & information: Intelligence gathering and social communication in India, 1780–1870* (New Delhi: Cambridge University Press).
Castle, J. (1878) Letter from Superintendent of Police, Ghazipur, to Magistrate of Ghazipur, 23 April, in UPSA/A/COV/119/12.

Chakrabarty, Dipesh (1991) Open space/public place: Garbage, modernity and India. *South Asia* 14(1), pp. 15–31.
Chatterjee, Indrani (1999) *Gender, slavery and law in colonial India* (New Delhi: Oxford University Press).
Chatterjee, Indrani (2000) A slave's quest for selfhood in eighteenth-century Hindustan. *Indian Economic and Social History Review* 37(1), pp. 53–86.
Colvin, A. (1875) Letter from Secretary, NWP, to Inspector-General of Police, NWP, 12 August, in BL/IOR/P/97.
Connell, C.J. (1884) Letter from Secretary, NWP&O, to Inspector-General of Police, NWP&O, 23 September, in BL/IOR/P/2208.
Couper, G. (1861) Letter from Secretary, NWP, to NWP Member, Legislative Council, 12 February, in BL/IOR/P/235/33.
Crooke, William (1896) *The tribes and castes of the North-Western Provinces and Oudh* (Calcutta: Office of the Superintendent of Government Printing, India).
Dalmahoy, P.C. (1865a) Report on a case of kidnapping by Superintendent of Police, Etawah, 9 December, in BL/IOR/P/438/61.
Dalmahoy, P.C. (1865b) Statement of Mussumat Mutheria by Superintendent of Police, Etawah, in BL/IOR/P/438/61.
Doron, Assa (2009) Ferrying the gods: Myth, performance and the question of "invented traditions" in the city of Banaras. *Sites* 6, pp. 1–22.
Drummond, R. (1865a) General Remarks to Cases No. 79 of 1864, Nos. 16, 17, 18, and 19 of 1865, by Sessions Judge, Shahjahanpur, in BL/IOR/P/438/61.
Drummond, R. (1865b) Letter from Commissioner Allahabad, to Secretary, NWP, 9 August, in BL/IOR/P/438/61.
Dutta, Aniruddha (2012) An epistemology of collusion: *Hijras*, *kothis* and the historical (dis)continuity of gender/sexual identities in eastern India. *Gender & History* 24(3), pp. 825–49.
Elliot, C.A. (1871a) Abstract of Replies, by Officiating Secretary, NWP, 21 April, in BL/IOR/P/92.
Elliot, C.A. (1871b) Letter from Officiating Secretary, NWP, to Officiating Secretary, Government of India, 21 April, in BL/IOR/P/92.
Elliot, C.A. (1873) Letter from Secretary, NWP, to Commissioner of Allahabad, 19 March, in UPSA/A/COV/119/12.
Ebden, H. (1856) A few notes, with reference to "the eunuchs", to be found in the large households of the state of Rajpootana. *Indian Annals of Medical Science* 3(6), pp. 520–25.
Enthoven, R.E. (1997 [1922]) *The tribes and castes of Bombay* (New Delhi: D.K. Publishers Distributors).
Faiz Bakhsh, Muhammad (1889) *Memoirs of Delhi and Faizábád, being a translation of the Tarikh Farahbakhsh of Muhammad Faiz-Bakhsh*, trans. William Hoey, Vol. 2 (Allahabad: Government Press).
Foucault, Michel (1991) Governmentality, in Graham Burchell, Colin Gordon and Peter Miller (eds), *The Foucault effect: Studies in governmentality, with two lectures and an interview with Michel Foucault*, pp. 87–104 (Hertfordshire: Harvester Wheatsheaf).
Freitag, Sandria B. (1991a) Crime in the social order of colonial North India. *Modern Asian Studies* 25(2), pp. 227–61.
Freitag, Sandria B. (1991b) Introduction: Aspects of "the public" in colonial South Asia. *South Asia* 14(1), pp. 1–13.
Gannon, Shane Patrick (2009) Translating the *hijra*: The symbolic reconstruction of the British Empire in India. Unpublished PhD thesis. University of Alberta, Canada.
Ghosh, Anindita (2007) Introduction, in Anindita Ghosh (ed.), *Behind the veil: Resistance, women and the everyday in colonial South Asia*, pp. 1–20 (Ranikhet: Permanent Black).
Glover, William J. (2008) *Making Lahore modern: Constructing and imagining a colonial city* (Minneapolis: University of Minnesota Press).
Goldman, Robert P. (1993) Transsexualism, gender, and anxiety in traditional India. *Journal of the American Oriental Society* 113(3), pp. 374–401.
Government of India (1871) Act XXVII of 1871, in BL/IOR/V/8/42.
Government of India (1911) Act III of 1911, in BL/IOR/L/PJ/5/82.
Griffin, L.H. (1870) Letter from Under-Secretary, Punjab, to Secretary, Government of India, 25 February, in BL/IOR/P/147.
Griffin, L.H. (1872) Letter from Secretary, Punjab, to Secretary, Government of India, 8 November, in NAI/HD/JB 12/1872 #72-3.

Gupta, Charu (2010) Feminine, criminal or manly?: Imagining Dalit masculinities in colonial North India. *Indian Economic and Social History Review* 47, pp. 309–42.
Hall, Kira (1997) "Go suck your husband's sugarcane!": Hijras and the use of sexual insult, in Anna Livia and Kira Hall (eds), *Queerly phrased: Language, gender, and sexuality*, pp. 430–60 (New York: Oxford University Press).
Hall, Kira and Veronica O'Donovan (1996) Shifting gender positions among Hindi-speaking hijras, in Victoria Lee Bergvall, Janet Muelle Bing and Alice F. Freed (eds), *Rethinking language and gender research: Theory and practice*, pp. 228–66 (London: Longman).
Hansen, Kathryn (2004) Theatrical transvestism in the Parsi, Gujarati and Marathi theatres (1850–1940), in Sanjay Srivastava (ed.), *Sexual sites, seminal attitudes: Sexualities, masculinities and culture in South Asia*, pp. 99–122 (New Delhi: Sage Publications).
Haynes, Douglas and Gyan Prakash (1991) Introduction: The entanglement of power and resistance, in Douglas Haynes and Gyan Prakash (eds), *Contesting power: Resistance and everyday social relations in South Asia*, pp. 1–22 (Berkeley: University of California Press).
Heath, Deana (2010) *Purifying empire: Obscenity and the politics of moral regulation in Britain, India and Australia* (Cambridge: Cambridge University Press).
Hobart, R.T. (1875) Letter from Deputy Inspector-General of Police, NWP, to Inspector-General of Police, NWP, 4 May, in BL/IOR/P/97.
Hobart, R.T. (1876a) Letter from Deputy Inspector-General of Police, NWP, to Inspector-General of Police, NWP, 21 June, in UPSA/A/COV/119/12.
Hobart, R.T. (1876b) Letter from Deputy Inspector-General of Police, NWP, to Inspector-General of Police, NWP, 28 June, in BL/IOR/P/839.
Hobart, R.T. (1877) Letter from Deputy Inspector-General of Police, NWP&O, to Inspector-General of Police, NWP&O, 11 September, in BL/IOR/P/840.
Hobart, R.T. (1882) Letter from Inspector-General of Police, NWP&O, to Secretary, NWP&O, in BL/IOR/P/1816.
Holderness, T.W. (1896) Letter from Secretary, NWP&O, to Inspector-General of Police, NWP&O, 7 August, in UPSA/A/COA/18/5.
Hossain, Adnan (2012) Beyond emasculation: Being Muslim and becoming *hijra* in South Asia. *Asian Studies Review* 36(4), pp. 495–513.
Jenkins, J.L. (1910) Statement of Objects and Reasons, 21 May, in BL/IOR/L/PJ/5/82.
Kaviraj, Sudipta (1997) Filth and the public sphere: Concepts and practices about space in Calcutta. *Public Culture* 10(1), pp. 83–113.
Khan, Syed Ahmed (1870) Letter to John Strachey, 14 April, in NAI/HD/JB 30/07/1870 #53-4.
Kidambi, Prashant (2007) *The making of an Indian metropolis: Colonial governance and public culture in Bombay, 1890–1920* (Aldershot, Hampshire: Ashgate Publishing).
Kirparam, Bhimbhai (1988 [1901]) Pavávás, in James M. Campbell (ed.), *Hindu castes and tribes of Gujarat*, pp. 506–08 (Haryana: Vintage Books).
Lal, Ruby (2005) *Domesticity and power in the early Mughal world* (New Delhi: Cambridge University Press).
Lal, Vinay (1999) Not this, not that: The hijras of India and the cultural politics of sexuality. *Social Text* 17, pp. 119–40.
Legg, Stephen (2007) *Spaces of colonialism: Delhi's urban governmentalities* (Oxford: Blackwell Publishing).
Levine, Philippa (2003) *Prostitution, race, and politics: Policing venereal disease in the British Empire* (New York: Routledge).
Low, J. (1836) Letter from Resident at Lucknow to Political Secretary, Government of India, 23 September, in NAI/F/PC 6/03/1837 #92.
Low, G.J. (1882) Report by Superintendent of Police, Lucknow, 14 September, in BL/IOR/P/2002.
Metcalf, Thomas R. (1994) *Ideologies of the Raj* (Cambridge: Cambridge University Press).
Mills, Sara (2005) *Gender and colonial space* (Manchester: Manchester University Press).
Mort, Frank (2000) *Dangerous sexualities: Medico-moral politics in England since 1830* (London: Routledge).
Nair, Janaki (2009) Beyond nationalism: Modernity, governance and a new urban history for India. *Urban History* 36(2), pp. 327–41.
Nanda, Serena (1989) *Neither man nor woman: The hijras of India* (Belmont, CA: Wadsworth Publishing Company).

Narrain, Arvind (2008) "That despicable specimen of humanity": Policing of homosexuality in India, in Kalpana Kannabiran and Ranbir Singh (eds), *Challenging the rule(s) of law: Colonialism, criminology and human rights in India*, pp. 48–77 (New Delhi: SAGE India).

Nazir ud-Daula (1874) Petition to Chief Commissioner, Oudh, 4 January, in UPSA/L/BR/LD #1140.

North-Western Provinces Government (1873) Matters of Routine Records, in BL/IOR/P/95, NWP Judicial Proceedings, Part B, March, #75.

North-Western Provinces Government (1880a) Matters of Routine Records, in BL/IOR/P/1467, NWP Judicial Proceedings, Part B, February, #87.

North-Western Provinces Government (1880b) Matters of Routine Records, in BL/IOR/P/1467, NWP Judicial Proceedings, Part B, September, #77.

North-Western Provinces Government (1881) Matters of Routine Records, in BL/IOR/P/1614, NWP Judicial Proceedings, Part B, January, #12.

North-Western Provinces Nizamut Adawlut (1852) Government versus Ali Buksh, in *Nizamut Adawlut Decisions NWP* 3.

Oldenburg, Veena Talwar (1984) *The making of colonial Lucknow, 1856–1877* (Princeton: Princeton University Press).

Oldham, W. (1875) Letter from Officiating Magistrate of Ghazipur to Commissioner of Benares, 6 February, in UPSA/A/COV/119/12.

Osella, Caroline, Filippo Osella and Radhika Chopra (2004) Introduction: Towards a more nuanced approach to masculinity, towards a richer understanding of South Asian men, in Radhika Chopra, Caroline Osella and Filippo Osella (eds), *South Asian masculinities*, pp. 1–33 (New Delhi: Women Unlimited).

Outram, J. (1855) Letter from Resident at Lucknow to Secretary to Government of India, 21 June, in NAI/FD/PC 28/12/1855 #335.

O'Flaherty, Wendy Doniger (1980) *Women, androgynes, and other mythical beasts* (Chicago: Chicago University Press).

O'Hanlon, Rosalind (1988) Recovering the subject: Subaltern Studies and histories of resistance in colonial South Asia. *Modern Asian Studies* 22(1), pp. 189–224.

Padshah of Awadh (1848) Written Agreement to Prohibit Eunuchs, Singers and Other Improper Persons from Holding Office, 22 June, in NAI/FD/PC 08/07/1848 #65.

People's Union for Civil Liberties, Karnataka (2004) Human rights violations against the transgender community: A study of kothi and hijra sex workers in Bangalore, India – September 2003. Available at http://ai.eecs.umich.edu/people/conway/TS/PUCL/PUCL%20Report.html, accessed 24 August 2012.

Phillips, Richard (2006) *Sex, politics and empire: A postcolonial geography* (Manchester: Manchester University Press).

Prakash, Gyan (2002) The colonial genealogy of society: Community and political modernity in India, in Patrick Joyce (ed.), *The social in question: New bearings in history and the social sciences*, pp. 81–96 (London: Routledge).

Prasad, Nita Verma (2007) The litigious widow: Inheritance disputes in colonial North India, 1875–1911, in Anindita Ghosh (ed.), *Behind the veil: Resistance, women and the everyday in colonial South Asia*, pp. 161–90 (Ranikhet, India: Permanent Black).

Preston, Laurence W. (1987) A right to exist: Eunuchs and the state in nineteenth-century India. *Modern Asian Studies* 21, pp. 371–87.

Rai, Mahtab (1889) Letter from Pleader, Delhi, to Private Secretary to Governor General India, 1 November, in NAI/HD/JB 02/1890 #110-2.

Reddy, Gayatri (2005a) Geographies of contagion: *Hijras, kothis*, and the politics of sexual marginality in Hyderabad. *Anthropology & Medicine* 12, pp. 255–70.

Reddy, Gayatri (2005b) *With respect to sex: Negotiating hijra identity in South Asia* (Chicago: University of Chicago Press).

Richmond, A.F. (1848) Letter from Resident at Lucknow to Secretary to Government of India, 22 June, in NAI/FD/PC 08/07/1848 #64.

Roberts, W. and R. Spankie (1866) Draft Act, by NWP Nizamut Adawlut Judges, 24 March, in BL/IOR/P/438/62.

Robertson, C. (1866) Letter from Commissioner of Allahabad to Secretary, NWP, 27 June, in BL/IOR/P/438/62.

Robertson, C. (1878) Letter from Secretary, NWP&O, to all Magistrates and Deputy Commissioners, NWP&O, 17 June, in BL/IOR/P/1138.

Robertson, C. (1879) Letter from Secretary, NWP&O, to Inspector-General of Police, NWP&O, 25 July, in BL/IOR/P/1281.

Robertson, C. (1880) Letter from Secretary, NWP&O, to Inspector-General of Police, NWP&O, 12 July, in BL/IOR/P/1467.

Robertson, C. (1881) Letter from Secretary, NWP&O, to Inspector-General of Police, NWP&O, 19 September, in BL/IOR/P/1614.

Rose, H.A. (1907) Muhammadan birth observances in the Punjab. *The Journal of the Anthropological Institute of Great Britain and Ireland* 37(1), pp. 237–60.

Rose, H.A. (1911) *A glossary of the tribes and castes of the Punjab and North-West Frontier Province: Based on the Census Report for the Punjab, 1883, by the late Sir DENZIL IBBETSON, K.C.S.I., and the Census Report for the Punjab, 1892, by the Hon. Mr. E.D. MacLAGAN, C.S.I., and compiled by H.A. ROSE* (Lahore: The Civil and Military Gazette Press).

Russell, R.V. (1916) *The tribes and castes of the central provinces of India* (London: Macmillan and Co., Limited).

Sapte, B. (1865) Letter from Commissioner Agra, to Secretary to Government, NWP, 16 September, in BL/IOR/P/438/61.

Short, W.A. (1873) List of Eunuchs in the District of Muzaffarnagar, by Superintendent of Police, Muzaffarnagar, circa January, in UPSA/A/COM/29/8.

Shortt, John (1873) The *kojahs* of southern India. *The Journal of the Anthropological Institute of Great Britain and Ireland* 2, pp. 402–07.

Simson, J. (1860) Letter from Register of NWP Nizamut Adawlut to Secretary, NWP, 31 December, in BL/IOR/P/235.

Simson, R. (1865) Letter from Secretary, NWP, to Inspector-General of Police, NWP, 9 June, in BL/IOR/P/438/6.

Simson, J. (1866) Letter from Register, NWP Nizamut Adawlut, to Secretary, NWP, 'Replies to the Court's Circular Letter, No. 4', 20 April, in BL/IOR/P/438/62.

Singha, Radhika (2003) Colonial law and infrastructural power: Reconstructing community, locating the female subject. *Studies in History* 19, pp. 87–126.

Sinha, Mrinalini (1995) *Colonial masculinity: The "manly" Englishman and the "effeminate" Bengali in the late nineteenth century* (Manchester: Manchester University Press).

Sinha, Nitin (2008) Mobility, control and criminality in early colonial India, 1760s–1850s. *Indian Economic and Social History Review* 45(1), pp. 1–33.

Smith, O.L. (1881) Letter from Deputy Inspector-General of Police, NWP&O, to Inspector-General of Police, NWP&O, 6 July, in BL/IOR/P/1614.

Smith, O.L. (1882) Letter from Deputy Inspector-General of Police, NWP&O, to Officiating Inspector-General of Police, NWP&O, 15 May, in BL/IOR/P/1816.

Smith, O.L. (1883) Letter from Deputy Inspector-General of Police, NWP&O, to Inspector-General of Police, NWP&O, 4 June, in BL/IOR/P/2002.

Smith, O.L. (1884) Letter from Deputy Inspector-General of Police, NWP&O, to Inspector-General of Police, NWP&O, 26 June, in BL/IOR/P/2208.

Solomon, Rakesh H. (1994) Culture, imperialism, and nationalist resistance: Performance in colonial India. *Theatre Journal* 46(3), pp. 323–47.

Solvyns, Balthazar (1808–12) *Les Hindoos* (Paris: Chez l'auteur; Chez H. Nicolle).

Sparks, H.J. (1877) Letter from Secretary, NWP&O, to all Deputy Commissioners, Oudh, 19 November, in BL/IOR/P/840.

Tambe, Ashwini (2010) *Codes of misconduct: Regulating prostitution in late colonial Bombay* (New Delhi: Zubaan).

Tiernan (1871) Letter from Inspector-General of Police, NWP, to Superintendent of Police, Gorakhpur, 26 May, in BL/IOR/P/92.

Tyrwhitt, E. (1874) Letter from Inspector-General of Police, NWP, to Secretary, NWP, 26 June, in BL/IOR/P/96.

Tyrwhitt, E. (1878) Letter from Inspector-General of Police, NWP&O, to Secretary, NWP&O, 28 May, in BL/IOR/P/1138.

Tyrwhitt, E. (1879) Letter from Inspector-General of Police, NWP&O, to Secretary, NWP&O, 5 July, in BL/IOR/P/1281.

Van der Veer, Peter (1988) *Gods on earth: The management of religious experience and identity in a North Indian pilgrimage centre* (London: Athlone Press).
Webster, H.B. (1880) Letter from Inspector-General of Police, NWP&O, to Secretary, NWP&O, 31 May, in BL/IOR/P/1467.
Webster, H.B. (1884) Letter from Inspector-General of Police, NWP&O, to Secretary to Government, NWP&O, 15 July, in BL IOR/P/2208.
Williams F. (1865) Letter from Commissioner of Meerut, to Secretary, NWP, 20 November, in BL/IOR/P/438/62.
Willock, H.D. (1873a) Letter from Magistrate of Bulandshahr to Commissioner of Meerut, 6 January, in UPSA/A/COM/29/8.
Willock, H.D. (1873b) Letter from Magistrate of Bulandshahr to Commissioner of Meerut, 9 January, in UPSA/COM/29/8.
Wise, James (1883) *Notes on the races, castes and trades of Eastern Bengal* (London: Harrison and Sons).

Index

Note: Page numbers in *italics* represent *tables*
Page numbers followed by 'n' refer to notes

abusive relationships 43–4
actors 3, 8, 19, 47; individual 7; sexually autonomous 3; social 3, 75–7
adultery 48
agency: cultural politics 5–22; everyday 1–4; older women's (rural China) 23–41; sexual 8–9, 14, 18–20
Agency of Women in Asia, The (Parker) 1
Ahearn, L. 2, 74
Aisyah, S.: and Parker, L. 1–3, 42–60
alms-collecting 116–17
American–Colonial Manila: modernity and urban transportation 90–110
An Zi 12–13
anthropology 2; feminist 2, 8
anti-colonialism 82
anti-marriage ideology 76
anti-polygyny 49
arranged marriage 2, 49–50, 56
Asia 80–9; masculinity 80–9
Asian Studies Review 1
Australia 51, 58n(3)
automobiles 93–5, 102–3
autonomy 2, 17, 30–4, 57, 62; financial 56; personal 2; sexual 3, 16

baby-boomer generation 72
Bachrach, E. 95–6
Banerjee, S. 113
Bangladesh 85
Barlow, T. 15
Batam (Indonesia) 85
Bei Mei (Sheng) 9
Beijing (China) 11
Bengal 115–17
Bengalis 112–13
Bennett, L.R.: and Idrus, N.I. 51
Beyonce (Knowles) 78n(8)
Blackburn, S. 58n(2)

Blanc-Szanton, C. 91
blogging 13
bodies: obscene/contagious 117–19
British Empire 114, 118
Buddhism 81, 88n(1)
Burma 83
Butt, L.: and Munro, J. 45, 57

Cambodia 84–5
capitalism 37
capitalist growth 24
Carroll, K. 36
caste 113, 114
Chakraborty, C. 82–3
Chattopadhyay, B. 82
childbearing 61, 69
Children's Day (9 September) 24
China 1–3, 5–22; Beijing 11; Dalian 11; Dongguan 6, 12, 21n(3); Guangdong Province 9; Hong Kong 9; Hunan Province 15–18; Maoist 31–2; New Year festival 27–9, 39n(8); Ningxia 23–5; older women's agency 23–41; Pearl River Delta 6, 12, 35; rural development 23–41; rural migrant women 1, 6–10; Rural Migrant Women's Home 10–11; Shanghai 14; Shenzhen 7–9, 12, 21n(3); Sichuan Province 6; South migrant literature 5–22; subaltern genre 12–15, 19; Suzhou 21n(4); women's living arrangements 28, *28*; women's workloads 29, *29*; Wuhan 33
Chinese coolies 100
citizenship 30
class: lower 55, 98; middle 3, 14, 55, 81, 92–8, 106, 115; upper 101
cochero 103–5
colonial control 120, 123

133

INDEX

colonial ideology 122
colonial masculinity 112
colonial transmission: elite response 95–8
colonialism 87; American–Colonial Manila 90–110; India 82, 111–31
conceptualising development (rural China) 23–41
conjugations: problematic 42–60
Connell, R.W. 81, 87; Hearn, J. and Kimmel, M.S. 80
consumerism 66
contagious bodies 117–19
control: colonial 120, 123
Cool Women are Good at Being Single (Haishi) 63
Criminal Tribes Act (CTA, India 1871) 111–25
criminalisation 122, 125
criminality 116, 124
cross-dressing 111, 115–23
cultural politics of agency 5–22
culture: popular 9, 19, 50; public 7–8

Da Peng Wai (magazine) 15
dagongmei (migrant women workers) 9–12, 20
Dales, L. 1, 4, 61–79; and Parker, L. 1–4
Dalian (China) 11
Dapengwan (magazine) 12
debauchery 119
deity 116
democracy 35, 58n(2)
democratisation 13, 45
dependants: passive 28–30
development: conceptualising (rural China) 23–41
diaspora 84
dichotomy 32, 37, 43, 101, 106
discrimination 106
disempowerment 34, 57, 85
domestic violence, Indonesia 3–4, 42–60; women's response to 55–7, 57
Dongguan (China) 6, 12, 21n(3)
Dulkha, I.M.: et al. 53–4

effeminacy 106, 119
eighteenth century 115–17
elite 95–8
elopement 48
emasculation 113
embodiment: transgressive gender 123–4
empowerment 4, 11, 36–8, 44, 77
England 14
English language 70, 75, 77n(7), 99
Environmental Protection Association (EPA) 35–6
equality: gender 34–6
Era of the Parasite Single, The (Yamada) 61

eroticism 85
ethnicity 3
eunuchs 112–14, 118; *hijras* 111–31
Europe 98
everyday agency of women 1–4

Fajardo, K.B. 83–4
Fang Yimeng 6–8, 13
Fee, M. 101
feminine ideal 62–4, 77
femininity 2, 62–9, 73–5, 121
feminisation 34, 62
feminism 44
feminist anthropology 2, 8
fertility 112, 116, 122
Filipino Crosscurrents (Fajardo) 83
financial autonomy 56
First World 25
Forbes, W.C. 96
Ford, M.: and Lyons, L. 85–6
Foucault, M. 125n(5)
Fraser, N.: and Gordon, L. 31–2
Freitag, S. 117
Fu, D. 10–11
Fushan Wenyin (journal) 12

Gandhi, M. 82
Gannon, S. 126n(6)
gender: roles 47–9, 51–3
gender-crossing 115
globalisation 2, 80–7
Gordon, L.: and Fraser, N. 31–2
governmentality 125n(5)
Greene, W. 96
Guangdong Province (China) 9
Guangzhou Wenyin (journal) 12
Gupta, C. 113–14

Haishi Kaori 63–5, 68, 74–6, 77n(2)
harassment: sexual 10–11
Hearn, J.: Kimmel, M.S. and Connell, R.W. 80
Heath, D. 117
hegemony 2, 15, 50, 70
heroism 10, 84
Hershatter, G. 14
Hertog, E. 67, 75
heterosexuality 85–7
hijras 111–31
Hilsdon, A-M. 62
Hinchy, J. 83, 111–31
Hindu Right 82–3
Hinduism 82, 112, 115
homoeroticism 81
homosexuality 112
Hong Kong (China) 9
Horn, F. 97

INDEX

Huacheng (journal) 12
Hunan Province (China) 15–18
hyperfemininity 84
hypermasculinity 85, 105

I am a Floating Flower (Fang) 6–8, 13
ideal: feminine 62–4, 77; masculine 112; social 77
ideal marriage 46–7, 63
ideal masculinity 95
identity: gender 81, 111–13, 123–4; self- 52–3; social 9, 15
ideology 37, 43, 47, 70, 80–1, 117; anti-marriage 76; colonial 122; gender 58, 86; modernist 94; neoliberal 37; patriarchal gender 50; swadeshi 82
Idrus, N.I. 55; and Bennett, L.R. 51
Ikeya, C. 80–9
immorality 5, 119
imperialism 91, 103, 106
impotency 113
India 85–7, 105; Bengal 115–17; colonial and postcolonial 82; Criminal Tribes Act (CTA, 1871) 111–25; *hijras* 111–31; North Western Provinces (NWP) 113, 117
Indian Penal Code (1860) 116, 125n(3)
individual actors 7
Indonesia 1–3, 42–60, 84–6; Bugis-Makassarese society 47–8; Butam 85; domestic violence 42–60; family foundation ideology (*azas kekeluargaan*) 47; gender relations of marriage 46–50; Jakarta 86; *Kekerasan Dalam Rumah Tangga* (KDRT) 45; Law on Domestic Violence (2004) 4, 49; Makassar 1–3, 42, 46–55; Makassar State Islamic University 46; Marriage Law (1974) 47–50, 55; Medan 54; Suharto 45; Sulawesi 1, 42, 46
industrialisation 12
inequality: gender 3, 28, 35
international NGOs 9, 19
International Women's Day (8 March) 24
Internet 1, 13
Islam 48, 51–3
Iwashita Kumiko 63–71, 74–6, 77n(5)

Jacka, T. 1–3, 23–41
Jacobsen, T. 85
Jakarta (Indonesia) 86
Japan 1–3, 61–79; Okinawa 66; singlehood for women 1, 4, 61–79; Tokyo 66–9

Kekerasan Dalam Rumah Tangga (KDRT, Indonesia) 45
Kimmel, M.S.: Connell, R.W. and Hearn, J. 80
Knowles, Beyonce 78n(8)

Kramer, P. 91, 98
Kyoto for the Ohitorisama (Haishi) 63

lesbian, gay, bisexual and transgender (LGBT) 91
living arrangements: rural Chinese women 28, *28*
Living Senior Years Alone (Ueno) 64
Loach (You) 18
Louie, K. 81
love marriage 2, 42, 56
lower class 55, 98
Lyons, L.: and Ford, M. 85–6

McCoy, A.: and Owen, N. 88n(4)
McNay, L. 73
Madrid International Plan of Action on Ageing (UN, 2002) 38
Mahmood, S. 44
Makassar (Indonesia) 1–3, 42, 46–55; State Islamic University 46
Malay Muslim men 86–7
Manila Electric Railroad and Light Company (Meralco) 92–3, 99–100, **99**, 103–5
Manila (Philippines): American–Colonial 90–110
Manila Times 101, 104, 107n(2, 4, 7, 10–14, 16, 25–7)
Maoist China 31–2
marginalisation 23, 74–6, 86
marital rape 51, 55
marriage: arranged 2, 49–50, 56; gender relations 46–50; ideal 46–7, 63; Indonesia 42–60; love 2, 42, 56; virilocal system 30
Marriage in Your 30s can be Happy! (Haishi) 63
masculine ideal 112
masculinity 42–3, 48, 52; American colonial Manila 90–110; Asia 80–9; colonial 112; and *hijras* 111–31; ideal 95; middle class 81; white 94
Masculinity, Asceticism, Hinduism: Past and Present Imaginings of India (Chakraborty) 82
Mayo, K. 100
Medan (Indonesia) 54
Mian Mian 14
microblogging 13
middle class 3, 14, 55, 92–8, 106, 115; masculinity 81
migrant literature: women in rural south China 1, 5–22
migration 12
mobility 14–15
modernisation 23, 92–3, 97
modernism: techno- 94, 98, 101, 106

INDEX

modernist ideology 94
modernity: in American–Colonial Manila 90–110
monogamy 54
moral contagion: northern India 111–31
moral economy: sexual 9, 19
morality 48, 121–2; sexual 10, 20
motorisation 91–8, 104–6
Mughal Empire (1500s–1600s) 114
Munro, J.: and Butt, L. 45, 57
Muslim men: Malay 86–7
Muslims 46, 49–50, 83, 112
Myrttinen, H. 86
mythology 115, 123

Nanfang Dushi Bao (Nanfang Metropolitan News) 7
nation state 45–7, 86, 91
nationalism 84, 87, 91, 114
neoliberal ideology 37
neologism 64
New Man 81
New Year festival (China) 27–9, 39n(8)
nineteenth century 65, 82, 91–7, 111–12, 115–16, 121, 124–5
Ningxia (China) 23–5
non-gender characteristics 3
nongovernmental organisations (NGOs) 9, 19, 21n(4), 35, 46, 58n(3); international 9, 19
Northern Girls (Sheng) 13–16, 20
Nurasiah, F.S.: et al. 53–4
Nurmila, N. 49
Nussbaum, M. 23–6, 33–7

obscene/contagious bodies 117–19
obscenity: colonial India 111–31
ohitorisama 61–79
Okinawa (Japan) 66
Oldenburg, V. 116
older women's agency (rural China) 23–41
Orientalist discourses 83
Ortner, S. 7, 20, 44, 70
Other 2
Owen, N.: and McCoy, A. 88n(4)

Pakistan 86
Pante, M.D. 83, 90–110
Parker, L. 44, 75; and Aisyah, S. 1–3, 42–60; and Dales, L. 1–4
passive dependants 28–30
Pathans 112
patriarchal gender ideology 50
patriarchal order 10, 14, 17
patriarchy 43–5, 72, 122
patriotism 86
Pearl River Delta (China) 6, 12, 35

personal autonomy 2
Philippine Commission (1901) 92
Philippine Motor Association (PMA) 96
Philippines: American–Colonial Manila 90–110; Manila Electric Railroad and Light Company (Meralco) 92–3, 99–100, **99**, 103–5
Philippines Free Press 102–4, 107–8n(6, 9, 15, 17, 30, 32–3, 34)
philosophy 26, 63
politics: cultural 5–22
polygyny 42, 46, 49, 54; anti 49
popular culture 9, 19, 50
post–Enlightenment 116
postcolonial India 82
poverty 27–8, 33, 38, 69; gendered 35
power relations 35–6, 45
Powers, J. 81
problematic conjugations 42–60
promiscuity 3
prostitution 10–14, 20, 118
public culture 7–8
public space 111–31
public sphere 49, 118
Pun, N. 9
Punjab (India) 113

Quezon, M. 97

Ram, K. 44, 115
rape: marital 51, 55
Reddy, W.M. 55, 125
reforestations 30
relations: social 2, 14, 62, 80–1
relationships: abusive 43–4
remasculinisation 83
repression: sexual 10–13
Reyes, R. 91
Robb, W. 96–7
Roberson, J.E.: and Suzuki, N. 81
Rockwell, J. 96
Rofel, L. 12
Roosevelt, T. 95
Roper, M.: and Tosh, J. 87
Rosenberg, H.J. 95
Roseneil, S. 74
Rowe, W.S.: et al. 53–4
Roxas, F. 96
rural development: China 23–41
rural migrant women (China) 1, 5–22; self-ethnography 15–19
Rural Migrant Women's Home (China) 10–11

Sakai, J. 64, 73
Sciortino, R.: and Smyth, I. 58n(2)
Scott, J.C. 58n(6)
self-ethnography of migrant women 15–19

INDEX

self-identity 52–3
Sen, A. 23–6, 33–6
Senior's Day (1 June) 24
sex industry 9–11
sex workers 9, 12, 17, 21n(1), 55
sexual agency 8–9, 14, 18–20
sexual autonomy 16
sexual harassment 10–11
sexual morality 10, 20
sexual repression 10–13
sexual violence 10, 51
sexual-moral economy 9, 19
sexuality 5–15, 18, 112–14, 119–24, 126n(6)
sexually autonomous actors 3
Shanghai Baby (Wei) 14
Shanghai (China) 14
Sheng Keyi 9, 13–15, 20, 21n(5)
Shenzen (China) 7–9, 12, 21n(3)
Shenzen Special Zone Daily 12
Sichuan Province (China) 6
Sikhism 112
Singapore 84–7
Single Ladies song (Beyonce) 78n(8)
singlehood for women: Japan 1, 4, 61–79
Sinha, M. 106, 112–13
Smyth, I.: and Sciortino, R. 58n(2)
social actors 3, 75–7
social contract theory 34
social ideal 77
social identity 9, 15
social relations 2, 14, 62, 80–1
sociology 2
sodomites 111
sodomy 117–18, 125n(3)
Solinger, D. 33
South China's migrant literature 5–22
space: public 111–31
Spain 91–2; Madrid International Plan of Action on Ageing (UN, 2002) 38
Special Zone Literature 12
sphere: public 49, 118
stereotypes 1, 17, 25, 69
stigmatisation 55
Subaltern Genre (China) 12–15, 19
Sugar (Mian) 14
Suhandjati, S. 49, 55
Suharto, President (Indonesia) 45; New Order 45–6
Sulawesi (Indonesia) 1, 42, 46
Sun, W. 1–3, 5–22
Suzhou (China) 21n(4)
Suzuki, N.: and Roberson, J.E. 81
swadeshi ideology 82

Taft, W. 96
Tagore, R. 82
Taiwan 9
TBS 66–9, 76
techno–modernism 94, 98, 101, 106
Thailand 63, 84–6
third gender 114
Third World 25
Timor-Leste 84–6
Tokyo (Japan) 66–9
Tosh, J.: and Roper, M. 87
transgender 83–4, 111
transgenderism 81
transgressive gender embodiment 123–4
transportation: urban 90–110
transvestism 112–13, 116, 119–24
twentieth century 14, 49, 66, 82, 92, 95, 98, 103
twenty-first century 24, 83
tyranny 119

Ueno Chizuko 64–8, 71, 74–6, 77n(3)
unionism 103
United Nations (UN) 25–6, 38; Madrid International Plan of Action on Ageing (2002) 38
United States of America (USA) 31–3, 39n(2), 85, 92, 98, 101; Roosevelt 95; TBS 66–9, 76
upper class 101
upper-caste 114
urban transportation: in American-Colonial Manila 90–110; sector occupations (1939) 92–3, *93*

victimisation 44
Vietnam 84–5
violence: domestic 1–4, 42–60, *57*; sexual 10, 51
virginity 18
virilocal marriage system 30

Wang Haiyan 6
Wang Lei 6
Wei Hui 14
West 2, 30, 78n(10), 83, 92–4; liberal thought 71
white masculinity 94
Wieringa, S.E. 55
Williams, S. 85
Wilson, I. 86
women: living arrangements (China) 28, *28*; singlehood for (Japan) 1, 4, 61–79; workloads (China) 29, *29*
women's agency: Indonesia 42–60
Woodman, S. 35
Worcester, D. 96
working class 2, 31, 73, 83–4, 91, 94
workloads: Chinese women 29, *29*

INDEX

World Bank 25
Wuhan (China) 33

Xie Fenzhu 30, 34

Yamada Masahiro 61–2
Yamamoto, B. 67

Yang Yulan 26–30, 34, 39n(5)
Yangco, T. 96
You Fenwei 18
Young, I. 31, 39n(2)

Zheng, T. 11–12
Zheng Xiaoqiong 13